THE
ROYAL NAVY
AND THE WAR AT SEA
1914–1919

DESPATCHES FROM THE FRONT

The Commanding Officers' Reports From the Field and At Sea.

THE
ROYAL NAVY
AND THE WAR AT SEA
1914–1919

Introduced and compiled by
Martin Mace and John Grehan
With additional research by
Sara Mitchell

Pen & Sword
MARITIME

First published in Great Britain in 2014 by
Pen & Sword Maritime
an imprint of
Pen & Sword Books Ltd
47 Church Street
Barnsley
South Yorkshire
S70 2AS

ISBN 978 1 78159 317 2

Printed and bound by CPI Group (UK) Ltd, Croydon, CR0 4YY

Pen & Sword Books Ltd incorporates the Imprints of Pen & Sword
Aviation, Pen & Sword Maritime, Pen & Sword Military, Wharncliffe Local
History, Pen and Sword Select, Pen and Sword Military Classics and Leo
Cooper.

For a complete list of Pen & Sword titles please contact:
PEN & SWORD BOOKS LIMITED
47 Church Street, Barnsley, South Yorkshire, S70 2AS, England
E-mail: enquiries@pen-and-sword.co.uk
Website: www.pen-and-sword.co.uk

CONTENTS

INTRODUCTION

The First World War is principally remembered as a land war, and this is because the Royal Navy was so dominant that the German naval threat was quickly and efficiently neutralised. Indeed, in some respects it was because of the Royal Navy's supremacy at sea that war between Britain and Germany at some point in the early twentieth century was inevitable.

The might of the Royal Navy had been emphatically displayed at the famous Spithead Review of 1897. The ships reviewed by Queen Victoria had stretched for five miles and included twenty-one battleships, forty-two cruisers, thirty destroyers and seventy-two other craft. Staggering though these numbers were, they represented only half of Britain's navy. The absent craft, 165 in total, were guarding the British Empire which, by the end of the nineteenth century, encompassed a quarter of the globe.

In stark contrast to this naval might the new major European power, Germany, could count only sixty-eight ships in its fleet. If Germany was ever to rival Britain in world affairs it needed a comparable naval force, and a huge warship-building programme was put in hand. Britain, acutely aware of German intentions followed with the building, in 1906, of the mightiest battleship the world had seen – HMS *Dreadnought*.

Faster, more heavily armed and armoured than any preceding battleship, HMS *Dreadnought* was so superior to any other warship that all others were instantly rendered obsolete. But it also meant that Britain was now only one ship of any importance ahead of Germany. As a result an arms race on an unprecedented scale ensued between the two countries. At the outbreak of war in 1914 Germany had built an impressive fleet of battleships, but she still lagged behind the UK, especially with regards to smaller warships.

The objective of the Royal Navy during the war was to blockade the German ships within their own harbours. By contrast, the Germans sought to entice a part of the numerically superior Royal Navy's Grand Fleet into action with its High Seas Fleet. As the German battle squadrons awaited their opportunity to strike, operations were conducted with smaller craft and the first naval engagement took place in the Heligoland Bight off the German coast when a large British destroyer force engaged a much smaller German patrol. The Germans lost six ships, including three cruisers with another six ships damaged.

The Battle of Heligoland Bight immediately established the Royal Navy's dominance, the Germans being restricted to coastal operations and attempts at disrupting Britain's maritime trade with submarine and surface raiders. The latter included the SMS *Königsberg*, which operated off German East Africa, and SMS *Emden*, which was one of the most successful surface raiders of all time having captured seventeen British or neutral merchant ships in the Indian Ocean before she ran aground after being engaged by HMAS *Sydney* in November 1914.

Another notable action in the early stages of the war was the Battle of the Falkland Islands. A German cruiser squadron which had defeated a Royal Navy squadron at the Battle of the Coronel, off the coast of Chile, was tracked down by a larger British squadron near the Falkland Islands. The resulting battle cost the Germans two heavy and two light cruisers and two supporting transport ships.

The Battle of the Falkland Islands confirmed the Royal Navy's superiority and no more German squadrons were permitted to take to the high seas. Until the two great navies met at the Battle of Jutland in 1916, the Imperial German Navy limited its operations to submarine warfare and the laying of mines, though still hoping to draw part of the Grand Fleet into the guns of its battleships.

The German plan almost succeeded at the end of May 1916 when the High Seas Fleet engaged one of the Grand Fleet's battle cruiser squadrons off Jutland on the Danish coast. Admiral Sir John Jellicoe's subsequent report on the Battle of Jutland is, as would be expected, one of the longest despatches in this compilation. This battle was the only opportunity of the war for the Grand Fleet to strike a decisive blow against the German navy; it was one that was squandered.

Jellicoe was criticized for failing to press home his attack in the traditional fashion of the Royal Navy. Nevertheless, both sides claimed victory, though in reality, neither side achieved what they desired. In his despatch, completed more than three weeks after the battle, Jellicoe wrote: "A review of all the reports which I have received leads me to conclude that the enemy's losses were considerably greater than those which we had sustained, in spite of their superiority, and included battleships, battle-cruisers, light cruisers, and destroyers."

Later it was learnt that it was Jellicoe who commanded a considerably greater force than admirals Scheer and Hipper and that the Royal Navy lost far more ships, and almost three times more men, than the German High Seas Fleet.

The main defensive formation on Britain's east coast throughout the war was the Dover Patrol. Based at Dover and Dunkirk, it was originally formed in July 1914 with a number of old destroyers and developed into a powerful and important force which included a wide range of vessel types, as well as seaplanes, land-based aircraft and airships. Its functions were correspondingly varied, but included anti-submarine patrols, minesweeping, the sowing of mines, escorting transports and merchantmen, as well as bombarding the German Army positions close to the Belgian coast.

The Dover Patrol also helped conduct raids against Ostend and the famous Zeebrugge raid of April 1918. Eight Victoria Crosses were awarded for the attempt at blocking the canal exit at Zeebrugge, yet as Vice Admiral Roger Keyes wrote in his despatch: "It seems almost invidious to mention names when every officer and man who took part was animated by one spirit, ardently welcoming the opportunity of achieving a feat of arms against odds in order that honour and merit might be added to that which our Service has gained in the past." Of the 1,700 men involved in the Zeebrugge operation, 300 men were wounded while more than 200 were killed.

The eclectic nature of the Royal Navy despatches is exemplified by one of the earliest in this volume – that relating to the defence of Antwerp in 1914. Also referred to the Siege of Antwerp, this land action, sometimes criticised as a foolhardy gesture, drew in men from the Royal Marines and Royal Navy.

On 1 October 1914, the Belgian government sent a telegram to the British announcing that they would retreat from Antwerp in three days' time. The British government allowed the First Lord of the Admiralty, Winston Churchill, to travel to the Continent to establish what assistance would be required to strengthen the Belgian defences.

On 2 October the Germans succeeded in penetrating two of the city's forts. Leaving London that night Churchill spent three days in trenches and fortifications around the city. He reported back to Kitchener on 4 October that Belgian resistance was weakening with morale low. He also telegrammed that Antwerp would have to be reinforced and then relieved.

On the night of 3 October, a brigade of Royal Marines arrived as the first element of the Royal Naval Division. Receiving a request from the Belgian government for more assistance, the British had also despatched a further 6,000 Royal Navy personnel; 2,000 on 4 October and 4,000 on the following day. The original division of 22,000 troops were also en route for Ostend. However, landing at Ostend on 6 October the British naval forces were too late. Whilst the Marines' arrival was undoubtedly a morale boost to the Belgians, it failed to alter the predicament of the city.

*

In November 1918 the guns fell silent on the Western Front, but fighting in Russia still continued. In October 1917, following heavy defeats at the hands of the Germans, a revolution in Russia resulted in the formation of a Bolshevik-led Communist government. The Communist leader, Lenin, sought peace with Germany and the end of hostilities between the two countries was formalized in March 1918, the terms of the treaty being hugely disadvantageous to the Russians. This also allowed large numbers of German troops which had been fighting the Russians to be transferred to the Western Front.

With Germany and Russia no longer at war, it was feared that the vast quantities of war material which the Allies had given to the Russians might fall into German hands. It was also thought that the 50,000-strong Czechoslovak Legions which had been fighting with Russia against the Germans would be trapped inside Russia. The Czechs wanted to continue fighting the Germans and it was intended that they would be transferred to the Western Front. Finally, it was hoped that if the Bolsheviks could be defeated and the monarchy restored, the Eastern Front against Germany could be re-established.

An Allied force, principally consisting of British troops with a large Royal Navy flotilla of more than twenty ships, was despatched to North Russia. Operations, which were never supported on a scale that could influence events in Russia, continued until the close of 1919. It was only then that, for the men of the Royal Navy if no one else, the First World War truly came to an end.

*

The objective of this book is to reproduce the despatches of the admirals and captains who led the Royal Navy's operations in the First World War as they first appeared to the general public. They have not been modified, edited or interpreted in any way and are therefore the original and unique words of the commanding officers as they saw things at the time. Any grammatical, typographical or spelling errors have been left uncorrected to retain the authenticity of the documents, including the occasional idiosyncratic use of apostrophes.

For example it will be noticed that in the despatch regarding the capture of the SMS *Emden* that the paragraphs run numerically up to paragraph 9 and that the next paragraph is number 13. This is how the despatch was published, just as the others were in this compilation, almost 100 years ago.

Martin Mace and John Grehan
Storrington, 2013

LIST OF ILLUSTRATIONS

1   HMS *Dreadnought* pictured before the outbreak of the First World War. *Dreadnought*'s entry into service in 1906 represented such a marked advance in naval technology that her name came to be associated with an entire generation of battleships, the "dreadnoughts", as well as the class of ships named after her, while the generation of ships she made obsolete became known as "pre-dreadnoughts". She was the sixth ship of that name in the Royal Navy.

2   Two of HMS *Dreadnought*'s BL 12-inch Mk X naval guns. A pair of QF 12-pounder anti-torpedo boat guns are mounted on the turret roof. *Dreadnought* did not participate in any of the First World War naval battles; she was being refitted at the time of the Battle of Jutland. However, *Dreadnought* became the only battleship ever to sink a submarine when she rammed *U-29* when it unexpectedly broke the surface after firing a torpedo at another dreadnought in 1915. (US Library of Congress)

3   On 30 October 1914, the Royal Navy seaplane carrier HMS *Hermes* docked at Dunkirk with a cargo of seaplanes having sailed from Portsmouth earlier the same day. Early the next morning she set out on the return journey. However, *Hermes* had barely left harbour when it was sighted by *U-29*, which then fired two torpedoes. Both struck the former cruiser with devastating effect. Despite remaining afloat for nearly two hours, HMS *Hermes* eventually slipped beneath the waves. Twenty-two of the ship's crew (including four members of the Royal Marine Light Infantry) were lost; all but two have no known grave. (HMP)

4   An artist's depiction of either *Scharnhorst* or *Gneisenau* sinking during the Battle of the Falkland Islands. Casualties and damage during the engagement were extremely disproportionate; the British suffered only very lightly. German survivors, on the otherhand, amounted to just 215 men. (HMP)

5   Taken from HMS *Invincible*, this photograph shows HMS *Inflexible* standing by to pick up survivors from SMS *Gneisenau* on 8 December 1914, during the Battle of the Falkland Islands. Such was the decisive nature of this British victory, German commerce raiding on the high seas by regular warships of the Imperial German Navy was brought to an end. (HMP)

6   A view of the King George V-class battleship HMS *Audacious* slowly settling

in the water after hitting a mine off the north coast of Ireland on 27 October 1914. HMS *Audacious* was the first principal naval casualty of the First World War, a victim of a mine laid by the converted German Norddeutscher Lloyd liner SS *Berlin*. The mine exploded on her port side just forward of her aft engine room bulkhead. After laying the mines *Berlin* attempted to return to Germany, but in the end was forced to put in to Trondheim where the ship was interned for the duration of the war. (HMP)

7   Passengers on the RMS *Olympic*, on the far right, watch the attempts to recover the sinking HMS *Audacious*. Despite the presence of these witnesses, the decision was taken by the Admiralty to maintain a veil of secrecy of the loss of the battleship. This situation was maintained until 14 November 1918, when the following notice was published in *The Times*: "The Secretary of the Admiralty makes the following announcement: HMS *Audacious* sank after striking a mine off the North Irish coast on October 27, 1914. This was kept secret at the urgent request of the Commander-in-Chief, Grand Fleet, and the Press loyally refrained from giving it any publicity." (HMP)

8   HMS *Pegasus* encountered the German heavy cruiser *Königsberg* on 20 September 1914 off the east coast of Africa. The original captain states: "During the action the flag of the *Pegasus* was shot away from its staff. A Marine at once ran forward, picked it up, and waved it aloft. He was struck down while standing on the deck exposed to the enemy's fire, but another came forward to take his place. Until the end the flag was kept flying." This illustration was one of a number produced during the First World War in an attempt to obscure the fact that *Pegasus* had actually struck the colours. (HMP)

9   The Formidable-class pre-dreadnought battleship HMS *Irresistible* listing and sinking in the Dardanelles, 18 March 1915 – an image taken from the battleship HMS *Lord Nelson*. Having struck a mine at 16.16 hours, the badly-damaged *Irresistible* was left without power, causing her to drift within range of Turkish guns which laid down a heavy barrage on her. HMS *Irresistible* finally sank at about 19.30 hours, her crew suffering about 150 casualties. (HMP)

10   It was at about 18.30 hours that the German battlecruisers *Lützow* and *Derfflinger* then fired three salvoes each at HMS *Invincible* during the Battle of Jutland. At least one 12-inch shell from the third German salvo is believed to have penetrated HMS *Invincible*'s midships 'Q' turret, which blew off its roof and detonated the midships magazines. This photograph itself was taken from the deck of HMS *Inflexible*, the next ship astern.

11   The original caption to this image states that it shows the damage caused to a British light cruiser during the Battle of Jutland. Unfortunately, it is not known which of the light cruisers this is. Two, HMS *Black Prince* and HMS *Tipperary*, were sunk, whilst HMS *Southampton* was the light cruiser hit the most times – with eighteen shells striking her. (HMP)

battleships, two at *Derfflinger* and one at the light cruiser *Wiesbaden* without success. (HMP)

16 By the latter half of the First World War the German surface fleet was limited to hit and run raids across the Channel and in response British destroyers were deployed to guard the Dover Strait. One night in April 1917 the opposing forces met. The British ships were outnumbered, but the German ships were outfought. This contemporary artist's depiction was "based on the accounts of eyewitnesses" and depicts the hand-to-hand fighting on board the Faulknor-class destroyer HMS *Broke* following the ramming of the German destroyer G.42 on 20 April 1917. (HMP)

17 Launched on 9 December 1897, and completed in 1899, the *Arrogant*-class protected cruiser HMS *Vindictive* is best remembered for its part in the Zeebrugge Raid in April 1918. In preparation for the attack, most of *Vindictive*'s guns were removed and replaced by howitzers, flamethrowers and mortars. On 23 April 1918 she was involved in the fierce action at Zeebrugge when she went alongside the Mole, and her upperworks were badly damaged by gunfire. The battered and badly-damaged HMS *Vindictive* is seen here after the attack at Dover. (HMP)

18 Some of the crew of HMS *Vindictive* inspecting equipment and souvenirs from the raid upon their return to Dover. The sailor on the far right is holding a lump of concrete from the Mole. Sir Roger Keyes once wrote that "over a hundredweight of concrete fell on the deck of the *Vindictive* while she was alongside the Mole ... Pieces of it were carried away as souvenirs by many of the crew after the ship returned". (HMP)

19 An unusual relic of the attacks on Zeebrugge and Ostend in 1918 – the bow section of HMS *Vindictive*, which was sunk as a blockship at Ostend on 10 May 1918. The wreck was raised on 16 August 1920 and subsequently broken up. The bow section was preserved as a memorial and can be seen today near the bridge at the end of the De Smet-De Naeyer Avenue in Ostend. One of the protected cruiser's 7.5-inch howitzers was also saved, and is now in the care of the Imperial War Museum. (With the kind permission of Peter De Rycke)

20 One of those awarded the Victoria Cross for his participation in the attack on Zeebrugge – in this case decided by a ballot of Royal Navy officers – was Captain Alfred Carpenter RN, the commander of HMS *Vindictive*. The announcement of his award included the following: "He set a magnificent example to all those under his command by his calm composure when navigating mined waters, bringing his ship alongside the mole in darkness. When 'Vindictive' was within a few yards of the mole the enemy started and maintained a heavy fire from batteries, machine guns and rifles on to the bridge. He showed most conspicuous bravery ..." Carpenter is pictured here being received by King George V and Queen Mary at a garden party for holders of the VC held at Buckingham Palace, July 1920. (HMP)

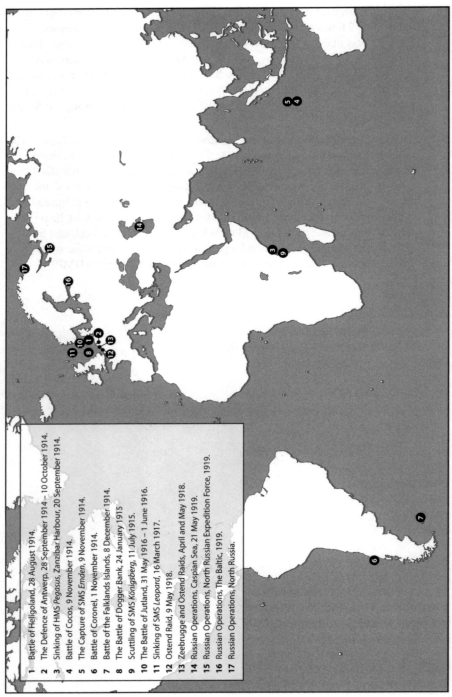

1   Battle of Heligoland, 28 August 1914.
2   The Defence of Antwerp, 28 September 1914 – 10 October 1914.
3   Sinking of HMS *Pegasus*, Zanzibar Harbour, 20 September 1914.
4   Battle of Cocos, 9 November 1914.
5   The Capture of SMS *Emden*, 9 November 1914.
6   Battle of Coronel, 1 November 1914.
7   Battle of the Falklands Islands, 8 December 1914.
8   The Battle of Dogger Bank, 24 January 1915
9   Scuttling of SMS *Königsberg*, 11 July 1915.
10 The Battle of Jutland, 31 May 1916 – 1 June 1916.
11 Sinking of SMS *Leopard*, 16 March 1917.
12 Ostend Raid, 9 May 1918.
13 Zeebrugge and Ostend Raids, April and May 1918.
14 Russian Operations, Caspian Sea, 21 May 1919.
15 Russian Operations, North Russian Expedition Force, 1919.
16 Russian Operations, The Baltic, 1919.
17 Russian Operations, North Russia.

A map showing the location of some of the main naval actions of the First World War.

1

BATTLE OF HELIGOLAND, 28 AUGUST 1914

FRIDAY, 23 OCTOBER, 1914.

Admiralty,
21st October, 1914.

The following despatches have been received from Vice-Admiral (Acting) Sir David Beatty, K.C.B., M.V.O., D.S.O., H.M.S. "Lion," Rear-Admiral Arthur H. Christian, M.V.O., H.M.S. "Euryalus," Commodore Reginald Y. Tyrwhitt, Commodore (T.), H.M.S. "Arethusa," and Commodore Roger J.B. Keyes, C.B., M.V.O., Commodore (S.), reporting the engagement off Heligoland on Friday, the 28th August.

A memorandum by the Director of the Air Department, Admiralty, is annexed.

H.M.S. "Lion,"
1st September, 1914.

Sir, – I have the honour to report that on Thursday, 27th August, at 5 a.m., I proceeded with the First Battle Cruiser Squadron and First Light Cruiser Squadron in company, to rendezvous with the Rear-Admiral, "Invincible."

At 4 a.m., 28th August, the movements of the Flotillas commenced as previously arranged, the Battle Cruiser Squadron and Light Cruiser Squadron supporting. The Rear-Admiral, "Invincible," with "New Zealand" and four Destroyers having joined my flag, the Squadron passed through the pre-arranged rendezvous.

At 8.10 a.m. I received a signal from the Commodore (T), informing me that the Flotilla was in action with the enemy. This was presumably in the vicinity of their pre-arranged rendezvous. From this time until 11 a.m. I remained about the vicinity ready to support as necessary, intercepting various signals, which contained no information on which I could act.

At 11 a.m. the Squadron was attacked by three Submarines. The attack was frustrated by rapid manoeuvring and the four Destroyers were ordered to attack them. Shortly after 11 a.m., various signals having been received indicating that the Commodore (T) and Commodore (S) were both in need of assistance, I ordered the Light Cruiser Squadron to support the Torpedo Flotillas.

Later I received a signal from the Commodore (T), stating that he was being attacked by a large Cruiser, and a further signal informing me that he was being hard pressed and asking for assistance. The Captain (D), First Flotilla, also signalled that he was in need of help.

From the foregoing the situation appeared to me critical. The Flotillas had advanced only ten miles since 8 a.m., and were only about twenty-five miles from two enemy bases on their flank and rear respectively. Commodore Goodenough had detached two of his Light Cruisers to assist some Destroyers earlier in the day, and these had not yet re-joined. (They rejoined at 2.30 p.m.) As the reports indicated the presence of many enemy ships – one a large Cruiser – I considered that his force might not be strong enough to deal with the situation sufficiently rapidly, so at 11.30 a.m. the Battle Cruisers turned to E.S.E., and worked up to full speed. It was evident that to be of any value the support must be overwhelming and carried out at the highest speed possible.

I had not lost sight of the risk of Submarines, and possible sortie in force from the enemy's base, especially in view of the mist to the South-East.

Our high speed, however, made submarine attack difficult, and the smoothness of the sea made their detection comparatively easy. I considered that we were powerful enough to deal with any sortie except by a Battle Squadron, which was unlikely to come out in time, provided our stroke was sufficiently rapid.

At 12.15 p.m. "Fearless" and First Flotilla were sighted retiring West. At the same time the Light Cruiser Squadron was observed to be engaging an enemy ship ahead. They appeared to have her beat.

I then steered N.E. to sounds of firing ahead, and at 12.30 p.m. sighted "Arethusa" and Third Flotilla retiring to the Westward engaging a Cruiser of the "Kolberg" class on our Port Bow. I steered to cut her off from Heligoland, and at 12.37 p.m. opened fire. At 12.42 the enemy turned to N.E., and we chased at 27 knots.

At 12.56 p.m. sighted and engaged a two-funnelled Cruiser ahead. "Lion" fired two salvoes at her, which took effect, and she disappeared into the mist, burning furiously and in a sinking condition. In view of the mist and that she was steering at high speed at right angles to "Lion," who was herself steaming at 28 knots, the "Lion's" firing was very creditable.

Our Destroyers had reported the presence of floating mines to the Eastward and I considered it inadvisable to pursue her. It was also essential that the Squadrons should remain concentrated, and I accordingly ordered a withdrawal. The Battle Cruisers turned North and circled to port to complete the destruction of the vessel first engaged. She was sighted again at 1.25 p.m. steaming S.E. with colours still flying. "Lion" opened fire with two turrets, and at 1.35 p.m., after receiving two salvoes, she sank.

The four attached Destroyers were sent to pick up survivors, but I deeply regret that they subsequently reported that they searched the area but found none.

At 1.40 p.m. the Battle Cruisers turned to the Northward, and "Queen Mary" was again attacked by a Submarine. The attack was avoided by the use of the helm. "Lowestoft" was also unsuccessfully attacked. The Battle Cruisers covered the retirement until nightfall. By 6 p.m., the retirement having been well executed and all Destroyers accounted for, I altered course, spread the Light Cruisers, and swept northwards in accordance with the Commander-in-Chief's orders. At 7.45 p.m. I detached "Liverpool" to Rosyth with German prisoners, 7 officers and 79 men, survivors from "Mainz." No further incident occurred. – I have the honour to be, Sir, your obedient Servant,

(Signed) DAVID BEATTY,
Vice-Admiral.
The Secretary of the Admiralty.

"Euryalus,"
28th September, 1914.

Sir, – I have the honour to report that in accordance with your orders a reconnaissance in force was carried out in the Heligoland Bight on the 28th August, with the object of attacking the enemy's Light Cruisers and Destroyers.

The forces under my orders (viz., the Cruiser Force, under Rear-Admiral H.H. Campbell, C.V.O., "Euryalus," "Amethyst," First and Third Destroyer Flotillas and the Submarines) took up the positions assigned to them on the evening of the 27th August, and, in accordance with directions given, proceeded during the night to approach the Heligoland Bight.

The Cruiser Force under Rear-Admiral Campbell, with "Euryalus" (my Flagship) and "Amethyst," was stationed to intercept any enemy vessels chased to the westward. At 4.30 p.m. on the 28th August these Cruisers, having proceeded to the eastward, fell in with "Lurcher" and three other Destroyers, and the wounded and prisoners in these vessels were transferred in boats to "Bacchante" and "Cressy," which left for the Nore. "Amethyst" took "Laurel" in tow, and at 9.30 p.m. "Hogue" was detached to take "Arethusa" in tow. This latter is referred to in Commodore R.Y. Tyrwhitt's report, and I quite concur in his remarks as to the skill and rapidity with which this was done in the dark with no lights permissible.

Commodore Reginald Y. Tyrwhitt was in command of the Destroyer Flotillas, and his report is enclosed herewith. His attack was delivered with great skill and gallantry, and he was most ably seconded by Captain William F. Blunt, in "Fearless," and the Officers in command of the Destroyers, who handled their vessels in a manner worthy of the best traditions of the British Navy.

Commodore Roger J.B. Keyes, in "Lurcher," had on the 27th August, escorted some Submarines into positions allotted to them in the immediate vicinity of the enemy's coast. On the morning of the 28th August, in company with "Firedrake," he searched the area to the southward of the Battle Cruisers for the enemy's Submarines, and subsequently, having been detached, was present at the sinking of the German Cruiser "Mainz," when he gallantly proceeded alongside her and rescued 220 of her crew, many of whom were wounded. Subsequently he escorted "Laurel" and "Liberty" out of action, and kept them company till Rear-Admiral Campbell's Cruisers were sighted.

As regards the Submarine Officers, I would specially mention the names of:-

(a) Lieutenant-Commander Ernest W. Leir. His coolness and resource in rescuing the crews of the "Goshawk's" and "Defender's" boats at a critical time of the action were admirable.

(b) Lieutenant-Commander Cecil P. Talbot. In my opinion, the bravery and resource of the Officers in command of Submarines since the war commenced are worthy of the highest commendation.

I have the honour to be, Sir,
Your obedient Servant,
A.H. CHRISTIAN,
Rear-Admiral.
The Secretary, Admiralty.

H.M.S. "Lowestoft,"
26th September, 1914.

Sir, – I have the honour to report that at 5 a.m. on Thursday, 27th August, in accordance with orders received from Their Lordships, I sailed in "Arethusa," in company with the First and Third Flotillas, except "Hornet," "Tigress," "Hydra," and "Loyal," to carry out the prearranged operations. H.M.S. "Fearless" joined the Flotillas at sea that afternoon.

At 6.53 a.m. on Friday, 28th August, an enemy's Destroyer was sighted, and was chased by the 4th Division of the Third Flotilla.

From 7.20 to 7.57 a.m. "Arethusa" and the Third Flotilla were engaged with numerous Destroyers and Torpedo Boats which were making for Heligoland; course was altered to port to cut them off.

Two Cruisers, with 4 and 2 funnels respectively, were sighted on the port bow at 7.57 a.m., the nearest of which was engaged. "Arethusa" received a heavy fire from both Cruisers and several Destroyers until 8.15 a.m., when the four-funnelled Cruiser transferred her fire to "Fearless."

Close action was continued with the two-funnelled Cruiser on converging courses until 8.25 a.m., when a 6-inch projectile from "Arethusa" wrecked the fore bridge of the enemy, who at once turned away in the direction of Heligoland, which was sighted slightly on the starboard bow at about the same time.

All ships were at once ordered to turn to the westward, and shortly afterwards speed was reduced to 20 knots.

During this action "Arethusa" had been hit many times, and was considerably damaged; only one 6-inch gun remained in action, all other guns and torpedo tubes having been temporarily disabled.

Lieutenant Eric W.P. Westmacott (Signal Officer) was killed at my side during this action. I cannot refrain from adding that he carried out his duties calmly and collectedly, and was of the greatest assistance to me.

A fire occurred opposite No. 2 gun port side caused by a shell exploding some ammunition, resulting in a terrific blaze for a short period and leaving the deck burning. This was very promptly dealt with and extinguished by Chief Petty Officer Frederick W. Wrench, O.N. 158630.

The Flotillas were reformed in Divisions and proceeded at 20 knots. It was now noticed that "Arethusa's" speed had been reduced.

"Fearless" reported that the 3rd and 5th Divisions of the First Flotilla had sunk the German Commodore's Destroyer and that two boats' crews belonging to "Defender" had been left behind, as our Destroyers had been fired upon by a German Cruiser during their act of mercy in saving the survivors of the German Destroyer.

At 10 a.m., hearing that Commodore (S) in "Lurcher" and "Firedrake" were being chased by Light Cruisers, I proceeded to his assistance with "Fearless" and the First Flotilla until 10.37 a.m., when, having received no news and being in the vicinity of Heligoland, I ordered the ships in company to turn to the westward.

All guns except two 4-inch were again in working order, and the upper deck supply of ammunition was replenished.

At 10.55 a.m. a four-funnelled German Cruiser was sighted, and opened a very heavy fire at about 11 o'clock.

Our position being somewhat critical, I ordered "Fearless" to attack, and the First Flotilla to attack with torpedoes, which they proceeded to do with great spirit. The Cruiser at once turned away, disappeared in the haze and evaded the attack.

About 10 minutes later the same Cruiser appeared on our starboard quarter. Opened fire on her with both 6-inch guns; "Fearless" also engaged her, and one Division of Destroyers attacked her with torpedoes without success.

The state of affairs and our position was then reported to the Admiral Commanding Battle Cruiser Squadron.

We received a very severe and almost accurate fire from this Cruiser; salvo after salvo was falling between 10 and 30 yards short, but not a single shell struck; two torpedoes were also fired at us, being well directed, but short.

The Cruiser was badly damaged by "Arethusa's" 6-inch guns and a splendidly directed fire from "Fearless," and she shortly afterwards turned away in the direction of Heligoland. Proceeded, and four minutes later sighted the three-funnelled Cruiser "Mainz." She endured a heavy fire from "Arethusa" and "Fearless" and many Destroyers. After an action of approximately 25 minutes she was seen to be sinking by the head, her engines stopped, besides being on fire.

At this moment the Light Cruiser Squadron appeared, and they very speedily reduced the "Mainz" to a condition which must have been indescribable.

I then recalled "Fearless" and the Destroyers, and ordered cease fire.

We then exchanged broadsides with a large, four-funnelled Cruiser on the starboard quarter at long range, without visible effect.

The Battle Cruiser Squadron now arrived, and I pointed out this Cruiser to the Admiral Commanding, and was shortly afterwards informed by him that the Cruiser in question had been sunk and another set on fire.

The weather during the day was fine, sea calm, but visibility poor, not more than 3 miles at any time when the various actions were taking place, and was such that ranging and spotting were rendered difficult.

I then proceeded with 14 Destroyers of the Third Flotilla and 9 of the First Flotilla.

"Arethusa's" speed was about 6 knots until 7 p.m., when it was impossible to proceed any further, and fires were drawn in all boilers except two, and assistance called for.

At 9.30 p.m. Captain Wilmot S. Nicholson, of the "Hogue," took my ship in tow in a most seamanlike manner, and, observing that the night was pitch dark and the only lights showing were two small hand lanterns, I consider his action was one which deserves special notice from Their Lordships.

I would also specially recommend Lieutenant-Commander Arthur P.N. Thorowgood, of "Arethusa," for the able manner he prepared the ship for being towed in the dark.

H.M. Ship under my command was then towed to the Nore, arriving at 5 p.m. on the 29th August. Steam was then available for slow speed, and the ship was able to proceed to Chatham under her own steam.

I beg again to call attention to the services rendered by Captain W.F. Blunt, of H.M.S. "Fearless," and the Commanding Officers of the Destroyers of the First and Third Flotillas, whose gallant attacks on the German Cruisers at critical moments undoubtedly saved "Arethusa" from more severe punishment and possible capture.

I cannot adequately express my satisfaction and pride at the spirit and ardour of my Officers and Ship's Company, who carried out their orders with the greatest alacrity under the most trying conditions, especially in view of the fact that the ship, newly built, had not been 48 hours out of the Dockyard before she was in action.

It is difficult to specially pick out individuals but the following came under my special observation:-

H.M.S. "Arethusa."

Lieutenant-Commander Arthur P.N. Thorowgood, First Lieutenant, and in charge of the After Control.

Lieutenant-Commander Ernest K. Arbuthnot (G.), in charge of the Fore Control.

Sub-Lieutenant Clive A. Robinson, who worked the range-finder throughout the entire action with extraordinary coolness.

Assistant Paymaster Kenneth E. Badcock, my Secretary, who attended me on the bridge throughout the entire action.

Mr. James D. Godfrey, Gunner (T.), who was in charge of the torpedo tubes.

The following men were specially noted:-

Armourer Arthur F. Hayes, O.N.34202G6 (Ch.).

Second Sick Berth Steward George Trolley, O.N. M. 296 (Ch.).

Chief Yeoman of Signals Albert Fox, O.N.194656 (Po.), on fore bridge during entire action.

Chief Petty Officer Frederick W. Wrench, O.N.158630 (Ch.) (for ready resource in extinguishing fire caused by explosion of cordite).

Private Thomas Millington, R.M.L.I., No. Ch. 17417.

Private William J. Beirne, R.M.L.I., No. Ch. 13540.

First Writer Albert W. Stone, O.N. 346080 (Po.).

I also beg to record the services rendered by the following Officers and Men of H.M. Ships under my orders:-

H.M.S. "Fearless."

Mr. Robert M. Taylor, Gunner, for coolness in action under heavy fire.

The following Officers also displayed great resource and energy in effecting repairs to "Fearless" after her return to harbour, and they were ably seconded by the whole of their staffs:-

Engineer Lieutenant-Commander Charles de F. Messervy.

Mr. William Morrissey, Carpenter.

H.M.S. "Goshawk."

Commander The Hon. Herbert Meade, who took his Division into action with great coolness and nerve, and was instrumental in sinking the German Destroyer "V. 187," and, with the boats of his Division, saved the survivors in a most chivalrous manner.

H.M.S. "Ferret."

Commander Geoffrey Mackworth, who, with his Division, most gallantly seconded Commander Meade, of "Goshawk."

H.M.S. "Laertes."

Lieutenant-Commander Malcolm L. Goldsmith, whose ship was seriously damaged, taken in tow, and towed out of action by "Fearless."

Engineer Lieutenant-Commander Alexander Hill, for repairing steering gear and engines under fire.

Sub-Lieutenant George H. Faulkner, who continued to fight his gun after being wounded.

Mr. Charles Powell, Acting Boatswain, O.N. 209388, who was gunlayer of the centre gun, which made many hits. He behaved very coolly, and set a good example when getting in tow and clearing away the wreckage after the action.

Edward Naylor, Petty Officer, Torpedo Gunner's Mate, O.N. 189136, who fired a torpedo which the Commanding Officer of "Laertes" reports undoubtedly hit the "Mainz," and so helped materially to put her out of action.

Stephen Pritchard, Stoker Petty Officer, O.N. 285152, who very gallantly dived into the cabin flat immediately after a shell had exploded there, and worked a fire hose.

Frederick Pierce, Stoker Petty Officer, O.N. 307943, who was on watch in the engine room and behaved with conspicuous coolness and resource when a shell exploded in No. 2 boiler.

H.M.S. "Laurel."

Commander Frank F. Rose, who most ably commanded his vessel throughout the early part of the action, and after having been wounded in both legs, remained on the bridge until 6 p.m., displaying great devotion to duty.

Lieutenant Charles R. Peploe, First Lieutenant, who took command after Commander Rose was wounded, and continued the action till its close, bringing his Destroyer out in an able and gallant manner under most trying conditions.

Engineer Lieutenant-Commander Edward H.T. Meeson, who behaved with great coolness during the action, and steamed the ship out of action, although she had been very severely damaged by explosion of her own lyddite, by which the after funnel was nearly demolished. He subsequently assisted to carry out repairs to the vessel.

Sam Palmer, Leading Seaman (G.L. 2) O.N. 179529, who continued to fight his gun until the end of the action, although severely wounded in the leg.

Albert Edmund Sellens, Able Seaman (L.T.O.), O.N. 217245, who was stationed at the fore torpedo tubes; he remained at his post throughout the entire action, although wounded in the arm, and then rendered first aid in a very able manner before being attended to himself.

George H. Sturdy, Chief Stoker, O.N. 285547, and

Alfred Britton, Stoker Petty Officer, O.N. 289893, who both showed great coolness in putting out a fire near the centre gun after an explosion had occurred there; several lyddite shells were lying in the immediate vicinity.

William R. Boiston, Engine Room Artificer, 3rd class, O.N. M.1369, who showed great ability and coolness in taking charge of the after boiler room during the action, when an explosion blew in the after funnel and a shell carried away pipes and seriously damaged the main steam pipe.

William H. Gorst, Stoker Petty Officer, O.N. 305616.

Edward Crane, Stoker Petty Officer, O.N. 307275.

Harry Wilfred Hawkes, Stoker 1st class, O.N. K.12086.

John W. Bateman, Stoker 1st class, O.N. K.12100.

These men were stationed in the after boiler room and conducted themselves with great coolness during the action, when an explosion blew in the after funnel, and shell carried away pipes and seriously damaged the main steam pipe.

H.M.S. "Liberty."

The late Lieutenant-Commander Nigel K.W. Barttelot commanded the "Liberty" with great skill and gallantry throughout the action. He was a most promising and able Officer, and I consider his death is a great loss to the Navy.

Engineer Lieutenant-Commander Frank A. Butler, who showed much resource in effecting repairs during the action.

Lieutenant Henry E. Horan, First Lieutenant, who took command after the death of Lieutenant-Commander Barttelot, and brought his ship out of action in an extremely able and gallant manner under most trying conditions.

Mr. Harry Morgan, Gunner (T), who carried out his duties with exceptional coolness under fire.

Chief Petty Officer James Samuel Beadle, O.N. 171735, who remained at his post at the wheel for over an hour after being wounded in the kidneys.

John Galvin, Stoker, Petty Officer, O.N. 279946, who took entire charge, under the Engineer Officer, of the party who stopped leaks, and accomplished his task although working up to his chest in water.

H.M.S. "Laforey."

Mr. Ernest Roper, Chief Gunner, who carried out his duties with exceptional coolness under fire.

I have the honour to be, Sir,
Your obedient Servant,
R.Y. TYRWHITT,
Commodore (T).

2

SUBMARINE OPERATIONS AUGUST - OCTOBER 1914

H.M.S. "Maidstone,"
17th October, 1914.

Sir, – In compliance with Their Lordships' directions, I have the honour to report as follows upon the services performed by Submarines since the commencement of hostilities:-

Three hours after the outbreak of war, Submarines "E. 6" (Lieutenant-Commander Cecil P. Talbot), and "E.8" (Lieutenant-Commander Francis H.H. Goodhart), proceeded unaccompanied to carry out a reconnaissance in the Heligoland Bight. These two vessels returned with useful information, and had the privilege of being the pioneers on a service which is attended by some risk.

During the transportation of the Expeditionary Force the "Lurcher" and "Firedrake" and all the Submarines of the Eighth Submarine Flotilla occupied positions from which they could have attacked the High Sea Fleet, had it emerged to dispute the passage of our transports. This patrol was maintained day and night without relief, until the personnel of our Army had been transported and all chance of effective interference had disappeared.

These Submarines have since been incessantly employed on the Enemy's Coast in the Heligoland Bight and elsewhere, and have obtained much valuable information regarding the composition and movement of his patrols. They have occupied his waters and reconnoitred his anchorages, and, while so engaged, have been subjected to skilful and well executed anti-submarine tactics; hunted for hours at a time by Torpedo Craft and attacked by gunfire and torpedoes.

At midnight on the 26th August, I embarked in the "Lurcher," and, in company with "Firedrake" and Submarines "D.2," "D.8," "E.4." "E.5," "E.6," "E.7," "E.8," and "E.9" of the Eighth Submarine Flotilla, proceeded to take part in the operations in the Heligoland Bight arranged for the 28th August. The Destroyers scouted for the

Submarines until nightfall on the 27th, when the latter proceeded independently to take up various positions from which they could co-operate with the Destroyer Flotillas on the following morning.

At daylight on the 28th August the "Lurcher" and "Firedrake" searched the area, through which the Battle Cruisers were to advance, for hostile Submarines, and then proceeded towards Heligoland in the wake of Submarines "E.6," "E.7," and "E.8," which were exposing themselves with the object of inducing the enemy to chase them to the westward.

On approaching Heligoland, the visibility, which had been very good to seaward, reduced to 5,000 to 6,000 yards, and this added considerably to the anxieties and responsibilities of the Commanding Officers of Submarines, who handled their vessels with coolness and judgment in an area which was necessarily occupied by friends as well as foes.

Low visibility and calm sea are the most unfavourable conditions under which Submarines can operate, and no opportunity occurred of closing with the Enemy's Cruisers to within torpedo range.

Lieutenant-Commander Ernest W. Leir, Commanding Submarine "E.4," witnessed the sinking of the German Torpedo Boat Destroyer "V.187" through his periscope, and, observing a Cruiser of the "Stettin" class close, and open fire on the British Destroyers which had lowered their boats to pick up the survivors, he proceeded to attack the Cruiser, but she altered course before he could get within range. After covering the retirement of our Destroyers, which had had to abandon their boats, he returned to the latter, and embarked a Lieutenant and nine men of "Defender," who had been left behind. The boats also contained two Officers and eight men of "V.187," who were unwounded, and eighteen men who were badly wounded. As he could not embark the latter, Lieutenant-Commander Leir left one of the Officers and six unwounded men to navigate the British boats to Heligoland. Before leaving he saw that they were provided with water, biscuit, and a compass. One German Officer and two men were made prisoners of war.

Lieutenant-Commander Leir's action in remaining on the surface in the vicinity of the enemy and in a visibility which would have placed his vessel within easy gun range of an enemy appearing out of the mist, was altogether admirable.

This enterprising and gallant Officer took part in the reconnaisance which supplied the information on which these operations were based, and I beg to submit his name, and that of Lieutenant-Commander Talbot, the Commanding Officer of "E.6," who exercised patience, judgment and skill in a dangerous position, for the favourable consideration of Their Lordships.

On the 13th September, "E.9" (Lieutenant-Commander Max K. Horton), torpedoed and sank the German Light Cruiser "Hela" six miles South of Heligoland.

A number of Destroyers were evidently called to the scene after "E.9" had delivered her attack, and these hunted her for several hours.

On the 14th September, in accordance with his orders, Lieutenant-Commander Horton examined the outer anchorage of Heligoland, a service attended by considerable risk.

On the 25th September, Submarine "E.6" (Lieutenant-Commander C.P. Talbot), while diving, fouled the moorings of a mine laid by the enemy. On rising to the surface she weighed the mine and sinker; the former was securely fixed between the hydroplane and its guard; fortunately, however, the horns of the mine were pointed outboard. The weight of the sinker made it a difficult and dangerous matter to lift the mine clear without exploding it. After half an hour's patient work this was effected by Lieutenant Frederick A.P. Williams-Freeman and Able Seaman Ernest Randall Cremer, Official Number 214235, and the released mine descended to its original depth.

On the 6th October, "E.9" (Lieutenant-Commander Max K. Horton), when patrolling off the Ems, torpedoed and sank the enemy's destroyer, "S.126."

The enemy's Torpedo Craft pursue tactics, which, in connection with their shallow draft, make them exceedingly difficult to attack with torpedo, and Lieutenant-Commander Horton's success was the result of much patient and skilful zeal. He is a most enterprising submarine officer, and I beg to submit his name for favourable consideration.

Lieutenant Charles M.S. Chapman, the Second in Command of "E.9," is also deserving of credit.

Against an enemy whose capital vessels have never, and Light Cruisers have seldom, emerged from their fortified harbours, opportunities of delivering Submarine attacks have necessarily been few, and on one occasion only, prior to the 13th September, has one of our Submarines been within torpedo range of a Cruiser during daylight hours.

During the exceptionally heavy westerly gales which prevailed between the 14th and 21st September, the position of the Submarines on a lee shore, within a few miles of the Enemy's coast, was an unpleasant one.

The short steep seas which accompany westerly gales in the Heligoland Bight made it difficult to keep the conning tower hatches open. There was no rest to be obtained, and even when cruising at a depth of 60 feet, the Submarines were rolling considerably, and pumping – *i.e.,* vertically moving about twenty feet.

I submit that it was creditable to the Commanding Officers that they should have maintained their stations under such conditions.

Service in the Heligoland Bight is keenly sought after by the Commanding Officers of the Eighth Submarine Flotilla, and they have all shown daring and enterprise in the execution of their duties. These Officers have unanimously expressed to me their admiration of the cool and gallant behaviour of the Officers and men under their command. They are, however, of the opinion that it is impossible to single out individuals when all have performed their duties so admirably, and in this I concur.

The following Submarines have been in contact with the enemy during these operations:-

"D.I" (Lieutenant-Commander Archibald D. Cochrane).
"D.2" (Lieutenant-Commander Arthur G. Jameson).
"D.3" (Lieutenant-Commander Edward C. Boyle).
"D.5" (Lieutenant-Commander Godfrey Herbert).

"E.4" (Lieutenant-Commander Ernest W. Leir).
"E.5" (Lieutenant-Commander Charles S. Benning).
"E.6" (Lieutenant-Commander Cecil P. Talbot).
"E.7" (Lieutenant-Commander Ferdinand E.B. Feilmann).
"E.9" (Lieutenant-Commander Max K. Horton).

> I have the honour to be, Sir,
> Your obedient Servant,
> (Signed) ROGER KEYES,
> Commodore (S).

3

THE DEFENCE OF ANTWERP, OCTOBER 1914

SATURDAY, 5 DECEMBER, 1914.

Admiralty, 5th December, 1914.

The following despatch has been received from Field-Marshal Sir J.D.P. French, G.C.B., G.C.V.O., K.C.M.G., covering a despatch from Major-General A. Paris, C.B., R.M.A., relating to the operations round Antwerp from the 3rd to the 9th October.

From Sir J.D.P. French, Field-Marshal, Commanding-in-Chief, to the Secretary of the Admiralty.

In forwarding this report to the Army Council at the request of the Lords Commissioners of the Admiralty, I have to state that, from a comprehensive review of all the circumstances, the force of Marines and Naval Brigades which assisted in the defence of Antwerp was handled by General Paris with great skill and boldness.

Although the results did not include the actual saving of the fortress, the action of the force under General Paris certainly delayed the enemy for a considerable time, and assisted the Belgian Army to be withdrawn in a condition to enable it to reorganize and refit, and regain its value as a fighting force. The destruction of war material and ammunition – which, but for the intervention of this force would have proved of great value to the enemy – was thus able to be carried out.

The assistance which the Belgian Army has rendered throughout the subsequent course of the operations on the canal and the Yeser river has been a valuable asset to the allied cause, and such help must be regarded as an outcome of the intervention of General Paris's force. I am further of opinion that the moral effect produced on the minds of the Belgian Army by this necessarily desperate attempt to bring them succour, before it was too late, has been of great value to their use and efficiency as a fighting force.

J.D.P. FRENCH,
Field-Marshal,
Commanding-in-Chief.

*From the Secretary of the Admiralty to Field Marshal Sir J.D.P. French,
Commanding-in-Chief. (Enclosure in No. 1.)*
Admiralty,
2nd November, 1914.

Sir,

I am commanded by My Lords Commissioners of the Admiralty to transmit herewith a despatch from Major-General Paris, reporting the proceedings of the Division round Antwerp from the 3rd to 9th October, with a view to its being considered by you and forwarded to the Army Council with your survey of the operations as a whole.

I am, etc.,
W. GRAHAM GEEENE.

*From Major-General A. Paris, C.B., Commanding Royal Naval Division,
to the Secretary of the Admiralty. (Sub-enclosure in No. 1.)*
31st October, 1914.

Regarding the operations round Antwerp from 3rd to 9th October, I have the honour to report as follows:-

The Brigade (2,200 all ranks) reached Antwerp during the night 3rd-4th October, and early on the 4th occupied, with the 7th Belgian Regiment, the trenches facing Lierre, with advanced post on the River Nethe, relieving some exhausted Belgian troops.

The outer forts on this front had already fallen and bombardment of the trenches was in progress. This increased in violence during the night and early morning of 5th October, when the advanced posts were driven in and the enemy effected a crossing of the river, which was not under fire from the trenches.

About midday the 7th Belgian Regiment was forced to retire, thus exposing my right flank. A vigorous counter-attack, gallantly led by Colonel Tierchon, 2nd Chasseurs, assisted by our aeroplanes, restored the position late in the afternoon.

Unfortunately, an attempt made by the Belgian troops during the night (5th-6th October) to drive the enemy across the river failed, and resulted in the evacuation of practically the whole of the Belgian trenches.

The few troops now capable of another counter-attack were unable to make any impression, and the position of the Marine Brigade became untenable.

The bombardment, too, was very violent, but the retirement of the Brigade was well carried out, and soon after midday (6th October) an intermediate position, which had been hastily prepared, was occupied.

The two Naval Brigades reached Antwerp during the night, 5th-6th October. The 1st Brigade moved out in the afternoon of 5th to assist the withdrawal to the main 2nd Line of Defence.

The retirement was carried out during the night, 6th-7th October, without opposition, and the Naval Division occupied the intervals between the forts on the 2nd Line of Defence.

The bombardment of the town, forts and trenches began at midnight, 7th-8th October, and continued with increasing intensity until the evacuation of the fortress.

As the water supply had been cut, no attempt could be made to subdue the flames, and soon 100 houses were burning. Fortunately, there was no wind, or the whole town and bridges must have been destroyed.

During the day (8th October) it appeared evident that the Belgian Army could not hold the forts any longer. About 5.20 p.m. I considered that if the Naval Division was to avoid disaster an immediate retirement under cover of darkness was necessary. General De Guise, the Belgian Commander, was in complete agreement. He was most chivalrous and gallant, insisting on giving orders that the roads and bridges were to be cleared for the passage of the British troops.

The retirement began about 7.30 p.m., and was carried out under very difficult conditions.

The enemy were reported in force (a Division plus a Reserve Brigade) on our immediate line of retreat, rendering necessary a detour of 15 miles to the north.

All the roads were crowded with Belgian troops, refugees, herds of cattle, and all kinds of vehicles, making inter-communication a practical impossibility. Partly for these reasons, partly on account of fatigue, and partly from at present unexplained causes large numbers of the 1st Naval Brigade became detached, and I regret to say are either prisoners or interned in Holland.

Marching all night (8th to 9th October), one battalion of 1st Brigade, the 2nd Brigade and Royal Marine Brigade, less one battalion, entrained at St. Gillies Waes and effected their retreat without further incident.

The Battalion (Royal Marine Brigade) Rear Guard of the whole force, also entrained late in the afternoon together with many hundreds of refugees, but at Morbeke the line was cut, the engine derailed, and the enemy opened fire.

There was considerable confusion. It was dark and the agitation of the refugees made it difficult to pass any orders. However, the battalion behaved admirably, and succeeded in fighting its way through, but with a loss in missing of more than half its number. They then marched another 10 miles to Selzaate and entrained there.

Colonel Seely and Colonel Bridges were not part of my command, but they rendered most skilful and helpful services during the evacuation.

The casualties are approximately-

1st Naval Brigade and 2nd Naval Brigade, 5 killed, 64 wounded, 2,040 missing.
Royal Marine Brigade, 23 killed, 103 wounded, 388 missing.

4

THE CAPTURE
OF SMS *EMDEN*

FRIDAY, 1 JANUARY, 1915.

Admiralty,
1st January, 1915.

The following despatch has been received from Captain John C.T. Glossop, reporting the capture of the German Cruiser "Emden" by H.M.A.S. "Sydney."

A memorandum is also appended by the Director of the Air Department, Admiralty, containing a report on the aerial attack on the airship sheds and factory at Friedrichshafen.

Despatch from Captain Glossop.
H.M.A.S. "Sydney" at Colombo,
15th November, 1914.

Sir,

I have the honour to report that whilst on escort duty with the Convoy under the charge of Captain Silver, H.M.A.S. "Melbourne," at 6.30 a.m., on Monday, 9th November, a wireless message from Cocos was heard reporting that a foreign warship was off the entrance. I was ordered to raise steam for full speed at 7.0 a.m. and proceeded thither. I worked up to 20 knots, and at 9.15 a.m. sighted land ahead and almost immediately the smoke of a ship, which proved to be H.I.G.M.S. "Emden" coming out towards me at a great rate. At 9.40 a.m., fire was opened, she firing the first shot. I kept my distance as much as possible to obtain the advantage of my guns. Her fire was very accurate and rapid to begin with, but seemed to slacken very quickly, all casualties occurring in this ship almost immediately. First the foremost funnel of her went, secondly the foremast, and she was badly on fire aft, then the second funnel went, and lastly the third funnel, and I saw she was making for the beach on North Keeling Island, where she grounded at 11.20 a.m. I gave her two more broadsides and left her to pursue a merchant ship which had come up during the action.

2. Although I had guns on this merchant ship at odd times during the action I had not fired, and as she was making off fast I pursued and overtook her at 12.10, firing a gun across her bows, and hoisting International Code Signal to stop, which she did. I sent an armed boat and found her to be the S. S. "Buresk," a captured British collier, with 18 Chinese crew, 1 English Steward, 1 Norwegian Cook, and a German Prize Crew of 3 Officers, 1 Warrant Officer and 12 men. The ship unfortunately was sinking, the Kingston knocked out and damaged to prevent repairing, so I took all on board, fired 4 shells into her and returned to "Emden" passing men swimming in the water, for whom I left 2 boats I was towing from "Buresk."

3. On arriving again off "Emden" she still had her colours up at mainmast head. I enquired by signal, International Code, "Will you surrender?" and received a reply in Morse "What signal? No signal books." I then made in Morse "Do you surrender?" and subsequently "Have you received my signal?" to neither of which did I get an answer. The German Officers on board gave me to understand that the Captain would never surrender, and therefore, though very reluctantly, I again fired at her at 4.30 p.m., ceasing at 4.35, as she showed white flags and hauled down her ensign by sending a man aloft.

4. I then left "Emden" and returned and picked up the "Buresk's" two boats, rescuing 2 sailors (5.0 p.m.), who had been in the water all day. I returned and sent in one boat to "Emden," manned by her own prize crew from "Buresk," and 1 Officer, and stating I would return to their assistance next morning. This I had to do, as I was desirous to find out the condition of cables and Wireless Station at Direction Island. On the passage over I was again delayed by rescuing another sailor (6.30 p.m.), and by the time I was again ready and approaching Direction Island it was too late for the night.

5. I lay on and off all night and communicated with Direction Island at 8.0 a.m., 10th November, to find that the "Emden's" party consisting of 3 officers and 40 men, 1 launch and 2 cutters had seized and provisioned a 70 tons schooner (the "Ayesha"), having 4 Maxims, with 2 belts to each. They left the previous night at six o'clock. The Wireless Station was entirely destroyed, 1 cable cut, 1 damaged, and 1 intact. I borrowed a Doctor and 2 Assistants, and proceeded as fast as possible to "Emden's" assistance.

6. I sent an Officer on board to see the Captain, and in view of the large number of prisoners and wounded and lack of accommodation, &c., in this ship, and the absolute impossibility of leaving them where they were, he agreed that if I received his Officers and men and all wounded, "then as for such time as they remained in 'Sydney' they would cause no interference with ship or fittings, and would be amenable to the ship's discipline." I therefore set to work at once to tranship them – a most difficult operation, the ship being on weather side of Island and the send alongside very heavy. The conditions in the "Emden" were indescribable. I received

the last from her at 5.0 p.m., then had to go round to the lee side to pick up 20 more men who had managed to get ashore from the ship.

7. Darkness came on before this could be accomplished, and the ship again stood off and on all night, resuming operations at 5.0 a.m. on 11th November, a cutter's crew having to land with stretchers to bring wounded round to embarking point. A German Officer, a Doctor, died ashore the previous day. The ship in the meantime ran over to Direction Island to return their Doctor and Assistants, send cables, and was back again at 10.0 a.m., embarked the remainder of wounded, and proceeded for Colombo by 10.35 a.m. Wednesday, 11th November.

8. Total casualties in "Sydney": Killed 3, severely wounded (since dead) 1, severely wounded 4, wounded 4, slightly wounded 4. In the "Emden" I can only approximately state the killed at 7 Officers and 108 men from Captain's statement. I had on board 11 Officers, 9 Warrant Officers, and 191 men, of whom 3 Officers and 53 men were wounded, and of this number 1 Officer and 3 men have since died of wounds.

9. The damage to "Sydney's" hull and fittings was surprisingly small; in all about 10 hits seem to have been made. The engine and boiler rooms and funnels escaped entirely.

13. I have great pleasure in stating that the behaviour of the ship's company was excellent in every way, and with such a large proportion of young hands and people under training it is all the more gratifying. The engines worked magnificently, and higher results than trials were obtained, and I cannot speak too highly of the Medical Staff and arrangements on subsequent trip, the ship being nothing but a hospital of a most painful description.

I have the honour to be,
Sir,
Your obedient Servant,
JOHN C.T. GLOSSOP,
Captain.
The Secretary of the Admiralty.

5

EAST COAST MINESWEEPING OPERATIONS, DECEMBER 1914

FRIDAY, 19 FEBRUARY, 1915.

Admiralty, 19th February, 1915.

The following Memorandum has been furnished by the Admiral Commanding the East Coast Minesweepers, detailing the recent mine-sweeping operations off Scarborough.

From the 19th to the 31st December sweeping operations were conducted by the East Coast Mine sweepers with the object of clearing the minefield which had been laid by the enemy off Scarborough.

At the beginning there was no indication of the position of the mines, although owing to losses of passing merchant ships it was known that a minefield had been laid.

In order to ascertain how the mines lay it was necessary to work at all times of tide with a consequent large increase in the element of danger.

The following officers are specially noticed for their services during the operations -

Commander Richard H. Walters, R.N.,

A M S Staff, was in charge of the whole of the mine sweeping operations from 19th to 31st December. During this period a large number of mines were swept up and destroyed. By the 25th December, a channel had been cleared, and traffic was able to pass through by daylight.

Commander (now Captain) Lionel G. Preston, R.N.,

H.M.S. "Skipjack," on the 19th December, proceeded at once into the middle of the area where the mines had exploded to give assistance to the damaged trawlers. He anchored between the trawlers and the mines which had been brought to the surface, and proceeded to sink them.

Lieutenant Godfrey Craik Parsons, R.N.,

H.M.S. "Pekin," displayed, great skill and devotion to duty in continuing to command his group of trawlers after having been mined in Trawler No. 58 on 19th December. On this day his group exploded eight mines, and brought to the surface six more, Trawler No. 99 being blown up and Nos. 58 and 465 damaged, all in the space of about 10 minutes.

Lieutenant H. Boothby, R.N.R.,

H.M.S. "Pekin". When Trawler No. 99 ("Orianda") in which he was serving was blown up by a mine on the 19th December, Lieutenant Boothby successfully got all his crew (except one who was killed) into safety. Lieutenant Boothby was again blown up on 6th January, 1915, in Trawler No. 450 ("The Banyers").

Lieutenant C.V. Crossley, R.N.R.,

H.M.S. "Pekin." Whilst sweeping on 19th December, three violent explosions occurred close under the stern of his ship, Trawler No. 465 (Star of Britain). He controlled the crew, and himself crawled into a confined space near the screw shaft, discovered the damage, and temporarily stopped the leak sufficiently to enable the pumps to keep the water down and save the ship.

Skipper T. Tringall, R.N.T.R.,

Trawler "Solon," No. 55, on his own responsibility went to the assistance of the Steamer "Gallier," which had just been mined on the night of 25th December. It was low water at the time and dark, and the "Gallier" was showing no lights, so had to be searched for in the mine field.

Skipper Ernest V. Snowline, R.N.T.R.,

Drifter "Hilda and Ernest," No. 201, carried out his duties as Commodore of the Flotilla of Lowestoft drifters under Chief Gunner Franklin, R.N., in a most satisfactory manner. He kept to his station in heavy weather, standing by the S.S. "Gallier" after she had been damaged by a mine.

Lieutenant W.G. Wood, R.N.R.,

Trawler "Restrivo," No. 48, did excellent work in going to the assistance of damaged trawlers on 19th December, and performed the risky duty of crossing the mine field at low water when sent to bring in the "Valiant," which had been disabled by a mine.

Skipper George W. Thornton, R.N.T.R.,

Trawler "Passing," No. 58, displayed great coolness and rendered valuable assistance to Lieutenant Parsons in controlling the crew when No. 58 had been mined.

Skipper William Allerton, R.N.T.R.,

Drifter "Eager," No. 202, kept to his station in heavy weather, standing by the S.S. "Gallier" after she had been damaged by a mine.

Sub-Lieutenant W. L. Scott, R.N.R.,

Drifter "Principal," went alongside the Trawler "Garmo" in a dinghy to rescue a man at considerable risk to himself and his boat, as the vessel was floating nearly vertical at the time, with only the forecastle above water. She turned completely over and sank a few minutes after he left her.

Skipper Thomas B. Belton, R.N.T.R.,

Drifter "Retriever," No. 223, kept to his station, marking the safe channel for shipping when all other drifters were driven in by the weather.

The following are also commended for Good Service done under dangerous conditions:-

Robert A. Gray, Engineman, R.N.R. No. 694ES, M.S.Tr. No.465.
William A. Lewis, P.O., Icl., O.N. 178498,. M.S.Tr. No.450.
Christopher Briggs, Engineman, R.N.R. No. 1542ES, M.S.Tr. No.450.
William Gladding, Cook, R.N.R. No. 223T.C., M.S.Tr. No.450.
Robert Frost, Second Hand, R.N.Ri No. 81D.A., M.S.Tr. No.43.
Edwin F. Frankland, Deck Hand, R.N.R. No. 2481D.A., M.S.Tr. No.49.
George Newman, Engineman, R.N.R; No. 625ES, M.S.Tr. No.451.
William R. Kemp, Engineman, R.N.R. No. 846ES, M.S.Tr. No.49.

6

NAVAL SEAPLANE OPERATIONS IN HELIGOLAND BIGHT, 25 DECEMBER 1914

Admiralty, 19th February, 1915.

ADMIRALTY MEMORANDUM
on the combined operations by H.M. Ships and
Naval Seaplanes on the 25th December, 1914.

On the 25th December, 1914, an air reconnaissance of the Heligoland Bight, including Cuxhaven, Heligoland, and Wilhelmshaven, was made by naval seaplanes, and the opportunity was taken at the same time of attacking with bombs points of military importance. The reconnaissance involved combined operations by light cruisers, destroyers and seaplane carriers, under Commodore Reginald Y. Tyrwhitt, C.B., and submarines acting under the orders of Commodore Roger Keyes, C.B., M.V.O.

The vessels detailed for the operations arrived at their rendezvous before daylight, and as soon as the light was sufficient the seaplanes were hoisted out and despatched. The following Air Service officers and observers took part in the reconnaissance:-

Pilots.

> Flight Commander (now Squadron Commander) Douglas Austin Oliver.
> Flight Commander Francis Esme Theodore Hewlett.
> Flight Commander Robert Peel Ross.
> Flight Commander Cecil Francis Kilner.
> Flight Lieutenant (now Flight Commander) Arnold John Miley.
> Flight Lieutenant Charles Humphrey Kingsman Edmonds.
> Flight Sub-Lieutenant (now Flight Lieutenant) Vivian Gaskell Blackburn.

Observers.

Lieutenant Erskine Childers, R.N.V.R.
C.P.O. Mechanic James W. Bell.
C.P.O. Mechanic Gilbert H.W. Budds.
The seaplane-carriers were commanded by:-
Squadron Commander Cecil J. L'Estrange Malone.
Flight Commander Edmund D.M. Robertson.
Flight Commander Frederick W. Bowhill.

At the beginning of the flight the weather was clear, but on nearing the land the seaplanes met with thick weather, and were compelled to fly low, thus becoming exposed to a heavy fire at short range from ships and shore batteries. Several machines were hit, but all remained in the air for over three hours, and succeeded in obtaining valuable information regarding the disposition of the enemy's ships and defences. Bombs were also dropped on military points. In the meanwhile German submarines, seaplanes and Zeppelins delivered a combined attack upon the light cruisers, destroyers and seaplane-carriers, but were driven off.

Flight Commanders Kilner and Ross and Flight Lieutenant Edmonds regained their ships. Flight Commander Oliver, Flight Lieutenant Miley and Flight Sub-Lieutenant Blackburn became short of fuel, and were compelled to descend near Submarine E.11, which with other submarine vessels was watching inshore to assist any seaplane that might be in difficulties. Lieutenant-Commander Martin E. Nasmith, commanding E.11, although attacked by an airship, succeeded, by his coolness and resource, in rescuing the three pilots. Flight Commander Hewlett, after a flight of 3½ hours, was compelled to descend on account of engine trouble, but was rescued by a Dutch trawler, landed in Holland, and returned safely to England.

An expression of their Lordships' appreciation has been conveyed to Commodore Keyes (Commodore S.), Commodore Tyrwhitt (Commodore T.), and to Captain Sueter (Director of the Air Department), for their share in the combined operations which resulted in this successful reconnaissance.

BATTLE OF THE FALKLAND ISLANDS, 8 DECEMBER 1914

WEDNESDAY, 3 MARCH, 1915.

Admiralty, 3rd March, 1915.

The following despatch has been received from Vice-Admiral Sir F.C. Doveton Sturdee, K.C.B., C.V.O., C.M.G., reporting the action off the Falkland Islands on Tuesday, the 8th of December, 1914:-

Invincible at Sea,
December 19th, 1914.

SIR,

I have the honour to forward a report on the action which took place on 8th December, 1914, against a German Squadron off the Falkland Islands.

I have the honour to be, Sir,
Your obedient Servant,
F.C.D. STURDEE,
Vice-Admiral, Commander-in-Chief.
The Secretary, Admiralty.

(A.) – Preliminary Movements.
(B.) – Action with the Armoured Cruisers.
(C.) – Action with the Light Cruisers.
(D.) – Action with the Enemy's Transports.

(A.) PRELIMINARY MOVEMENTS.

The squadron, consisting of H.M. ships "Invincible," flying my flag, Flag Captain Percy T.H. Beamish; "Inflexible," Captain Richard F. Phillimore; "Carnarvon," flying the flag of Rear-Admiral Archibald P. Stoddart, Flag Captain Harry L. d'E. Skipwith; "Cornwall," Captain Walter M. Ellerton; "Kent," Captain John D. Allen; "Glasgow," Captain John Luce; "Bristol," Captain Basil H. Fanshawe; and "Macedonia," Captain Bertram S. Evans; arrived at Port Stanley, Falkland Islands, at 10.30 a.m. on Monday, the 7th December, 1914. Coaling was commenced at once, in order that the ships should be ready to resume the search for the enemy's squadron the next evening, the 8th December.

At 8 a.m. on Tuesday, the 8th December, a signal was received from the signal station on shore:-

"A four-funnel and two-funnel man-of-war in sight from Sapper Hill, steering northwards."

At this time, the positions of the various ships of the squadron were as follows:-

"Macedonia": At anchor as look-out ship.
"Kent" (guard ship): At anchor in Port William.
"Invincible" and "Inflexible": In Port William.
"Carnarvon": In Port William.
"Cornwall": In Port William.
"Glasgow": In Port Stanley.

"Bristol": In Port Stanley.

The "Kent" was at once ordered to weigh, and a general signal was made to raise steam for full speed.

At 8.20 a.m. the signal station reported another column of smoke in sight to the southward, and at 8.45 a.m. the "Kent" passed down the harbour and took up a station at the entrance.

The "Canopus," Captain Heathcoat S. Grant, reported at 8.47 a.m. that the first two ships were 8 miles off, and that the smoke reported at 8.20 a.m., appeared to be the smoke of two ships about 20 miles off.

At 8.50 a.m. the signal station reported a further column of smoke in sight to the southward.

The "Macedonia" was ordered to weigh anchor on the inner side of the other ships, and await orders.

At 9.20 a.m. the two leading ships of the enemy ("Gneisenau" and "Nürnberg"), with guns trained on the wireless station, came within range of the "Canopus," who opened fire at them across the low land at a range of 11,000 yards. The enemy at once hoisted their colours and turned away. At this time the masts and smoke of the enemy were visible from the upper bridge of the "Invincible" at a range of approximately 17,000 yards across the low land to the south of Port William.

A few minutes later the two cruisers altered course to port, as though to close the

"Kent" at the entrance to the harbour, but about this time it seems that the "Invincible" and "Inflexible" were seen over the land, as the enemy at once altered course and increased speed to join their consorts.

The "Glasgow" weighed and proceeded at 9.40 a.m. with orders to join the "Kent" and observe the enemy's movements.

At 9.45 a.m. the squadron – less the "Bristol" – weighed, and proceeded out of harbour in the following order: "Carnarvon," "Inflexible," "Invincible," and "Cornwall." On passing Cape Pembroke Light, the five ships of the enemy appeared clearly in sight to the south-east, hull down. The visibility was at its maximum, the sea was calm, with a bright sun, a clear sky, and a light breeze from the north-west.

At 10.20 a.m. the signal for a general chase was made. The battle cruisers quickly passed ahead of the "Carnarvon" and overtook the "Kent." The "Glasgow" was ordered to keep two miles from the "Invincible," and the "Inflexible" was stationed on the starboard quarter of the flagship. Speed was eased to 20 knots at 11.15 a.m. to enable the other cruisers to get into station.

At this time the enemy's funnels and bridges showed just above the horizon.

Information was received from the "Bristol" at 11.27 a.m. that three enemy ships had appeared off Port Pleasant, probably colliers or transports. The "Bristol" was therefore directed to take the "Macedonia" under his orders and destroy transports.

The enemy were still maintaining their distance, and I decided, at 12.20 p.m., to attack with the two battle cruisers and the "Glasgow."

At 12.47 p.m. the signal to "Open fire and engage the enemy" was made.

The "Inflexible" opened fire at 12.55 p.m. from her fore turret at the right-hand ship of the enemy, a light cruiser; a few minutes later the "Invincible" opened fire at the same ship.

The deliberate fire from a range of 16,500 to 15,000 yards at the right-hand light cruiser, who was dropping astern, became too threatening, and when a shell fell close alongside her at 1.20 p.m. she (the "Leipzig") turned away, with the "Nürnberg" and "Dresden" to the south-west. These light cruisers were at once followed by the "Kent," "Glasgow," and "Cornwall", in accordance with my instructions.

The action finally developed into three separate encounters, besides the subsidiary one dealing with the threatened landing.

(B.) ACTION WITH THE ARMOURED CRUISERS.

The fire of the battle cruisers was directed on the "Scharnhorst" and "Gneisenau." The effect of this was quickly seen, when at 1.25 p.m., with the "Scharnhorst" leading, they turned about 7 points to port in succession into line ahead and opened fire at 1.30 p.m. Shortly afterwards speed was eased to 24 knots, and the battle cruisers were ordered to turn together, bringing them into line ahead, with the "Invincible" leading.

The range was about 13,500 yards at the final turn, and increased, until, at 2 p.m., it had reached 16,450 yards.

The enemy then (2.10 p.m.) turned away about 10 points to starboard and a second chase ensued, until, at 2.45 p.m., the battle cruisers again opened fire; this caused the enemy, at 2.53 p.m., to turn into line ahead to port and open fire at 2.55 p.m.

The "Scharnhorst" caught fire forward, but not seriously, and her fire slackened perceptibly; the "Gneisenau" was badly hit by the "Inflexible."

At 3.30 p.m. the "Scharnhorst" led round about 10 points to starboard; just previously her fire had slackened perceptibly, and one shell had shot away her third funnel; some guns were not firing, and it would appear that the turn was dictated by a desire to bring her starboard guns into action. The effect of the fire on the "Scharnhorst" became more and more apparent in consequence of smoke from fires, and also escaping steam; at times a shell would cause a large hole to appear in her side, through which could be seen a dull red glow of flame. At 4.4 p.m. the "Scharnhorst," whose flag remained flying to the last, suddenly listed heavily to port, and within a minute it became clear that she was a doomed ship; for the list increased very rapidly until she lay on her beam ends, and at 4.17 p.m. she disappeared.

The "Gneisenau" passed on the far side of her late flagship, and continued a determined but ineffectual effort to fight the two battle cruisers.

At 5.8 p.m. the forward funnel was knocked over and remained resting against the second funnel. She was evidently in serious straits, and her fire slackened very much.

At 5.15 p.m. one of the "Gneisenau's" shells struck the "Invincible"; this was her last effective effort.

At 5.30 p.m. she turned towards the flagship with a heavy list to starboard, and appeared stopped, with steam pouring from her escape-pipes, and smoke from shell and fires rising everywhere. About this time I ordered the signal "Cease fire," but before it was hoisted the "Gneisenau" opened fire again, and continued to fire from time to time with a single gun.

At 5.40 p.m. the three ships closed in on the "Gneisenau," and, at this time, the flag flying at her fore truck was apparently hauled down, but the flag at the peak continued flying.

At 5.50 p.m. "Cease fire" was made.

At 6 p.m. the "Gneisenau" heeled over very suddenly, showing the men gathered on her decks and then walking on her side as she lay for a minute on her beam ends before sinking.

The prisoners of war from the "Gneisenau" report that, by the time the ammunition was expended, some 600 men had been killed and wounded. The surviving officers and men were all ordered on deck and told to provide themselves with hammocks and any articles that could support them in the water.

When the ship capsized and sank there were probably some 200 unwounded survivors in the water, but, owing to the shock of the cold water, many were drowned within sight of the boats and ship.

Every effort was made to save life as quickly as possible, both by boats and from the ships; life-buoys were thrown and ropes lowered, but only a proportion could be rescued. The "Invincible" alone rescued 108 men, fourteen of whom were found to be dead after being brought on board; these men were buried at sea the following day with full military honours.

(C.) ACTION WITH THE LIGHT CRUISERS.

At about 1 p.m., when the "Scharnhorst" and "Gneisenau" turned to port to engage the "Invincible" and "Inflexible" the enemy's light cruisers turned to starboard to escape; the "Dresden" was leading and the "Nürnberg" and "Leipzig" followed on each quarter.

In accordance with my instructions, the "Glasgow," "Kent," and "Cornwall" at once went in chase of these ships; the "Carnarvon," whose speed was insufficient to overtake them, closed the battle cruisers.

The "Glasgow" drew well ahead of the "Cornwall" and "Kent," and, at 3 p.m., shots were exchanged with the "Leipzig" at 12,000 yards. The "Glasgow's" object was to endeavour to outrange the "Leipzig" with her 6-inch guns and thus cause her to alter course and give the "Cornwall" and "Kent" a chance of coming into action.

At 4.17 p.m. the "Cornwall" opened fire, also on the "Leipzig."

At 7.17 p.m. the "Leipzig" was on fire fore and aft, and the "Cornwall" and "Glasgow" ceased fire.

The "Leipzig" turned over on her port side and disappeared at 9 p.m. Seven officers and eleven men were saved.

At 3.36 p.m. the "Cornwall" ordered the "Kent" to engage the "Nürnberg," the nearest cruiser to her.

Owing to the excellent and strenuous efforts of the engine room department, the "Kent" was able to get within range of the "Nürnberg" at 5 p.m. At 6.35 p.m. the "Nürnberg" was on fire forward and ceased firing. The "Kent" also ceased firing and closed to 3,300 yards; as the colours were still observed to be flying in the "Nürnberg," the "Kent" opened fire again. Fire was finally stopped five minutes later on the colours being hauled down, and every preparation was made to save life. The "Nürnberg" sank at 7.27 p.m., and, as she sank, a group of men were waving a German ensign attached to a staff. Twelve men were rescued, but only seven survived.

The "Kent" had four killed and twelve wounded, mostly caused by one shell.

During the time the three cruisers were engaged with the "Nürnberg" and "Leipzig," the "Dresden," who was beyond her consorts, effected her escape owing to her superior speed. The "Glasgow" was the only cruiser with sufficient speed to have had any chance of success. However, she was fully employed in engaging the "Leipzig" for over an hour before either the "Cornwall" or "Kent" could come up and get within range. During this time the "Dresden" was able to increase her distance and get out of sight.

The weather changed after 4 p.m., and the visibility was much reduced; further, the sky was overcast and cloudy, thus assisting the "Dresden" to get away unobserved.

(D.) ACTION WITH THE ENEMY'S TRANSPORTS.

A report was received at 11.27 a.m. from H.M.S. "Bristol" that three ships of the enemy, probably transports or colliers, had appeared off Port Pleasant. The "Bristol" was ordered to take the "Macedonia" under his orders and destroy the transports.

H.M.S. "Macedonia" reports that only two ships, steamships "Baden" and "Santa Isabel," were present; both ships were sunk after the removal of the crew.

I have pleasure in reporting that the officers and men under my orders carried out their duties with admirable efficiency and coolness, and great credit is due to the Engineer Officers of all the ships, several of which exceeded their normal full speed.

The names of the following are specially mentioned:-

Officers.

Commander Richard Herbert Denny Townsend, H.M.S. "Invincible."
Commander Arthur Edward Frederick Bedford, H.M.S. "Kent."
Lieutenant-Commander Wilfred Arthur Thompson, H.M.S. "Glasgow."
Lieutenant-Commander Hubert Edward Danreuther, First and Gunnery Lieutenant, H.M.S. "Invincible."
Engineer-Commander George Edward Andrew, H.M.S. "Kent."
Engineer-Commander Edward John Weeks, H.M.S. "Invincible."
Paymaster Cyril Sheldon Johnson, H.M.S. "Invincible."
Carpenter Thomas Andrew Walls, H.M.S. "Invincible."
Carpenter William Henry Venning, H.M.S. "Kent."
Carpenter George Henry Egford, H.M.S. "Cornwall."
Petty Officers and Men.
Chief Petty Officer David Leighton, O.N. 124238; H.M.S. "Kent."
Petty Officer, 2nd Class, Matthew J. Walton (R.F.R., A. 1756), O.N. 118358, H.M.S. "Kent."
Leading Seaman Frederick Sidney Martin, O.N. 233301, H.M.S. "Invincible," Gunner's Mate, Gunlayer, 1st Class.
Signalman Frank Glover, O.N. 225731, H.M.S. "Cornwall."
Chief Engine-Room Artificer, 2nd Class, John George Hill, O.N. 269646, H.M.S. "Cornwall."
Acting Chief Engine-Room Artificer, 2nd Class, Robert Snowdon, O.N. 270654, H.M.S. "Inflexible."
Engine-Room. Artificer, 1st Class, George Henry Francis McCarten, O.N. 270023, H.M.S. "Invincible."
Stoker Petty Officer George S. Brewer, O.N. 150950, H.M.S. "Kent."
Stoker Petty Officer William Alfred Townsend, O.N. 301650, H.M.S. "Cornwall."
Stoker, 1st Class, John Smith, O.N. SS 111915, H.M.S. "Cornwall."
Shipwright, 1st Class, Albert N.E. England, O.N. 341971, H.M.S. "Glasgow."
Shipwright. 2nd Class, Albert C.H. Dymott, O.N. M 8047, H.M.S. "Kent."
Portsmouth R.F.R.B. /3307 Sergeant Charles Mayes, H.M.S. "Kent."

F.C.D. STURDEE.

8

DOVER PATROL, OPERATIONS OFF THE BELGIAN COAST, OCTOBER-NOVEMBER 1914

TUESDAY, 13 APRIL, 1915.

Admiralty,
13th April 1915.

The following despatch has been received from Rear-Admiral the Hon. Horace L.A. Hood C.B., M.V.O., D.S.O. reporting the proceedings of the flotilla off the coast of Belgium between 17th October and 9th November 1914 -

Office of Rear-Admiral
Dover Patrol
11th November 1914.

SIR, – I have the honour to report the proceedings of the flotilla acting off the coast of Belgium between October 17th and November 9th.

The flotilla was organised to prevent the movement of large bodies of German troops along the coast roads from Ostend to Nieuport to support the left flank of the Belgian Army and to prevent any movement by sea of the enemy's troops.

Operations commenced during the night of October 17th when the "Attentive" flying my flag accompanied by the monitors "Severn", "Humber" and "Mersey" the light cruiser "Foresight" and several torpedo boat destroyers, arrived and anchored off Nieuport Pier.

Early on the morning of the 18th October information was received that German infantry were advancing on Westende village, and that a battery was in action at Westende Barns. The flotilla at once proceeded up past Westende and Middlekirke to draw the fire and endeavour to silence the guns.

A brisk shrapnel fire was opened from the shore which was immediately replied to and this commenced the naval operations on the coast which continued for more than three weeks without intermission.

During the first week the enemy's troops were endeavouring to push forward along the coast roads and a large accumulation of transport existed within reach of the naval guns.

On October 18th machine guns from the "Severn" were landed at Nieuport to assist in the defence, and Lieutenant E.S. Wise fell gallantly leading his men.

The "Amazon", flying my flag was badly holed on the waterline and was sent to England for repairs and during these early days most of the vessels suffered casualties, chiefly from shrapnel shell from the field guns of the enemy.

The presence of the ships on the coast soon caused alterations in the enemy's plans, less and less of their troops were seen, while more and more heavy guns were gradually mounted among the sand dunes that fringe the coast.

It soon became evident that more and heavier guns were required in the flotilla. The Scouts therefore returned to England, while H.M.S. "Venerable" and several older cruisers, sloops and gunboats arrived to carry on the operations.

Five French torpedo-boat destroyers were placed under my orders by Admiral Favereau, and on the 30th October I had the honour of hoisting my flag in the "Intrepide," and leading the French flotilla into action off Lombartzyde. The greatest harmony and enthusiasm existed between the allied flotillas.

As the heavier guns of the enemy came into play it was inevitable that the casualties of the flotilla increased, the most important being the disablement of the 6-inch turret and several shots on the waterline of the "Mersey," the death of the Commanding Officer and eight men and the disablement of 16 others in the "Falcon," which vessel came under a heavy fire when guarding the "Venerable" against submarine attack; the "Wildfire" and "Vestal" were badly holed, and a number of casualties caused in the "Brilliant" and "Rinaldo."

Enemy submarines were seen and torpedoes were fired, and during the latter part of the operations the work of the torpedo craft was chiefly confined to the protection of the larger ships.

It gradually became apparent that the rush of the enemy along the coast had been checked, that the operations were developing into a trench warfare, and that the work of the flotilla had, for the moment, ceased.

The arrival of allied reinforcements and the inundation of the country surrounding Nieuport rendered the further presence of the ships unnecessary.

The work of the squadron was much facilitated by the efforts of Colonel Bridges, attached to the Belgian Headquarters, and to him I am greatly indebted for his constant and unfailing support.

I would like especially to bring to your notice:-

Captaine de fregate Richard, of the "Dunois," Senior Officer of the French flotilla, whose courtesy and gallantry assisted to make the operations a success.

Captain C.D. Johnson, M.V.O., in charge of 6th Destroyer Flotilla.

Commander Eric J.A. Fullerton, in command of the monitors, whose ships were constantly engaged in the inshore fighting.

Commander A.D.M. Cherry, of the "Vestal," who commanded the sloops, which were constantly engaged for the whole period. He remained in command of the flotilla after my departure on 7th November, and continued the bombardment on 8th November, returing to England the next day.

Commander H.C. Halahan, of the "Bustard," whose gunboat was constantly in action close to the shore.

Commander A.L. Snagge, of the "Humber."

Commander H.G.L. Oliphant, of the "Amazon."

Lieutenant-Commander R.A. Wilson, of the "Mersey."

Lieutenant-Commander G.L.D. Gibbs, of the "Crusader," in which ship my flag was hoisted during most of the operations.

Lieutenant-Commander J.B. Adams, R.N.R., on my staff.

Lieutenant H.O. Wauton, of the "Falcon," who maintained his position in a heavy fire on the look-out for submarines, and was unfortunately killed.

Lieutenant H.O. Joyce, of the "Vestal," who was badly wounded by a shell, but rallied his men to attend to the wounded, and then got his gun again into action.

Sub-Lieutenant C.J.H. DuBoulay, of the "Falcon," who took command of his ship after the Captain and 24 men were killed and wounded.

Petty-Officer Robert Chappell, O.N. 207788, of the "Falcon," who, though both legs were shattered and he was dying, continued to try and assist in the tending of the wounded. He shortly afterwards died of his wounds.

Petty-Officer Fredk. William Motteram, of the "Falcon," O.N. 183216, for immediate attention to the wounded under fire on 28th October.

Able Seaman Ernest Dimmock, of the "Falcon," O.N. 204549, who directly the casualties occurred in "Falcon," finding himself the only person unwounded on deck, went immediately to the helm and conned the ship.

Herbert Edward Sturman, of the "Mersey," Boy, 1st class O.N.J. 24887, who, when wounded by shrapnel, continued to serve the guns.

Leading Seaman John Thos. Knott, O.N.J. 1186, of the "Brilliant," who, when all men at his gun being killed or wounded, and himself severely wounded, endeavoured to fight his gun.

The following are specially recommended by their Commanding Officers for their good behaviour and coolness under fire:-

Chief Engine Room Artificer William Ernest Brading, of the "Falcon," O.N. 268579.

Private R.M.L.I. Alfred J. Foster, of the "Brilliant," O.N. Ch./10605.

Petty-Officer Sydney Edric Murphy, of the "Mersey," O.N. 190841.
Petty-Officer Henry Sayce, of the "Mersey," O.N. 132956.
Herbert Edward Sturman (Boy), of the "Mersey," O.N.J. 24887.
Leading Signalman Cyril Henry Swan, of the "Sirius," R.F.R., O.N. 230592.
Petty-Officer James Weatherhead, of the "Rinaldo," O.N. 127747.
Leading Seaman John Keane, of the "Rinaldo," O.N. 204128.
Private R.M.L.I. Joseph Martin, of the "Humber" (who landed with Marine detachment), O.N. Ch./15582.
Stoker, 1st, Samuel Johnston, of the "Humber," O.N. Ch./282822 (R.F.R. Ch.B. 4090).
Petty-Officer Robt. Frederick Jennings, of the "Vestal," O.N. 157343 (R.F.R. Po. B. 1481).
Petty-Officer Charles Henry Sutton, of the "Vestal" O.N. 158086.
Leading Seaman Frederick Stanley Woodruff, of the "Vestal," O.N. 237062.
Able Seaman William Chapman, of the "Vestal," O.N. 183312 (R.F.R. Po. B. 1666).
Officer's Steward James Whiteman, of the "Vestal," O.N. L. 1275.
I beg to append a list of the vessels engaged.

I have the honour to be, Sir,
Your obedient servant,
HORACE HOOD,
Rear-Admiral, Dover Patrol.
The Secretary of the Admiralty.

9

OPERATIONS AGAINST SMS *KONIGSBERG*, 1915

WEDNESDAY, 8 DECEMBER, 1915.

Admiralty, 8th December, 1915.

The following Despatch has been received from the Commander-in-Chief, Cape of Good Hope Station:-

"Challenger,"
15th July, 1915.

Sir, – Be pleased to lay before their Lordships the following report of the operations against, the "Königsberg" on the 6th and 11th instant:-

In accordance with orders issued by me, the various vessels concerned took up their appointed stations on the 5th July, in readiness for the operations on the following day.

At 4.15 a.m. on the 6th July, H.M.S. "Severn," Captain Eric J.A. Fullerton, R.N., and H.M.S. "Mersey," Commander Robert A. Wilson, weighed and proceeded across the bar into the Kikunja branch of the Rufiji river, which they entered about 5.20 a.m.

The "Severn" was anchored head and stern and fire was opened on the "Königsberg" by 6.30 a.m. The "Mersey" was similarly moored and opened fire shortly after.

Both Monitors were fired on with 3-pounders, pom-poms and machine-guns when entering the river and on their way up, and they replied to the fire.

At 5.25 a.m. an aeroplane, with Flight-Commander Harold E.M. Watkins as pilot, and carrying six bombs, left the aerodrome on Mafia Island. The bombs were dropped at the "Königsberg" with the intention of hampering any interference she might attempt with the Monitors while they were getting into position.

At 5.40 a.m. another aeroplane, with Flight-Commander John T. Cull as pilot, and

Flight Sub-Lieutenant Harwood J. Arnold as observer, left the aerodrome for the purpose of spotting for the Monitors.

At 5.45 a.m. I transferred my Flag to the "Weymouth," Captain Denis B. Crampton, M.V.O., and at 6.30 a.m. proceeded across the bar, with the Whalers "Echo" and "Fly" sweeping, and the "Childers" sounding ahead; the "Pyramus," Commander Viscount Kelburn, being in company.

The "Weymouth" grounded on the bar for a few minutes on the way across, but soon came off with the rising tide, and advanced as far as the entrance to the river, where she anchored.

Fire from small guns was opened on her, and on the Whalers, from the shore, but beyond one shell, which struck the "Fly," no damage was sustained. A few rounds from the 6-inch guns put a stop to the firing, although it was impossible to locate the position of the guns owing to their being concealed amongst the trees and dense undergrowth.

After anchoring, the "Weymouth" did what was possible to assist the Monitors by bombarding at long range a position at Pemba, where a spotting and observation station was supposed to be, and by keeping down the enemy's fire at the aeroplanes. This was done very effectively.

At the same time the "Pioneer," Commander (Acting) Thomas W. Biddlecombe, R.A.N., under the orders of "Hyacinth," Captain David M. Anderson, M.V.O., engaged the defences at the Ssimba Uranga Mouth, her fire being returned until the defences were silenced.

Returning to the operations of the Monitors; fire was opened, as before stated, at 6.30 a.m., but as the "Königsberg" was out of sight it was very difficult to obtain satisfactory results, and the difficulties of the observers in the aeroplanes in marking the fall of the shots which fell amongst the trees were very great, and made systematic shooting most difficult.

There being only two aeroplanes available, considerable intervals elapsed between the departure of one and the arrival of its relief from the aerodrome 30 miles distant, and this resulted in a loss of shooting efficiency.

At 12.35 one of the aeroplanes broke down, and at 3.50 the second one also. I signalled to Captain Fullerton to move further up the river, which he did, until about 12.50 the tops of the "Königsberg's" masts were visible.

The "Königsberg" kept up a heavy fire on the Monitors until about 12.30, when her fire slackened. At 2.40 p.m. she ceased firing, having for some time limited her fire to one gun. At 3.30 p.m. the Monitors ceased fire, and retired out of the river, rejoining my Flag off Koma Island at 6 p.m. On their way out they were again attacked by the small guns from the banks.

I had returned over the bar in "Weymouth" at 12.30 p.m., and transferred to "Hyacinth" at 3.0 p.m.

The "Mersey" had four men killed and four wounded, two of whom have since died, and her foremost 6-in. gun, at which most of the casualties occurred, was put out of action. The "Severn" fortunately suffered no losses or damage.

The various ships, whalers, tugs, &c., anchored for the night off the Delta, and proceeded to their various stations for coaling, &c., the following morning.

In view of the many difficulties in the way, and the heavy and accurate fire to which the monitors were subjected, I consider that the operations on 6th July, though not a complete and final success, are creditable to Captain Fullerton and Commander Wilson.

As it was necessary to make a fresh attack on the "Königsberg" to complete her destruction, further operations were carried out on the 11th July, by which date the aeroplanes were again ready for service, and the monitors had made good certain defects and completed with coal.

I reinforced the crew of the "Severn" by Acting Sub-Lieutenant Arthur G. Mack, with six Petty Officers and men; and the crew of the "Mersey" by Lieutenant Richard Ussher and Lieutenant Rundle B. Watson, with six Petty Officers and men. All the above were drawn from "Hyacinth."

The attack was carried out on the same lines as on the previous occasion, and the same mouth of the river was used.

The monitors crossed the bar at 11.45 a.m., followed up to the entrance by "Weymouth" and "Pyramus," the latter proceeding three miles inside, and both searching the banks. "Hyacinth" and "Pioneer" bombarded the Ssimba Uranga entrance.

On this occasion the monitors did not fire simultaneously; the "Mersey" remained under way, and fired while "Severn" moored, and ceased fire when "Severn" commenced.

The "Severn" was moored in a position 1,000 yards closer to the enemy than on the 6th July, which made her fire much more effective.

The observers in the aeroplanes, by their excellent spotting, soon got the guns on the target, and hit after hit was rapidly signalled. At 12.50 it was reported that the "Königsberg" was on fire.

As previously arranged with Captain Fullerton, as soon as they had got the situation well in hand, the monitors moved up the river, and completed the destruction of the "Königsberg" by 2.30 p.m., when I ordered them to withdraw.

The "Königsberg" is now a complete wreck, having suffered from shells, fire and explosions, several of which latter were observed.

The only casualties sustained were three men slightly wounded in the "Mersey." There were no casualties in "Severn."

By 8.0 p.m. all ships, except those detached on patrol, had returned.

I have much pleasure in bringing to the notice of their Lordships the names of the following Officers and men:-

Captain Eric J.A. Fullerton, H.M.S. "Severn."
Commander Robert A. Wilson, H.M.S. "Mersey."
Captain Denis B. Crampton, M.V.O., H.M.S. "Weymouth."
Commander The Hon. Robert O.B. Bridgeman.
Squadron Commander Robert Gordon, in command of the Air Squadron.
Flight Commander John T. Cull.
Flight Lieutenant Vivian G. Blackburn.
Flight Sub-Lieutenant Harwood J. Arnold.
Flight Lieutenant Harold E.M. Watkins.

Assistant Paymaster Harold G. Badger, H.M.S. "Hyacinth." This Officer volunteered to observe during the first attack on the "Königsberg," though he had had no previous experience of flying.

Acting Lieutenant Alan G. Bishop, Royal Marine Light Infantry, of H.M.S. "Hyacinth." This Officer volunteered to observe during the second attack on the "Königsberg," though he had had no previous experience of flying.

Air Mechanic Ebenezer Henry Alexander Boggis, Chatham 14849, who went up on the 25th April with Flight Commander Cull, and photographed the "Königsberg" at a height of 700 feet. They were heavily fired on, and the engine of the machine was badly damaged.

Most serious risks have been run by the officers and men who have flown in this climate, where the effect of the atmosphere and the extreme heat of the sun are quite unknown to those whose flying experience is limited to moderate climates. "Bumps" of 250 feet have been experienced several times, and the temperature varies from extreme cold when flying at a height to a great heat, with burning, tropical sun, when on land.

In the operations against the "Königsberg" on the 6th July both the *personnel* and *materiel* of the Royal Naval Air Service were worked to the extreme limit of endurance. The total distance covered by the two available aeroplanes on that date was no less than 950 miles, and the time in the air, working watch and watch, was 13 hours.

I will sum up by saying that the Flying Officers, one and all, have earned my highest commendations.

Chief Carpenter William J. Leverett, H.M.S. "Hyacinth." This Officer was in charge of the fitting out of the two Monitors.

I also desire to bring to their Lordships' notice the Master of the tug "Revenger," John Osment Richards, and the following members of her crew, who most readily volunteered to serve in their tug and to proceed into the river to the assistance of the Monitors and tow them out if necessary:-

Frank Walker, Navigating Master.
George Edward Milton, Mate.
Frederick James Kennedy, Chief Engineer.
Lewis John Hills, Second Engineer.
Sidney Robert Rayner, Third Engineer.

The four tugs "Blackcock," "Revenger," "Sarah Joliffe," and "T.A. Joliffe" were manned by Naval Officers and men, with the exception of the above named, and although their services were not called for I consider the example they set was most praiseworthy.

I have the honour to be,
Sir,
Your obedient servant,
H. KING HALL,
Vice-Admiral,
Commander in Chief.

10

DOVER PATROL, OPERATIONS OFF THE BELGIAN COAST, AUGUST-NOVEMBER 1915

WEDNESDAY, 12 JANUARY, 1916.

Admiralty, 12th January, 1916.

The following Despatch has been received from Vice Admiral Reginald H.S. Bacon, K.C.B., C.V.O., D.S.O., commanding the Dover Patrol, reporting the operations off the Belgian coast between 22nd August and 19th November 1915-

Office of Vice Admiral,
Dover,
3rd December, 1915.

SIR-

In the summer and autumn of this year circumstances enabled offensive operations to be undertaken from the sea at certain points on the Belgian Coast. It is unnecessary to enter into the reasons for the various operations or the exact objectives attacked, since these are well known to Their Lordships.

In all cases great care has been taken to confine the fire of the guns to objectives of military or naval importance, so as to inflict the minimum of loss of life and distress on the civil population, the larger number of whom are our allies. In order to carry this principle into effect, it has at times been necessary to modify and even postpone projected attacks. The results therefore have been effective rather than sensational.

On the evening of the 22nd August I sailed with H.M. Ships "Sir John Moore"

(Commander S.B. Miller R.N.), "Lord Clive" (Commander N.H. Carter R.N.), "Prince Rupert" (Commander H.O. Remold, R.N.), and 76 other vessels and auxiliaries and on the following morning attacked the harbour and defences of Zeebrugge. The results were markedly successful all the objectives selected were damaged or destroyed.

It was satisfactory that extreme accuracy was obtained with the gun fire at the long ranges necessary for the best attack of such defences. This accuracy fully justifies the novel methods used and the careful training in attention to details to which the vessels are subjected. A similar organisation was employed in subsequent attacks.

On the 6th September I attacked Ostende with five monitors including "General Craufurd" (Commander E. Altham R.N.) and "M.25" (Lieutenant-Commander B.H. Ramsay, R.N.), and damage was done to submarine workshops and harbour works. The enemy returned our fire with heavy guns of calibre probably larger than our own, and with considerable accuracy. Again the shooting on the part of our vessels was remarkably good, and the assistance rendered by the Auxiliary Craft most valuable.

On the same day Westende was subjected to attack by H.M. Ships "Redoubtable" (Captain V.B. Molteno, R.N.), "Bustard" (Lieutenant O.H.K. Maguire, R.N.), and "Excellent" (Commander G.L. Saurin, R.N.), under the direction of Captain V.B. Molteno, and with results that reflected credit on all concerned.

On the 19th September, with several of the vessels, including H.M.S. "Marshal Ney"(Captain H.J. Tweedie, R.N.), I carried out an attack against certain defences in the neighbourhood of Middlekirke, Raversyde and Westende, which resulted in damaging and silencing the batteries. Valuable co-operation was received from the French batteries in the vicinity of Nieuport.

On the evening of the 24th September, I despatched H.M.S. "Prince Eugene" (Captain E. Wigram, R.N.) and one other monitor and the requisite auxiliary craft to bombard the following morning the coast of Knocke, Heyst, Zeebrugge and Blankenberghe (east of Ostende), while with the other vessels, including H.M.S. "Lord Clive" (Commander G.R.B. Blount, R.N.), on the same day I carried out an attack on the fortified positions west of that place. Again, during these attacks, considerable damage was done.

On the 26th, 27th and 30th September I made further attacks on the various batteries and strong positions at Middlekirke and Westende.

On the evening of the 2nd October I sailed with four monitors, and again attacked with satisfactory results the batteries at Zeebrugge on the morning of the 3rd. The whole coast during our passage was showing signs of considerable alarm and unrest as a result of the previous operations. Our advanced vessels were attacked by submarine boats, but without result.

On the 6th, 12th, 13th and 18th October and 16th-19th November other batteries or positions of military value have been attacked by the vessels under my command.

Up to the present, therefore, concerted operations of considerable magnitude have been carried out on six occasions, and on eight other days attacks on a smaller scale on fortified positions have taken place. The accuracy of the enemy's fire has been good.

The damage inflicted on the enemy is known to include the sinking of one torpedo boat, two submarines and one large dredger, the total destruction of three military factories and damage to a fourth, extensive damage to the locks at Zeebrugge and the destruction of thirteen guns of considerable calibre, in addition to the destruction of two ammunition depôts and several military storehouses, observation stations and signalling posts, damage to wharves, moles and other secondary places. Further, a considerable number of casualties are known to have been suffered by the enemy.

I regret that three vessels were lost during the operations:-

H.M. Armed Yacht "Sanda," sunk by gunfire;
H.M. Drifter "Great Heart," sunk by mine;
H.M. Mine Sweeper "Brighton Queen," sunk by mine.

Our total casualties numbered 34 killed and 24 wounded, which, considering the dangers to which the vessels were exposed by gun fire, aircraft, submarine boats and mines on an enemy's coast, may be looked upon as comparatively small in proportion to the number of officers and men taking part in the operations.

It is with regret that, among others, I have to report the death of Lieutenant-Commander H. T. Gartside-Tipping, R.N., of the Armed Yacht "Sanda," who was the oldest naval officer afloat. In spite of his advanced age, he rejoined, and with undemonstrative patriotism served at sea as a Lieutenant-Commander.

I cannot speak too highly of the manner in which the officers and men under my command have carried out the duties allotted to them. The work has been varied, and to a great extent novel, but in all particulars it has been entered into with a zeal and enthusiasm which could not have been surpassed. The gunnery results have exceeded my expectations.

Their Lordships will appreciate the difficulties attendant on the cruising in company by day and night under war conditions of a fleet of 80 vessels comprising several widely different classes, manned partly by trained naval ratings but more largely by officers of the Naval Reserve, whose fleet training has necessarily been scant, and by men whose work in life has hitherto been that of deep sea fishermen.

The protection of such a moving fleet by the destroyers in waters which are the natural home of the enemy's submarines has been admirable, and justifies the training and organisation of the personnel of the flotilla. But more remarkable still, in my opinion, is the aptitude shown by the officers and crews of the drifters and trawlers, who in difficult waters, under conditions totally strange to them, have maintained their allotted stations without a single accident. Moreover, these men under fire have exhibited a coolness well worthy of the personnel of a service inured by discipline. The results show how deeply sea adaptability is ingrained in the seafaring race of these islands.

It is to the excellent work done by the destroyers under Commodore C.D. Johnson, M.V.O., and the drifters under Captain F.G. Bird, that I ascribe our immunity from loss by submarine attack. The mine sweepers, under Commander W.G. Rigg, R.N., have indefatigably carried out their dangerous duties.

Throughout these operations attacks have been made on our vessels by the enemy's aircraft, but latterly the vigilance of our Dunkirk Aerodrome, under Wing-Commander A.M. Longmore, has considerably curtailed their activity.

I wish specially to mention the cordial assistance always tendered to me by the Vice-Admiral Favereau, Commanding the French Second Light Cruiser Squadron, whose patrol vessels under Commander Saillard have assisted to protect our ships from submarine dangers. In doing this, I regret to say, their patrols have lost three vessels and several gallant lives.

I would also bring to Their Lordships' attention the great assistance rendered to me by Brigadier-General T. Bridges, C.B., attached to the Belgian Mission.

Captain H.W. Bowring, throughout these operations, has acted most ably as my Chief of the Staff.

I have the honour to be,

Sir,

Your obedient Servant,

R.H. BACON,

Vice-Admiral, Dover Patrol.

The Secretary of the

Admiralty.

11

DOVER PATROL, OPERATIONS OFF THE BELGIAN COAST, DECEMBER 1915-MAY 1916

TUESDAY, 25 JULY, 1916.

Admiralty, 25th July, 1916.

The following despatch has been received from Vice-Admiral Sir Reginald H. S. Bacon, K.C.B., C.V.O., D.S.O., commanding the Dover Patrol, reporting the operations of the Dover Patrol since 3rd Dec. 1915:-

Office of the Vice-Admiral,
Dover,
29th May, 1916.

Sir,

Since my last Despatch to their Lordships on 3rd December, 1915, the varied duties of this Patrol have been carried out with unremitting energy on the part of the Officers and men under my command.

During the winter months offensive operations on the Belgian Coast were much impeded by the shortness of the daylight hours and by gales of wind and bad weather. These same factors that impeded offensive action facilitated the work of the enemy in laying mines and in attacking our commerce in these narrow waters, since it assisted them to elude our patrols of protective vessels.

The Services of the Dover Patrol can be best appreciated from the following facts:-

Over 21,000 Merchant Ships, apart from Men-of-War and Auxiliaries, have passed through this Patrol in the last six months. Of these twenty-one have been lost or have been seriously damaged by the enemy. The losses in Merchant Vessels, therefore, have been less than one per thousand. On the other hand, to effect this very considerable security to our Merchant Shipping I regret that over 4 per cent. of our Patrol Vessels have been sunk and the lives of 77 Officers and men lost to the Nation. No figures could emphasise more thoroughly the sacrifice made by the personnel of the Patrol and the relative immunity ensured to the commerce of their country.

Besides the foregoing the Patrol assists in the protection of the flank of all the sea Transport to and from our Army in France. The number of vessels that have passed and also of the troops that have been carried are known to Their Lordships, but it is well to call attention to the fact that this vast transport of troops has been so thoroughly safeguarded that not one single life has been lost during the sea passage.

The work of the Destroyer Flotilla throughout the winter has been incessant and arduous and thoroughly well carried out.

Certain opportunities have arisen of bombarding the enemy's positions in Belgium. On these occasions the necessary minor operations have been carried out.

In addition to the daily reconnaissance and protective work performed by the Royal Naval Air Service on the coast, eleven organised attacks against the enemy's Aerodromes and thirteen attacks on enemy vessels have been carried out. Nine enemy machines and one submarine have been destroyed by air attack and appreciable damage has been inflicted on military adjuncts.

The services rendered by the Naval Airmen in Flanders, under Acting Captain Lambe, have been most valuable.

It is equally advantageous to maintain the offensive in the air as it is to do so on land or at sea. It is with considerable satisfaction, therefore, that I am able to report that, with only one exception, all the aeroplanes destroyed were fought over the enemy's territory and that all the seaplanes were brought down into waters off the enemy's coast.

The advent of spring weather has lately enabled me to take measures to limit the extent to which the submarine and other vessels of the enemy had free access to the waters off the Belgian coast.

The success achieved has, so far, been considerable, and the activities of submarines operating from the Belgian Coast have been much reduced.

We have destroyed several of the enemy's submarines and some of his surface vessels.

Our losses, I regret to say, were four Officers killed, one wounded; men: 22 killed, two wounded.

It is to the energy and endurance of the Officers and men of the vessels that have been employed, and who are now daily on patrol that the success of these operations has been due. Whether of our Royal Navy, of the French Navy, of our Mercantile

Marine or our Fishermen, all have exhibited those qualities most valued at sea in time of war.

My cordial thanks are due to Rear-Admiral de Marliave for the hearty co-operation he has afforded me during the whole of the foregoing period.

During these operations I was afforded much assistance by Commodore R. Tyrwhitt, C.B., Commodore C.D. Johnson, M.V.O., D.S.O., and Captain F.S. Litchfield-Speer, as well as Commandant Excelman, of the French Navy.

Captain H.W. Bowring, D.S.O., acted most ably as Chief of my Staff throughout the operations.

Enclosed is a list of Officers and men I desire to bring to their Lordships' notice for distinguished and meritorious services, in addition to those of the Auxiliary patrol and Royal Naval Air Service previously specially forwarded by me during the period under report.

I have the honour to be,
Sir,
Your obedient Servant,
(Sd.) R.H. BACON,
Vice-Admiral Dover Patrol.
The Secretary of the Admiralty.

12

THE BATTLE OF JUTLAND, 31 MAY-1 JUNE 1916

THURSDAY, 6 JULY, 1916.

Admiralty, 6th July, 1916.

The following Despatch has been received from Admiral Sir John Jellicoe, G.C.B., G.C.V.O., Commander-in-Chief, Grand Fleet, reporting the action in the North Sea on 31st May, 1916*:-

"Iron Duke,"
24th June, 1916.

SIR, – Be pleased to inform the Lords Commissioners of the Admiralty that the German High Sea Fleet was brought to action on 31st May, 1916, to the westward of the Jutland Bank, off the coast of Denmark.

The ships of the Grand Fleet, in pursuance of the general policy of periodical sweeps through the North Sea, had left its bases on the previous day, in accordance with instructions issued by me.

In the early afternoon of Wednesday, 31 May, the 1st and 2nd Battle-cruiser Squadrons,1st, 2nd and 3rd Light-cruiser Squadrons and destroyers from the 1st, 9th, 10th and 13th Flotillas, supported by the 5th Battle Squadron, were, in accordance with my directions, scouting to the southward of the Battle Fleet, which was accompanied by the 3rd Battle-cruiser Squadron, 1st and 2nd Cruiser Squadrons, 4th Light-cruiser Squadron, 4th, 11th and 12th Flotillas.

The junction of the Battle Fleet with the scouting force after the enemy had been sighted was delayed owing to the southerly course steered by our advanced force during the first hour after commencing their action with the enemy battle-cruisers.

This was, of course, unavoidable, as had our battle-cruisers not followed the enemy to the southward the main fleets would never have been in contact.

The Battle-cruiser Fleet, gallantly led by Vice-Admiral Sir David Beatty, K.C.B., M.V.O., D.S.O., and admirably supported by the ships of the Fifth Battle Squadron under Rear-Admiral Hugh Evan-Thomas, M.V.O., fought an action under, at times, disadvantageous conditions, especially in regard to light, in a manner that was in keeping with the best traditions of the service.

The following extracts from the report of Sir David Beatty give the course of events before the Battle Fleet came upon the scene:-

"At 2.20 p.m. reports were received from 'Galatea' (Commodore Edwyn S. Alexander Sinclair, M.V.O., A.D.C.), indicating the presence of enemy vessels. The direction of advance was immediately altered to S.S.E., the course for Horn Reef, so as to place my force between the enemy and his base.

"At 2.35 p.m. a considerable amount of smoke was sighted to the eastward. This made it clear that the enemy was to the northward and eastward, and that it would be impossible for him to round the Horn Reef without being brought to action. Course was accordingly altered to the eastward and subsequently to north-eastward, the enemy being sighted at 3.31 p.m. Their force consisted of five battle-cruisers.

"After the first report of the enemy, the 1st and 3rd Light Cruiser Squadrons changed their direction, and, without waiting for orders, spread to the east, thereby forming a screen in advance of the Battle Cruiser Squadrons and 5th Battle Squadron by the time we had hauled up to the course of approach. They engaged enemy light cruisers at long range. In the meantime the 2nd Light Cruiser Squadron had come in at high speed, and was able to take station ahead of the battle cruisers by the time we turned to E.S.E., the course on which we first engaged the enemy. In this respect the work of the Light Cruiser Squadrons was excellent, and of great value.

"From a report from 'Galatea' at 2.25 p.m. it was evident that the enemy force was considerable, and not merely an isolated unit of light cruisers, so at 2.45 p.m. I ordered 'Engadine' (Lieutenant-Commander C.G. Robinson) to send up a seaplane and scout to N.N.E. This order was carried out very quickly, and by 3.8 p.m. a seaplane, with Flight Lieutenant F J. Rutland, R.N., as pilot, and Assistant Paymaster G.S. Trewin, R.N., as observer, was well under way; her first reports of the enemy were received in 'Engadine' about 3.30 p.m. Owing to clouds it was necessary to fly very low, and in order to identify four enemy light cruisers the seaplane had to fly at a height of 900 feet within 3,000 yards of them, the light cruisers opening fire on her with every gun that would bear. This in no way interfered with the clarity of their reports, and both Flight Lieutenant Rutland and Assistant Paymaster Trewin are to be congratulated on their achievement, which indicates that seaplanes under such circumstances are of distinct value.

"At 3.30 p.m. I increased speed to 25 knots, and formed line of battle, the 2nd Battle Cruiser Squadron forming astern of the 1st Battle Cruiser Squadron, with destroyers of the 13th and 9th Flotillas taking station ahead. I turned to E.S.E. slightly converging on the enemy, who were now at a range of 23,000 yards, and formed the ships on a line of bearing to clear the smoke. The 5th Battle Squadron, who had conformed to our movements, were now bearing N.N.W., 10,000 yards. The visibility at this time was good, the sun behind us and the wind S.E. Being between the enemy and his base, our situation was both tactically and strategically good.

"At 3.48 p.m. the action commenced at a range of 18,500 yards, both forces opening fire practically simultaneously. Course was altered to the southward, and subsequently the mean direction was S.S.E., the enemy steering a parallel course distant about 18,000 to 14,500 yards.

"At 4.8 p.m. the 5th Battle Squadron came into action and opened fire at a range of 20,000 yards. The enemy's fire now seemed to slacken. The destroyer 'Landrail' (Lieutenant-Commander Francis E.H.G. Hobart), of 9th Flotilla, who was on our port beam, trying to take station ahead, sighted the periscope of a submarine on her port quarter. Though causing considerable inconvenience from smoke, the presence of 'Lydiard' (Commander Malcolm L. Goldsmith) and 'Landrail' undoubtedly preserved the battle-cruisers from closer submarine attack. 'Nottingham' (Captain Charles B. Miller) also reported a submarine on the starboard beam.

"Eight destroyers of the 13th Flotilla, 'Nestor' (Commander the Hon. Edward B.S. Bingham), 'Nomad'(Lieutenant-Commander Paul Whitfield), 'Nicator' (Lieutenant Jack E.A. Mocatta), 'Narborough' (Lieutenant-Commander Geoffrey Corlett), 'Pelican' (Lieutenant-Commander Kenneth A. Beattie), 'Petard' (Lieutenant-Commander Evelyn C.O. Thomson), 'Obdurate' (Lieutenant-Commander Cecil H.H. Sams), 'Nerissa' (Lieutenant-Commander Montague C.B. Legge), with 'Moorsom' (Commander John C. Hodgson), and 'Morris' (Lieutenant-Commander Edward S. Graham), of 10th Flotilla, 'Turbulent' (Lieutenant-Commander Dudley Stuart), and 'Termagant' (Lieutenant-Commander Cuthbert P. Blake), of the 9th Flotilla, having been ordered to attack the enemy with torpedoes when opportunity offered, moved out at 4.15 p.m., simultaneously with a similar movement on the part of the enemy Destroyers. The attack was carried out in the most gallant manner, and with great determination. Before arriving at a favourable position to fire torpedoes, they intercepted an enemy force consisting of a light-cruiser and fifteen destroyers. A fierce engagement ensued at close quarters, with the result that the enemy were forced to retire on their battle-cruisers, having lost two destroyers sunk, and having their torpedo attack frustrated. Our destroyers sustained no loss in this engagement, but their attack on the enemy battle-cruisers was rendered less effective, owing to some of the destroyers having dropped astern during the fight. Their position was therefore unfavourable for torpedo attack.

" 'Nestor,' 'Nomad' and 'Nicator,' gallantly led by Commander the Hon. Edward B.S. Bingham, of Nestor,' pressed home their attack on the battle-cruisers and fired two torpedoes at them, being subjected to a heavy fire from the enemy's secondary armament. 'Nomad' was badly hit, and apparently remained stopped between the lines. Subsequently 'Nestor' and 'Nicator' altered course to the S.E., and in a short time, the opposing battle-cruisers having turned 16 points, found themselves within close range of a number of enemy battleships. Nothing daunted, though under a terrific fire, they stood on, and their position being favourable for torpedo attack fired a torpedo at the second ship of the enemy line at a range of 3,000 yards. Before they could fire their fourth torpedo, 'Nestor' was badly hit and swung to starboard, 'Nicator' altering course inside her to avoid collision, and thereby being prevented from firing the last torpedo. 'Nicator' made good her escape, and subsequently rejoined the Captain (D), 13th Flotilla. 'Nestor' remained stopped, but was afloat when last seen. 'Moorsom' also carried out an attack on the enemy's battle fleet.

" 'Petard,' 'Nerissa,' 'Turbulent', and 'Termagant' also pressed home their attack on the enemy battle-cruisers, firing torpedoes after the engagement with enemy destroyers. 'Petard' reports that all her torpedoes must have crossed the enemy's line, while 'Nerissa' states that one torpedo appeared to strike the rear ship. These destroyer attacks were indicative of the spirit pervading His Majesty's Navy, and were worthy of its highest traditions. I propose to bring to your notice a recommendation of Commander Bingham and other Officers for some recognition of their conspicuous gallantry.

"From 4.15 to 4.43 p.m. the conflict between the opposing battle-cruisers was of a very fierce and resolute character. The 5th Battle Squadron was engaging the enemy's rear ships, unfortunately at very long range. Our fire began to tell, the accuracy and rapidity of that of the enemy, depreciating considerably. At 4.18 p.m. the third enemy ship was seen to be on fire. The visibility to the north-eastward had become considerably reduced, and the outline of the ships very indistinct.

"At 4.38 p m. 'Southampton' (Commodore William E. Goodenough, M.V.O., A.D.C.) reported the enemy's Battle Fleet ahead. The destroyers were recalled, and at 4.42 p.m. the enemy's Battle Fleet was sighted S.E. Course was altered 16 points in succession to starboard, and I proceeded on a northerly course to lead them towards the Battle Fleet. The enemy battle-cruisers altered course shortly afterwards, and the action continued. 'Southampton,' with the 2nd Light-cruiser Squadron, held on to the southward to observe. They closed to within 13,000 yards of the enemy Battle Fleet, and came under a very heavy but ineffective fire. 'Southampton's' reports were most valuable. The 5th Battle Squadron were now closing on an opposite course and engaging the enemy battle-cruisers with all guns. The position of the enemy Battle Fleet was communicated to them, and I ordered them to alter course 16 points. Led by Rear-Admiral Evan-Thomas, in 'Barham' (Captain Arthur W. Craig), this squadron supported us brilliantly and effectively.

"At 4.57 p.m. the 5th Battle Squadron turned up astern of me and came under the fire of the leading ships of the enemy Battle Fleet. 'Fearless' (Captain (D) Charles D. Roper), with the destroyers of 1st Flotilla, joined the battle-cruisers, and, when speed admitted, took station ahead. 'Champion' (Captain (D) James U. Farie), with 13th Flotilla, took station on the 5th Battle Squadron. At 5 p.m. the 1st and 3rd Light-cruiser Squadrons, which had been following me on the southerly course, took station on my starboard bow; the 2nd Light-cruiser Squadron took station on my port quarter.

"The weather conditions now became unfavourable, our ships being silhouetted against a clear horizon to the westward, while the enemy were for the most part obscured by mist, only showing up clearly at intervals. These conditions prevailed until we had turned their van at about 6 p.m. Between 5 and 6 p.m. the action continued on a northerly course, the range being about 14,000 yards. During this time the enemy received very severe punishment, and one of their battle-cruisers quitted the line in a considerably damaged condition. This came under my personal observation, and was corroborated by 'Princess Royal' (Captain Walter H. Cowan, M.V.O., D.S.O.) and 'Tiger' (Captain Henry B. Pelly, M.V.O.). Other enemy ships also showed signs of increasing injury. At 5.5 p.m. 'Onslow' (Lieutenant-Commander John C. Tovey) and 'Moresby' (Lieutenant-Commander Roger V. Alison), who had been detached to assist 'Engadine' with the seaplane, rejoined the battle-cruiser squadrons and took station on the starboard (engaged) bow of 'Lion' (Captain Alfred E.M. Chatfield, C.V.O.). At 5.10 p.m. 'Moresby,' being 2 points before the beam of the leading enemy ship, fired a torpedo at a ship in their line. Eight minutes later she observed a hit with a torpedo on what was judged to be the sixth ship in the line. 'Moresby' then passed between the lines to clear the range of smoke, and rejoined 'Champion.' In corroboration of this, 'Fearless' reports having seen an enemy heavy ship heavily on fire at about 5.10 p.m., and shortly afterwards a huge cloud of smoke and steam.

"At 5.35 p.m. our course was N.N.E., and the estimated position of the Battle Fleet was N. 16 W., so we gradually hauled to the north-eastward, keeping the range of the enemy at 14,000 yards. He was gradually hauling to the eastward, receiving severe punishment at the head of his line, and probably acting on information received from his light-cruisers which had sighted and were engaged with the Third Battle-cruiser Squadron.

"Possibly Zeppelins were present also. At 5.50 p.m. British cruisers were sighted on the port bow, and at 5.56 p.m. the leading battleships of the Battle Fleet, bearing north 5 miles. I thereupon altered course to east, and proceeded at utmost speed. This brought the range of the enemy down to 12,000 yards. I made a report to you that the enemy battle-cruisers bore south-east. At this time only three of the enemy battle-cruisers were visible, closely followed by battleships of the 'Koenig' class.

"At about 6.5 p.m. 'Onslow,' being on the engaged bow of 'Lion,' sighted an enemy light-cruiser at a distance of 6,000 yards from us, apparently endeavouring to attack with torpedoes. 'Onslow' at once closed and engaged her, firing 58 rounds at a range of from 4,000 to 2,000 yards, scoring a number of hits. 'Onslow' then closed the enemy battle-cruisers, and orders were given for all torpedoes to be fired. At this moment she was struck amidships by a heavy shell, with the result that only one torpedo was fired. Thinking that all his torpedoes had gone, the Commanding Officer proceeded to retire at slow speed. Being informed that he still had three torpedoes, he closed with the light-cruiser previously engaged and torpedoed her. The enemy's Battle Fleet was then sighted, and the remaining torpedoes were fired at them and must have crossed the enemy's track. Damage then caused 'Onslow' to stop.

"At 7.15 p.m. 'Defender' (Lieutenant-Commander Lawrence R. Palmer), whose speed had been reduced to 10 knots, while on the disengaged side of the battle-cruisers, by a shell which damaged her foremost boiler, closed 'Onslow' and took her in tow. Shells were falling all round them during this operation, which, however, was successfully accomplished. During the heavy weather of the ensuing night the tow parted twice, but was re-secured. The two struggled on together until 1 p.m. 1st

June, when 'Onslow' was transferred to tugs. I consider the performances of these two destroyers to be gallant in the extreme, and I am recommending Lieutenant-Commander J.C. Tovey, of 'Onslow,' and Lieutenant-Commander L.R. Palmer, of 'Defender,' for special recognition. 'Onslow' was possibly the destroyer referred to by the Rear-Admiral Commanding 3rd Light Cruiser Squadron as follows:- 'Here I should like to bring to your notice the action of a destroyer (name unknown) which we passed close in a disabled condition soon after 6 p.m. She apparently was able to struggle ahead again, and made straight for the 'Derfflinger' to attack her.' "

Proceedings of Battle Fleet and Third Battle Cruiser Squadron.

On receipt of the information that the enemy had been sighted, the British Battle Fleet, with its accompanying cruiser and destroyer force, proceeded at full speed on a S.E.by S. course to close the Battle-cruiser Fleet. During the two hours that elapsed before the arrival of the Battle Fleet on the scene the steaming qualities of the older battleships were severely tested. Great credit is due to the engine-room departments for the manner in which they, as always, responded to the call, the whole Fleet maintaining a speed in excess of the trial speeds of some of the older vessels.

The Third Battle-cruiser Squadron, commanded by Rear-Admiral the Hon. Horace L.A. Hood, C.B., M.V.O., D.S.O., which was in advance of the Battle Fleet, was ordered to reinforce Sir David Beatty. At 5.30 p.m. this squadron observed flashes of gunfire and heard the sound of guns to the south-westward. Rear-Admiral Hood sent the 'Chester' (Captain Robert N. Lawson) to investigate, and this ship engaged three or four enemy light-cruisers at about 5.45 p.m. The engagement lasted for about twenty minutes, during which period Captain Lawson handled his vessel with great skill against heavy odds, and, although the ship suffered considerably in casualties, her fighting and steaming qualities were unimpaired, and at about 6.5 p.m. she rejoined the Third Battle-cruiser Squadron.

The Third Battle-cruiser Squadron had turned to the north-westward, and at 6.10 p.m. sighted our battle-cruisers, the squadron taking station ahead of the 'Lion' at 6.21 p.m. in accordance with the orders of the Vice-Admiral Commanding Battle-cruiser Fleet.

He reports as follows:-

"I ordered them to take station ahead, which was carried out magnificently, Rear-Admiral Hood bringing his squadron into action ahead in a most inspiring manner, worthy of his great naval ancestors. At 6.25 p.m. I altered course to the E.S.E. in support of the Third Battle-cruiser Squadron, who were at this time only 8,000 yards from the enemy's leading ship. They were pouring a hot fire into her and caused her to turn to the westward of south. At the same time I made a report to you of the bearing and distance of the enemy battle-fleet.

"By 6.50 p.m. the battle-cruisers were clear of our leading battle squadron then bearing about N.N.W. 3 miles, and I ordered the Third Battle-cruiser Squadron to prolong the line astern and reduced to 18 knots. The visibility at this time was very indifferent, not more than 4 miles, and the enemy ships were temporarily lost sight of. It is interesting to note that after 6 p.m., although the visibility became reduced, it was undoubtedly more favourable to us than to the enemy. At intervals their ships showed up clearly, enabling us to punish them very severely and establish a definite superiority over them. From the report of other ships and my own observation it was clear that the enemy suffered considerable damage, battle-cruisers and battleships alike. The head of their line was crumpled up, leaving battleships as targets for the majority of our battle-cruisers. Before leaving us the Fifth Battle Squadron was also engaging battleships. The report of Rear-Admiral Evan-Thomas shows that excellent results were obtained, and it can be safely said that his magnificent squadron wrought great execution.

"From the report of Rear-Admiral T.D.W. Napier, M.V.O., the Third Light-cruiser Squadron, which had maintained its station on our starboard bow well ahead of the enemy, at 6.25 p.m. attacked with the torpedo. 'Falmouth' (Captain John D. Edwards) and 'Yarmouth' (Captain Thomas D. Pratt) both fired torpedoes at the leading enemy battle-cruiser, and it is believed that one torpedo hit, as a heavy underwater explosion was observed. The Third Light-cruiser Squadron then gallantly attacked the heavy ships with gunfire, with impunity to themselves, thereby demonstrating that the fighting efficiency of the enemy had been seriously impaired. Rear-Admiral Napier deserves great credit for his determined and effective attack. 'Indomitable' (Captain Francis W. Kennedy) reports that about this time one of the 'Derfflinger' class fell out of the enemy's line."

Meanwhile, at 5.45 p.m., the report of guns had become audible to me, and at 5.55 p.m. flashes were visible from ahead round to the starboard beam, although in the mist no ships could be distinguished, and the position of the enemy's battle fleet could not be determined. The difference in estimated position by "reckoning" between 'Iron Duke' (Captain Frederic C. Dreyer, C.B.) and 'Lion,' which was inevitable under the circumstances, added to the uncertainty of the general situation.

Shortly after 5.55 p.m. some of the cruisers ahead, under Rear-Admirals Herbert L. Heath, M.V.O., and Sir Robert Arbuthnot, Bt., M.V.O., were seen to be in action, and reports received show that 'Defence,' flagship (Captain Stanley V. Ellis), and 'Warrior' (Captain Vincent B. Molteno), of the First Cruiser Squadron, engaged an enemy light-cruiser at this time. She was subsequently observed to sink.

At 6 p.m. 'Canterbury' (Captain Percy M.R. Royds), which ship was in company with the Third Battle Cruiser Squadron, had engaged enemy light-cruisers which were firing heavily on the torpedo-boat destroyer 'Shark' (Commander Loftus W. Jones), 'Acasta' (Lieutenant-Commander John O. Barron), and 'Christopher' (Lieutenant-Commander Fairfax M. Kerr); as a result of this engagement the 'Shark' was sunk.

At 6 p.m. vessels, afterwards seen to be our battle-cruisers, were sighted by 'Marlborough' bearing before the starboard beam of the battle fleet.

At the same time the Vice-Admiral Commanding, Battle-cruiser Fleet, reported to me the position of the enemy battle-cruisers, and at 6.14 p.m. reported the position of the enemy battle fleet.

At this period, when the battle fleet was meeting the battle-cruisers and the Fifth Battle Squadron, great care was necessary to ensure that our own ships were not mistaken for enemy vessels.

I formed the battle fleet in line of battle on receipt of Sir David Beatty's report, and during deployment the fleets became engaged. Sir David Beatty had meanwhile formed the battle-cruisers ahead of the battle fleet.

The divisions of the battle fleet were led by:-

The Commander-in-Chief.
Vice-Admiral Sir Cecil Burney, K.C.B., K.C.M.G.
Vice-Admiral Sir Thomas Jerram, K.C.B.
Vice-Admiral Sir Doveton Sturdee, Bt., K.C.B., C.V.O., C.M.G.
Rear-Admiral Alexander L. Duff, C.B.
Rear-Admiral Arthur C. Leveson, C.B.
Rear-Admiral Ernest F.A. Gaunt, C.M.G.

At 6.16 p.m. 'Defence' and 'Warrior' were observed passing down between the British and German Battle Fleets under a very heavy fire. 'Defence' disappeared, and 'Warrior' passed to the rear disabled.

It is probable that Sir Robert Arbuthnot, during his engagement with the enemy's light-cruisers and in his desire to complete their destruction, was not aware of the approach of the enemy's heavy ships, owing to the mist, until he found himself in close proximity to the main fleet, and before he could withdraw his ships' they were caught under a heavy fire and disabled. It is not known when 'Black Prince' (Captain Thomas P. Bonham), of the same squadron, was sunk, but a wireless signal was received from her between 8 and 9 p.m.

The First Battle Squadron became engaged during deployment, the Vice-Admiral opening fire at 6.17 p.m. on a battleship of the 'Kaiser' class. The other Battle Squadrons, which had previously been firing at an enemy light-cruiser, opened fire at 6.30 p.m. on battleships of the 'Koenig' class.

At 6.6 p.m. the Rear-Admiral Commanding Fifth Battle Squadron, then in company with the battle-cruisers, had sighted the starboard wing division of the battle-fleet on the port bow of 'Barham,' and the first intention of Rear-Admiral Evan-Thomas was to form ahead of the remainder of the battle-fleet, but on realising the direction of deployment he was compelled to form astern, a manoeuvre which was well executed by the squadron under a heavy fire from the enemy battle-fleet. An accident to 'Warspite's' steering gear caused her helm to become jammed temporarily and took the ship in the direction of the enemy's line, during which time she was hit several times. Clever handling enabled Captain Edward M. Phillpotts to extricate his ship from a somewhat awkward situation.

Owing principally to the mist, but partly to the smoke, it was possible to see only a few ships at a time in the enemy's battle line. Towards the van only some four or five ships were ever visible at once. More could be seen from the rear squadron, but never more than eight to twelve.

The action between the battle-fleets lasted intermittently from 6.17 p.m. to 8.20 p.m. at ranges between 9,000 and 12,000 yards, during which time the British Fleet made alterations of course from S.E. by E. to W. in the endeavour to close. The enemy constantly turned away and opened the range under cover of destroyer attacks and smoke screens as the effect of the British fire was felt, and the alterations of course had the effect of bringing the British Fleet (which commenced the action in a position of advantage on the bow of the enemy) to a quarterly bearing from the enemy battle line, but at the same time placed us between the enemy and his bases.

At 6.55 p.m. 'Iron Duke' passed the wreck of 'Invincible' (Captain Arthur L. Cay), with 'Badger' (Commander C.A. Fremantle) standing by.

During the somewhat brief periods that the ships of the High Sea Fleet were visible through the mist, the heavy and effective fire kept up by the battleships and battle-cruisers of the Grand Fleet caused me much satisfaction, and the enemy vessels were seen to be constantly hit, some being observed to haul out of the line and at least one to sink. The enemy's return fire at this period was not effective, and the damage caused to our ships was insignificant.

The Battle-cruisers in the Van.

Sir David Beatty reports:-

"At 7.6 p.m. I received a signal from you that the course of the Fleet was south. Subsequently signals were received up to 8.46 p.m. showing that the course of the Battle Fleet was to the south-westward.

"Between 7 and 7.12 p.m. we hauled round gradually to S.W. by S. to regain touch with the enemy, and at 7.14 p.m. again sighted them at a range of about 15,000 yards. The ships sighted at this time were two battle-cruisers and two battleships, apparently of the 'Koenig' class. No doubt more continued the line to the northward, but that was all that could be seen. The visibility having improved considerably as the sun descended below the clouds, we re-engaged at 7.17 p.m. and increased speed to 22 knots. At 7.32 p.m. my course was S.W., speed 18 knots, the leading enemy battleship bearing N. W. by W. Again, after a very short time, the enemy showed signs of punishment, one ship being on fire, while another appeared to drop right astern. The destroyers at the head of the enemy's line emitted volumes of grey smoke, covering their capital ships as with a pall, under cover of which they turned away, and at 7.45 p.m. we lost sight of them.

"At 7.58 p.m. I ordered the First and Third Light-cruiser Squadrons to sweep to the westward and locate the head of the enemy's line, and at 8.20 p.m. we altered course to west in support. We soon located two battle-cruisers and battleships, and were heavily engaged at a short range of about 10,000 yards. The leading ship was hit repeatedly by 'Lion' and turned away eight points, emitting very high flames and with a heavy list to port. 'Princess Royal' set fire to a three-funnelled battleship. 'New Zealand' (Captain John F.E. Green) and 'Indomitable' report that the third ship, which they both engaged, hauled out of the line, heeling over and on fire. The mist which now came down enveloped them, and 'Falmouth' reported they were last seen at 8.38 p.m. steaming to the westward.

"At 8.40 p.m. all our battle-cruisers felt a heavy shock as if struck by a mine or torpedo, or possibly sunken wreckage. As, however, examination of the bottoms reveals no sign of such an occurrence, it is assumed that it indicated the blowing up of a great vessel.

"I continued on a south-westerly course with my light cruisers spread until 9.24 p.m. Nothing further being sighted, I assumed that the enemy were to the north-westward, and that we had established ourselves well between him and his base. 'Minotaur' (Captain Arthur C.S.H. D'Aeth) was at this time bearing north 5 miles, and I asked her the position of the leading battle squadron of the Battle Fleet. Her reply was that it was not in sight, but was last seen bearing N.N.E. I kept you informed of my position, course, and speed, also of the bearing of the enemy.

"In view of the gathering darkness, and the fact that our strategical position was such as to make it appear certain that we should locate the enemy at daylight under most favourable circumstances, I did not consider it desirable or proper to close the enemy Battle Fleet during the dark hours. I therefore concluded that I should be carrying out your wishes by turning to the course of the Fleet, reporting to you that I had done so."

Details of Battle-fleet Action.

As was anticipated, the German Fleet appeared to rely very much on torpedo attacks, which were favoured by the low visibility and by the fact that we had arrived in the position of a "following" or "chasing" fleet. A large number of torpedoes were apparently fired, but only one took effect (on 'Marlborough'), and even in this case the ship was able to remain in the line and to continue the action. The enemy's efforts to keep out of effective gun range were aided by the weather conditions, which were ideal for the purpose. Two separate destroyer attacks were made by the enemy.

The First Battle Squadron, under Vice-Admiral Sir Cecil Burney, came into action at 6.17 p.m. with the enemy's Third Battle Squadron, at a range of about 11,000 yards, and administered severe punishment, both to the battleships and to the battle-cruisers and light-cruisers, which were also engaged. The fire of 'Marlborough' (Captain George P. Ross) was particularly rapid and effective. This ship commenced at 6.17 p.m. by firing seven salvoes at a ship of the 'Kaiser' class, then engaged a cruiser, and again a battleship, and at 6.54 she was hit by a torpedo and took up a considerable list to starboard, but reopened at 7.3 p.m. at a cruiser and at 7.12 p.m. fired fourteen rapid salvoes at a ship of the 'Koenig' class, hitting her frequently until she turned out of the line. The manner in which this effective fire was kept up in spite of the disadvantages due to the injury caused by the torpedo was most creditable to the ship and a very fine example to the squadron.

The range decreased during the course of the action to 9,000 yards. The First Battle Squadron received more of the enemy's return fire than the remainder of the battle-fleet, with the exception of the Fifth Battle Squadron. 'Colossus' (Captain Alfred

D.P.R. Pound) was hit but was not seriously damaged, and other ships were straddled with fair frequency.

In the Fourth Battle Squadron – in which squadron my flagship 'Iron Duke' was placed – Vice-Admiral Sir Doveton Sturdee leading one of the divisions – the enemy engaged was the squadron consisting of 'Koenig' and 'Kaiser' class and some of the battle-cruisers, as well as disabled cruisers and light-cruisers. The mist rendered range taking a difficult matter, but the fire of the squadron was effective. 'Iron Duke,' having previously fired at a light-cruiser between the lines, opened fire at 6.30 p.m. on a battleship of the 'Koenig' class at a range of 12,000 yards. The latter was very quickly straddled, and hitting commenced at the second salvo and only ceased when the target ship turned away. The rapidity with which hitting was established was most creditable to the excellent gunnery organisation of the flagship, so ably commanded by my Flag Captain, Captain Frederic C. Dreyer.

The fire of other ships of the squadron was principally directed at enemy battle-cruisers and cruisers as they appeared out of the mist. Hits were observed to take effect on several ships.

The ships of the Second Battle Squadron, under Vice-Admiral Sir Thomas Jerram, were in action with vessels of the 'Kaiser' or 'Koenig' classes between 6.30 and 7.20 p.m., and fired also at an enemy battle-cruiser which had dropped back apparently severely damaged.

During the action between the battle fleets the Second Cruiser Squadron, ably commanded by Rear-Admiral Herbert L. Heath, M.V.O., with the addition of 'Duke of Edinburgh' (Captain Henry Blackett) of the First Cruiser Squadron, occupied a position at the van, and acted as a connecting link between the battle fleet and the battle-cruiser fleet. This squadron, although it carried out useful work, did not have an opportunity of coming into action.

The attached cruisers 'Boadicea' (Captain Louis C.S. Woollcombe, M.V.O.), 'Active' (Captain Percy Withers), 'Blanche' (Captain John M. Casement), and 'Bellona' (Captain Arthur B. S. Dutton) carried out their duties as repeating-ships with remarkable rapidity and accuracy under difficult conditions.

The Fourth Light-cruiser Squadron, under Commodore Charles E. Le Mesurier, occupied a position in the van until ordered to attack enemy destroyers at 7.20 p.m., and again at 8.18 p.m., when they supported the Eleventh Flotilla, which had moved out under Commodore

James R.P. Hawksley, M.V.O., to attack. On each occasion the Fourth Light-cruiser Squadron was very well handled by Commodore Le Mesurier, his captains giving him excellent support, and their object was attained, although with some loss in the second attack, when the ships came under the heavy fire of the enemy battle fleet at between 6,500 and 8,000 yards. The 'Calliope' (Commodore Le Mesurier) was hit several times, but did not sustain serious damage, although, I regret to say, she had several casualties. The light-cruisers attacked the enemy's battleships with torpedoes at this time, and an explosion on board a ship of the 'Kaiser' class was seen at 8.40 p.m.

During these destroyer attacks four enemy torpedo-boat destroyers were sunk by the gunfire of battleships, light-cruisers and destroyers.

After the arrival of the British Battle Fleet the enemy's tactics were of a nature generally to avoid further action, in which they were favoured by the conditions of visibility.

Night Dispositions.

At 9 p.m. the enemy was entirely out of sight, and the threat of torpedoboat-destroyer attacks during the rapidly approaching darkness made it necessary for me to dispose the fleet for the night, with a view to its safety from such attacks, whilst providing for a renewal of action at daylight. I accordingly manoeuvred to remain between the enemy and his bases, placing our flotillas in a position in which they would afford protection to the fleet from destroyer attack, and at the same time be favourably situated for attacking the enemy's heavy ships.

Night Attacks by Flotillas.

During the night the British heavy ships were not attacked, but the Fourth, Eleventh and Twelfth Flotillas, under Commodore Hawkesley and Captains Charles J. Wintour and Anselan J.B. Stirling, delivered a series of very gallant and successful attacks on the enemy, causing him heavy losses.

It was during these attacks that severe losses in the Fourth Flotilla occurred, including that of 'Tipperary,' with the gallant leader of the Flotilla, Captain Wintour. He had brought his flotilla to a high pitch of perfection, and although suffering severely from the fire of the enemy, a heavy toll of enemy vessels was taken, and many gallant actions were performed by the flotilla.

Two torpedoes were seen to take effect on enemy vessels as the result of the attacks of the Fourth Flotilla, one being from 'Spitfire' (Lieutenant-Commander Clarence W.E. Trelawny), and the other from either 'Ardent' (Lieutenant-Commander Arthur Marsden), 'Ambuscade' (Lieutenant-Commander Gordon A. Coles) or 'Garland' (Lieutenant-Commander Reginald S. Goff).

The attack carried out by the Twelfth Flotilla (Captain Anselan J.B. Stirling) was admirably executed. The squadron attacked, which consisted of six large vessels, besides light-cruisers, and comprised vessels of the 'Kaiser' class, was taken by surprise. A large number of torpedoes was fired, including some at the second and third ships in the line; those fired at the third ship took effect, and she was observed to blow up. A second attack made twenty minutes later by 'Maenad' (Commander John P. Champion) on the five vessels still remaining, resulted in the fourth ship in the line being also hit.

The destroyers were under a heavy fire from the light-cruisers on reaching the rear of the line, but the 'Onslaught' (Lieutenant-Commander Arthur G. Onslow, D.S.C.) was the only vessel which received any material injuries. In the 'Onslaught' Sub-Lieutenant Harry W.A. Kemmis, assisted by Midshipman Reginald G. Arnot, R.N.R., the only executive officers not disabled, brought the ship successfully out of action and reached her home port.

During the attack carried out by the Eleventh Flotilla, 'Castor' (Commodore James R.P. Hawksley) leading the flotilla, engaged and sank an enemy torpedoboat-destroyer at point-blank range.

Sir David Beatty reports:-

"The Thirteenth Flotilla, under the command of Captain James U. Farie, in 'Champion,' took station astern of the battle fleet for the night. At 0.30 a.m. on Thursday, 1st June, a large vessel crossed the rear of the flotilla at high speed. She passed close to 'Petard' and 'Turbulent,' switched on searchlights and opened a heavy fire, which disabled 'Turbulent.'

At 3.30 a.m. 'Champion' was engaged for a few minutes with four enemy destroyers. 'Moresby' reports four ships of 'Deutschland' class sighted at 2.35 a.m., at whom she fired one torpedo. Two minutes later an explosion was felt by 'Moresby' and 'Obdurate.'

" 'Fearless' and the 1st Flotilla were very usefully employed as a submarine screen during the earlier part of the 31st May. At 6.10 p.m., when joining the Battle Fleet, 'Fearless' was unable to follow the battle cruisers without fouling the battleships, and therefore took station at the rear of the line. She sighted during the night a battleship of the 'Kaiser' class steaming fast and entirely alone. She was not able to engage her, but believes she was attacked by destroyers further astern. A heavy explosion was observed astern not long after."

There were many gallant deeds performed by the destroyer flotillas; they surpassed the very highest expectations that I had formed of them.

Apart from the proceedings of the flotillas, the Second Light-cruiser Squadron in the rear of the battle fleet was in close action for about 15 minutes at 10.20 p.m. with a squadron comprising one enemy cruiser and four light-cruisers, during which period 'Southampton' and 'Dublin' (Captain Albert C. Scott) suffered rather heavy casualties, although their steaming and fighting qualities were not impaired. The return fire of the squadron appeared to be very effective.

'Abdiel,' ably commanded by Commander Berwick Curtis, carried out her duties with the success which has always characterised her work.

Proceedings on 1st June.

At daylight, 1st June, the battle fleet, being then to the southward and westward of the Horn Reef, turned to the northward in search of enemy vessels and for the purpose of collecting our own cruisers and torpedo-boat destroyers. At 2.30 a.m. Vice-Admiral Sir Cecil Burney transferred his flag from 'Marlborough' to 'Revenge,' as the former ship had some difficulty in keeping up the speed of the squadron. 'Marlborough' was detached by my direction to a base, successfully driving off an enemy submarine attack en route. The visibility early on 1st June (three to four miles) was less than on 31st May, and the torpedoboat destroyers, being out of visual touch, did not rejoin until 9 a.m. The British Fleet remained in the proximity of the battlefield and near the line of approach to German ports until 11 a.m. on 1st June, in spite of the disadvantage of long distances from fleet bases and the danger incurred in waters adjacent to enemy coasts from submarines and torpedo craft. The enemy, however, made no sign, and I was reluctantly compelled to the conclusion that the High Sea Fleet had returned into port. Subsequent events proved this assumption to have been correct. Our position must have been known to the enemy, as at 4 a.m. the Fleet engaged a Zeppelin for about five minutes, during which time she had ample opportunity to note and subsequently report the position and course of the British Fleet.

The waters from the latitude of the Horn Reef to the scene of the action were thoroughly searched, and some survivors from the destroyers 'Ardent' (Lieutenant-Commander Arthur Marsden), 'Fortune' (Lieutenant-Commander Frank G. Terry), and 'Tipperary'(Captain (D) Charles J. Wintour), were picked up, and the 'Sparrowhawk' (Lieutenant-Commander (Sydney Hopkins),which had been in collision and was no longer seaworthy, was sunk after her crew had been taken off. A large amount of wreckage was seen, but no enemy ships, and at 1.15 p.m., it being evident that the German Fleet had succeeded in returning to port, course was shaped for our bases, which were reached without further incident on Friday, 2nd June. A cruiser squadron was detached to search for 'Warrior,' which vessel had been abandoned whilst in tow of 'Engadine' on her way to the base owing to bad weather setting in and the vessel becoming unseaworthy, but no trace of her was discovered, and a further subsequent search by a light-cruiser squadron having failed to locate her, it is evident that she foundered.

Sir David Beatty reports in regard to the 'Engadine' as follows:-

"The work of 'Engadine' appears to have been most praiseworthy throughout, and of great value. Lieutenant-Commander C.G. Robinson deserves great credit for the skilful and seamanlike manner in which he handled his ship. He actually towed 'Warrior' for 75 miles between 8.40 p.m., 31st May, and 7.15 a.m., 1st June, and was instrumental in saving the lives of her ship's company."

I fully endorse his remarks.

The Fleet fuelled and replenished with ammunition, and at 9.30 p.m. on 2nd June was reported ready for further action.

Losses.

The conditions of low visibility under which the day action took place and the approach of darkness enhance the difficulty of giving an accurate report of the damage inflicted or the names of the ships sunk by our forces, but after a most careful examination of the evidence of all officers, who testified to seeing enemy vessels actually sink, and personal interviews with a large number of these officers, I am of opinion that the list shown in the enclosure gives the minimum in regard to numbers, though it is possibly not entirely accurate as regards the particular class of vessel, especially those which were sunk during the night attacks. In addition to the vessels sunk, it is unquestionable that many other ships were very seriously damaged by gunfire and by torpedo attack.

I deeply regret to report the loss of H.M. ships 'Queen Mary,' 'Indefatigable' 'Invincible,' 'Defence,' 'Black Prince,' 'Warrior,' and of H.M. T.B.D.'s 'Tipperary,' 'Ardent,' 'Fortune,' 'Shark,' 'Sparrowhawk,' 'Nestor,' 'Nomad,' and 'Turbulent,' and still more do I regret the resultant heavy loss of life. The death of such gallant and distinguished officers as Rear-Admiral Sir Robert Arbuthnot, Bart., Rear-Admiral The Hon. Horace Hood, Captain Charles F. Sowerby, Captain Cecil I. Prowse, Captain Arthur L. Cay, Captain Thomas P. Bonham,

Captain Charles J. Wintour, and Captain Stanley V. Ellis, and those who perished with them, is a serious loss to the Navy and to the country. They led officers and men who were equally gallant, and whose death is mourned by their comrades in the Grand Fleet. They fell doing their duty nobly, a death which they would have been the first to desire.

The enemy fought with the gallantry that was expected of him. We particularly admired the conduct of those on board a disabled German light-cruiser which passed down the British line shortly after deployment, under a heavy fire, which was returned by the only gun left in action.

The Personnel of the Fleet.

The conduct of officers and men throughout the day and night actions was entirely beyond praise. No words of mine could do them justice. On all sides it is reported to me that the glorious traditions of the past were most worthily upheld – whether in heavy ships, cruisers, light-cruisers, or destroyers – the same admirable spirit prevailed. Officers and men were cool and determined, with a cheeriness that would have carried them through anything. The heroism of the wounded was the admiration of all.

I cannot adequately express the pride with which the spirit of the Fleet filled me.

Details of the work of the various ships during action have now been given. It must never be forgotten, however, that the prelude to action is the work of the engine-room department, and that during action the officers and men of that department perform their most important duties without the incentive which a knowledge of the course of the action gives to those on deck. The qualities of discipline and endurance are taxed to the utmost under these conditions, and they were, as always, most fully maintained throughout the operations under review. Several ships attained speeds that had never before been reached, thus showing very clearly their high state of steaming efficiency. Failures in material were conspicuous by their absence, and several instances are reported of magnificent work on the part of the engine-room departments of injured ships.

The artisan ratings also carried out much valuable work during and after the action; they could not have done better.

The work of the medical officers of the Fleet, carried out very largely under the most difficult conditions, was entirely admirable and invaluable. Lacking in many cases all the essentials for performing critical operations, and with their staff seriously depleted by casualties, they worked untiringly and with the greatest success. To them we owe a deep debt of gratitude.

It will be seen that the hardest fighting fell to the lot of the Battle-cruiser Fleet (the units of which were less heavily armoured than their opponents), the Fifth Battle Squadron, the First Cruiser Squadron, Fourth Light-cruiser Squadron and the Flotillas. This was inevitable under the conditions, and the squadrons and flotillas mentioned as well as the individual vessels composing them were handled with conspicuous ability, as were also the 1st, 2nd and 4th Squadrons of the Battle Fleet and the 2nd Cruiser Squadron.

I desire to place on record my high appreciation of the manner in which all the vessels were handled. The conditions were such as to call for great skill and ability, quick judgment and decisions, and this was conspicuous throughout the day.

I beg also to draw special attention to the services rendered by Vice-Admiral Sir Cecil Burney (Second in Command of the Grand Fleet), Vice-Admiral Sir Thomas Jerram, Vice-Admiral Sir Doveton Sturdee, Rear-Admiral Hugh Evan-Thomas, Rear-Admiral Alexander L. Duff, Rear-Admiral Arthur C. Leveson and Rear-Admiral Ernest F.A. Gaunt, commanding squadrons or divisions in the Battle Fleet. They acted throughout with skill and judgment. Sir Cecil Burney's squadron owing to its position was able to see more of the enemy Battle Fleet than the other battle squadrons, and under a leader who has rendered me most valuable and loyal assistance at all times the squadron did excellent work. The magnificent squadron commanded by Rear-Admiral Evan-Thomas formed a support of great value to Sir David Beatty during the afternoon, and was brought into action in rear of the Battle Fleet in the most judicious manner in the evening.

Sir David Beatty once again showed his fine qualities of gallant leadership, firm determination and correct strategic insight. He appreciated the situations at once on sighting first the enemy's lighter forces, then his battle-cruisers and finally his battle fleet. I can fully sympathise with his feelings when the evening mist and fading light robbed the Fleet of that complete victory for which he had manoeuvred, and for which the vessels in company with him had striven so hard. The services rendered by him, not only on this, but on two previous occasions, have been of the very greatest value.

Sir David Beatty brings to my notice the brilliant support afforded him by Rear-Admiral Hugh Evan-Thomas; the magnificent manner in which Rear-Admiral The Hon. Horace Hood brought his squadron into action, the able support afforded him by Rear-Admiral William C. Pakenham and Rear-Admiral Osmond de B. Brock, and the good work performed by the Light-cruiser Squadrons under the command respectively of Rear-Admiral Trevylyan D.W. Napier, Commodore William E. Goodenough and Commodore Edwyn S. Alexander-Sinclair. He states that on every occasion these officers anticipated his wishes and used their forces to the best possible effect.

I most fully endorse all his remarks, and I forward also the following extract from his report regarding the valuable services rendered by his staff:-

"I desire to record and bring to your notice the great assistance that I received on a day of great anxiety and strain from my Chief of the Staff,

Captain Rudolf W. Bentinck, whose good judgment was of the greatest help. He was a tower of strength. My Flag-Commander, the Hon. Reginald A.R. Plunkett, was most valuable in observing the effect of our fire, thereby enabling me to take advantage of the enemy's discomfiture; my Secretary, Frank T. Spickernell, who made accurate notes of events as they occurred, which proved of the utmost value in keeping the situation clearly before me; my Flag Lieutenant-Commander Ralph F. Seymour, who maintained efficient communications under the most difficult circumstances despite the fact that his signalling appliances were continually shot away. All these officers carried out their duties with great coolness on the manoeuvring platform, where they were fully exposed to the enemy's fire."

I cannot close this despatch without recording the brilliant work of my Chief of the Staff, Vice-Admiral Sir Charles Madden, K.C.B., C.V.O. Throughout a period of 21 months of war his services have been of inestimable value. His good judgment, his long experience in fleets, special gift for organisation, and his capacity for unlimited work, have all been of the greatest assistance to me, and have relieved me of much of the anxiety inseparable from the conduct of the Fleet during the war. In the stages leading up to the Fleet Action and during and after the action he was always at hand to assist, and his judgment never at fault. I owe him more than I can say.

My special thanks are due also to Commodore Lionel Halsey, C.M.G., the Captain of the Fleet, who also assists me in the working of the fleet at sea, and to whose good organisation is largely due the rapidity with which the fleet was fuelled and replenished with ammunition on return to its bases. He was of much assistance to me during the action.

Commander Charles M. Forbes, my flag-commander, and Commander Roger M. Bellairs, of my Staff, plotted the movements of the two fleets with rapidity and accuracy as reports were received; Commander the Hon. Matthew R. Best, M.V.O., of my Staff, acted as observer aloft throughout the action, and his services were of value. These officers carried out their duties with much efficiency during the action.

The signals were worked with smoothness and rapidity by Commander Alexander R.W. Woods, assisted by the other signal officers, and all ships responded remarkably well under difficult conditions. The signal departments in all ships deserve great credit for their work. My Flag-Lieutenant, Lieutenant-Commander Herbert Fitzherbert, was also of much service to me throughout the action.

The high state of efficiency of the W/T arrangements of the fleet, and the facility with which they were worked before, during and after the action, is a great testimony to the indefatigable work carried out by Commander Richard L. Nicholson. His services have been invaluable throughout the war.

A special word of praise is due to the wireless departments in all ships.

My Secretaries, Fleet Paymasters Hamnet H. Share, C.B., and Victor H.T. Weekes, recorded with accuracy salient features of the action. Their records have been of much assistance.

To the Master of the Fleet, Captain Oliver E. Leggett, I am indebted for the accuracy with which he kept the reckoning throughout the operations.

In a separate despatch I propose to bring to the notice of their Lordships the names of officers and men all of whom did not come under my personal observation, but who had the opportunity of specially distinguishing themselves.

I append the full text of Sir David Beatty's report to me, from which, as will be seen, I have made copious extracts in order to make my narrative continuous and complete.[†]

I am, Sir,
Your obedient Servant,
J.R. JELLICOE, Admiral,
Commander-in-Chief.

[ENCLOSURE.]

List of Enemy Vessels put out of action, 31 May – 1 June, 1916.

Battleships or Battle-cruisers.
2 Battleships, "Dreadnought" type.
1 Battleship, "Deutschland" type.
(Seen to sink.)
1 Battle-cruiser.
(Sunk – 'Lützow' admitted by Germans.)
1 Battleship, "Dreadnought" type.
1 Battle-cruiser.
(Seen to be so severely damaged as to render it extremely doubtful if they could reach port.)
Light-cruisers.
5 Light-cruisers.
(Seen to sink; one of them had the appearance of being a larger type, and might have been a battleship.)
Torpedo-boat Destroyers.
6 Torpedo-boat Destroyers.
(Seen to sink.)
3 Torpedo-boat Destroyers.
(Seen to be so severely damaged as to render it extremely doubtful if they could reach port.)
Submarines.
1 Submarine.
(Sunk.)

APPENDIX.

"Lion,"
19th June, 1916.

Sir, – I have the honour to report that at 2.37 p.m. on 31st May, 1916, I was cruising and steering to the northward to join your Flag.

The Light Cruiser Screen was disposed from E. to W.

At 2.20 p.m. reports were received from 'Galatea' (Commodore Edwyn S. Alexander-Sinclair, M.V.O., A.D.C.) indicating the presence of enemy vessels. The direction of advance was immediately altered to S.S.E., the course for Horn Reef, so as to place my force between the enemy and his base. At 2.35 p.m. a considerable amount of smoke was sighted to the eastward. This made it clear that the enemy was to the northward and eastward, and that it would be impossible for him to round the Horn Reef without being brought to action. Course was accordingly altered to the eastward, and subsequently to north-eastward, the enemy being sighted at 3.31 p.m. Their force consisted of five battle cruisers.

After the first reports of the enemy the 1st and 3rd Light Cruiser Squadrons changed their direction, and, without waiting for orders, spread to the east, thereby forming a screen in advance of the Battle Cruiser Squadrons and 5th Battle Squadron by the time we had hauled up to the course of approach. They engaged enemy light cruisers at long range. In the meantime the 2nd Light Cruiser Squadron had come in at high speed, and was able to take station ahead of the battle cruisers by the time we turned to E.S.E., the course on which we first engaged the enemy. In this respect the work of the Light Cruiser Squadrons was excellent and of great value.

From a report from 'Galatea' at 2.25 p.m. it was evident that the enemy force was considerable, and not merely an isolated unit of light cruisers, so at 2.45 p.m. I ordered 'Engadine' (Lieutenant-Commander C.G. Robinson) to send up a seaplane and scout to N.N.E. This order was carried out very quickly, and by 3.8 p.m. a seaplane, with Flight Lieutenant F.J. Rutland, R.N., as pilot, and Assistant Paymaster G.S. Trewin, R.N., as observer, was well under way; her first reports of the enemy were received in 'Engadine' about 3.30 p.m. Owing to clouds it was necessary to fly very low, and in order to identify four enemy light cruisers the seaplane had to fly at a height of 900 ft. within 3,000 yards of them, the light cruisers opening fire on her with every gun that would bear. This in no way interfered with the clarity of their reports, and both Flight Lieutenant Rutland and Assistant Paymaster Trewin are to be congratulated on their achievement, which indicates that seaplanes under such circumstances are of distinct value.

At 3.30 p.m. I increased speed to 25 knots and formed line of battle, the 2nd Battle Cruiser Squadron forming astern of the 1st Battle Cruiser Squadron, with destroyers of the 13th and 9th Flotillas taking station ahead. I turned to E.S.E., slightly converging on the enemy, who were now at a range of 23,000 yards, and formed the ships on a line of bearing to clear the smoke. The 5th Battle Squadron, who had conformed to our movements, were now bearing N.N.W., 10,000 yards. The visibility at this time was good, the sun behind us and the wind S.E. Being between the enemy and his base, our situation was both tactically and strategically good.

At 3.48 p.m. the action commenced at a range of 18,500 yards, both forces opening fire practically simultaneously. Course was altered to the southward, and subsequently the mean direction was S.S.E., the enemy steering a parallel course distant about 18,000 to 14,500 yards.

At 4.8 p.m. the 5th Battle Squadron came into action and opened fire at a range of 20,000 yards. The enemy's fire now seemed to slacken. The destroyer 'Landrail' (Lieutenant- Commander Francis E.H.G. Hobart), of the 9th Flotilla, which was on our port beam, trying to take station ahead, sighted the periscope of a submarine on her port quarter. Though causing considerable inconvenience from smoke, the presence of 'Lydiard' (Commander Malcolm L. Goldsmith) and 'Landrail' undoubtedly preserved the battle-cruisers from closer submarine attack. 'Nottingham' (Captain Charles B. Miller) also reported a submarine on the starboard beam.

Eight destroyers of the 13th Flotilla, 'Nestor' (Commander the Hon. Edward B.S. Bingham), 'Nomad' (Lieutenant-Commander Paul Whitfield), 'Nicator' (Lieutenant Jack E.A. Mocatta), 'Narborough' (Lieutenant-Commander Geoffrey Corlett), 'Pelican' (Lieutenant-Commander Kenneth A. Beattie), 'Petard' (Lieutenant-Commander Evelyn C.O. Thomson), 'Obdurate' (Lieutenant-Cecil H.H. Sams), 'Nerissa' (Lieutenant-Commander Montague C.B. Legge), with 'Moorsom' (Commander John C. Hodgson) and 'Morris' (Lieutenant-Commander Edward S. Graham), of 10th Flotilla, 'Turbulent' (Lieutenant-Commander Dudley Stuart), 'Termagant' (Lieutenant-Commander Cuthbert P. Blake), of the 9th Flotilla, having been ordered to attack the enemy with torpedoes when opportunity offered, moved out at 4.15 p.m. simultaneously with a similar movement on the part of the enemy's destroyers. The attack was carried out in the most gallant manner and with great determination. Before arriving at a favourable position to fire torpedoes they intercepted an enemy force consisting of a light cruiser and 15 destroyers. A fierce engagement ensued at close quarters, with the result that the enemy were forced to retire on their battle-cruisers, having lost two destroyers sunk and having their torpedo attack frustrated. Our destroyers sustained no loss in this engagement, but their attack on the enemy battle-cruisers was rendered less effective owing to some of the destroyers having dropped astern during the fight. Their position was therefore unfavourable for torpedo attack.

'Nestor,' 'Nomad' and 'Nicator,' gallantly led by Commander Hon. E.B.S.

Bingham, of 'Nestor,' pressed home their attack on the battle-cruisers and fired two torpedoes at them, being subjected to a heavy fire from the enemy's secondary armament. 'Nomad' was badly hit and apparently remained stopped between the lines. Subsequently 'Nestor' and 'Nicator' altered course to the S.E., and in a short time, the opposing battle-cruisers having turned 16 points, found themselves within close range of a number of enemy battleships. Nothing daunted, though under a terrific fire, they stood on, and their position being favourable for torpedo attack, fired a torpedo at the second ship of the enemy line at a range of 3,000 yards. Before they could fire their fourth torpedo 'Nestor' was badly hit and swung to starboard, 'Nicator' altering course inside her to avoid collision and thereby being prevented from firing the last torpedo. 'Nicator' made good her escape, and subsequently rejoined the Captain D, 13th Flotilla. 'Nestor' remained stopped, but was afloat when last seen. 'Moorsom' also carried out an attack on the enemy's Battle Fleet.

'Petard,' 'Nerissa,' 'Turbulent' and 'Termagant' also pressed home their attack on the enemy battle-cruisers, firing torpedoes after the engagement with enemy destroyers. 'Petard' reports that all her torpedoes must have crossed the enemy's line, while 'Nerissa' states that one torpedo appeared to strike the rear ship. These destroyer attacks were indicative of the spirit pervading His Majesty's Navy, and were worthy of its highest traditions. I propose to bring to your notice a recommendation of Commander Bingham and other Officers for some recognition of their conspicuous gallantry.

From 4.15 to 4.43 p.m. the conflict between the opposing battle-cruisers was of a very fierce and resolute character. The 5th Battle Squadron was engaging the enemy's rear ships, unfortunately at very long range. Our fire began to tell, the accuracy and rapidity of that of the enemy depreciating considerably. At 4.18 p.m. the third enemy ship was seen to be on fire. The visibility to the north-eastward had become considerably reduced, and the outline of the ships very indistinct.

At 4.38 p.m. 'Southampton' (Commodore William E. Goodenough, M.V.O., A.D.C.) reported the enemy's Battle Fleet ahead. The destroyers were recalled, and at 4.42 p.m. the enemy's Battle Fleet was sighted S.E. Course was altered 16 points in succession to starboard, and I proceeded on a northerly course to lead them towards the Battle Fleet. The enemy battle-cruisers altered course shortly afterwards, and the action continued. 'Southampton,' with the 2nd Light Cruiser Squadron, held on to the southward to observe. They closed to within 13,000 yards of the enemy Battle Fleet, and came under a very heavy but ineffective fire. 'Southampton's' reports were most valuable. The 5th Battle Squadron were now closing on an opposite course and engaging the enemy battle-cruisers with all guns. The position of the enemy Battle Fleet was communicated to them, and I ordered them to alter course 16 points. Led by Rear-Admiral Evan-Thomas in 'Barham' (Captain Arthur W. Craig), this squadron supported us brilliantly and effectively.

At 4.57 p.m. the 5th Battle Squadron turned up astern of me and came under the fire of the leading ships of the enemy Battle Fleet. 'Fearless' (Captain (D) Charles O. Roper), with the destroyers of 1st Flotilla, joined the battle-cruisers and, when speed admitted, took station ahead. 'Champion' (Captain (D) James U. Farie), with

13th Flotilla, took station on the 5th Battle Squadron. At 5 p.m. the 1st and 3rd Light Cruiser Squadrons, which had been following me on the southerly course, took station on my starboard bow; the 2nd Light Cruiser Squadron took station on my port quarter.

The weather conditions now became unfavourable, our ships being silhouetted against a clear horizon to the westward, while the enemy were for the most part obscured by mist, only showing up clearly at intervals. These conditions prevailed until we had turned their van at about 6 p.m. Between 5 and 6 p.m. the action continued on a northerly course, the range being about 14,000 yards. During this time the enemy received very severe punishment, and one of their battle-cruisers quitted the line in a considerably damaged condition. This came under my personal observation, and was corroborated by 'Princess Royal' (Captain Walter H. Cowan, M.V.O., D.S.O.) and 'Tiger' (Captain Henry B. Pelly, M.V.O.). Other enemy ships also showed signs of increasing injury. At 5.5 p.m. 'Onslow' (Lieutenant-Commander John C. Tovey), and 'Moresby' (Lieutenant-Commander Roger V. Alison), who had been detached to assist 'Engadine' with the seaplane, rejoined the Battle Cruiser Squadrons, and took station on the starboard (engaged) bow of 'Lion' (Captain Alfred E.M. Chatfield, C.V.O.). At 5.10 p.m. 'Moresby,' being 2 points before the beam of the leading enemy ship, fired a torpedo at a ship in their line. Eight minutes later she observed a hit with a torpedo on what was judged to be the sixth ship in the line. 'Moresby' then passed between the lines to clear the range of smoke and rejoined 'Champion.' In corroboration of this 'Fearless' reports having seen an enemy heavy ship heavily on fire at about 5.10 p.m. and shortly afterwards a huge cloud of smoke and steam.

At 5.35 p.m. our course was N.N.E., and the estimated position of the Battle Fleet was N. 16 W., so we gradually hauled to the north-eastward, keeping the range of the enemy at 14,000 yards. He was gradually hauling to the eastward, receiving severe punishment at the head of his line, and probably acting on information received from his light cruisers, which had sighted, and were engaged with, the Third Battle Cruiser Squadron. Possibly Zeppelins were present also. At 5.50 p.m. British cruisers were sighted on the port bow, and at 5.56 p.m. the leading battleships of the Battle Fleet, bearing north 5 miles. I thereupon altered course to east, and proceeded at utmost speed. This brought the range of the enemy down to 12,000 yards. I made a report to you that the enemy battle-cruisers bore south-east. At this time only three of the enemy battle-cruisers were visible, closely followed by battleships of the 'Koenig' class.

At about 6.5 p.m. 'Onslow,' being on the engaged bow of 'Lion,' sighted an enemy light cruiser at a distance of 6,000 yards from us, apparently endeavouring to attack with torpedoes. 'Onslow' at once closed and engaged her, firing 58 rounds at a range of from 4,000 to 2,000 yards, scoring a number of hits. 'Onslow' then closed the enemy battle-cruisers, and orders were given for all torpedoes to be fired. At this moment she was struck amidships by a heavy shell, with the result that only one torpedo was fired. Thinking that all his torpedoes had gone, the commanding officer proceeded to retire at slow speed. Being informed that he still had three torpedoes, he closed the light cruiser previously engaged, and torpedoed her. The enemy's Battle

Fleet was then sighted, and the remaining torpedoes were fired at them, and must have crossed the enemy's track. Damage then caused 'Onslow' to stop.

At 7.15 p.m. 'Defender' (Lieutenant-Commander Lawrence R. Palmer), whose speed had been reduced to 10 knots while on the disengaged side of the battle-cruisers by a 12-inch shell, which damaged her foremost boiler, closed 'Onslow' and took her in tow. Shells were falling all round them during this operation, which, however, was successfully accomplished. During the heavy weather of the ensuing night the tow parted twice, but was re-secured. The two struggled on together until 1 p.m. 1st June, when 'Onslow' was transferred to tugs. I consider the performances of these two destroyers to be gallant in the extreme, and I am recommending Lieut.-Commander J.C. Tovey of 'Onslow' and Lieut.-Commander L.R. Palmer of 'Defender' for special recognition. 'Onslow' was possibly the destroyer referred to by Rear-Admiral Commanding 3rd Light Cruiser Squadron as follows:- "Here I should like to bring to your notice the action of a destroyer (name unknown) which we passed close in a disabled condition soon after 6 p.m. She apparently was able to struggle ahead again and made straight for the 'Derfflinger' to attack her."

At 6.20 p.m. the Third Battle Cruiser Squadron appeared ahead, steaming South towards the enemy's van. I ordered them to take station ahead, which was carried out magnificently, Rear-Admiral Hood bringing his squadron into action ahead in a most inspiring manner, worthy of his great naval ancestors. At 6.25 p.m. I altered course to the E.S.E. in support of the Third Battle Cruiser Squadron, who were at this time only 8,000 yards from the enemy's leading ship. They were pouring a hot fire into her and caused her to turn to the Westward of South. At the same time I made a report to you of the bearing and distance of the enemy Battle Fleet.

By 6.50 p.m. the battle cruisers were clear of our leading Battle Squadron then bearing about N.N.W. 3 miles from 'Lion,' and I ordered the 3rd Battle Cruiser Squadron to prolong the line astern and reduced to 18 knots. The visibility at this time was very indifferent, not more than 4 miles, and the enemy ships were temporarily lost sight of. It is interesting to note that after 6 p.m., although the visibility became reduced, it was undoubtedly more favourable to us than to the enemy. At intervals their ships showed up clearly, enabling us to punish them very severely and establish a definite superiority over them. From the reports of other ships and my own observation it was clear that the enemy suffered considerable damage, battle-cruisers and battleships alike. The head of their line was crumpled up, leaving battleships as targets for the majority of our battle cruisers. Before leaving us the 5th Battle Squadron was also engaging battleships. The report of Rear-Admiral Evan-Thomas shows that excellent results were obtained, and it can be safely said that his magnificent squadron wrought great execution.

From the report of Rear-Admiral T.D.W. Napier, M.V.O., the 3rd Light Cruiser Squadron, which had maintained its station on our starboard bow well ahead of the enemy, at 6.25 p.m. attacked with the torpedo. 'Falmouth' (Captain John D. Edwards) and 'Yarmouth' (Captain Thomas D. Pratt) both fired torpedoes at the leading enemy battle-cruiser, and it is believed that one torpedo hit, as a heavy underwater explosion was observed. The 3rd Light Cruiser Squadron then gallantly attacked the heavy ships with gunfire, with impunity to themselves, thereby demonstrating that the fighting efficiency of the enemy had been seriously impaired. Rear-Admiral Napier deserves great credit for his determined and effective attack. 'Indomitable' (Captain Francis W. Kennedy) reports that about this time one of the 'Derfflinger' class fell out of the enemy's line.

At 7.6 p.m. I received a signal from you that the course of the Fleet was South. Subsequently signals were received up to 8.46 p.m. showing that the course of the Battle Fleet was to the south-westward. Between 7 and 7.12 p.m. we hauled round gradually to S.W. by S. to regain touch with the enemy, and at 7.14 p.m. again sighted them at a range of about 15,000 yards. The ships sighted at this time were two battle-cruisers and two battleships, apparently of the 'Koenig' class. No doubt more continued the line to the Northward, but that was all that could be seen. The visibility having improved considerably as the sun descended below the clouds, we re-engaged at 7.17 p.m. and increased speed to 22 knots. At 7.32 p.m. my course was S.W., speed 18 knots, the leading enemy battleship bearing N.W. by W. Again after a very short time the enemy showed signs of punishment, one ship being on fire, while another appeared to drop right astern. The destroyers at the head of the enemy's line emitted volumes of grey smoke, covering their capital ships as with a pall, under cover of which they turned away, and at 7.45 p.m. we lost sight of them.

At 7.58 p.m. I ordered the 1st and 3rd Light Cruiser Squadrons to sweep to the Westward and locate the head of the enemy's line, and at 8.20 p.m. we altered course to West in support. We soon located two battle-cruisers and battleships, and were heavily engaged at a short range of about 10,000 yards. The leading ship was hit repeatedly by 'Lion,' and turned away 8 points, emitting very high flames and with a heavy list to port. 'Princess Royal' set fire to a three-funnelled battleship; 'New Zealand' (Captain John F.E Green) and 'Indomitable' report that the third ship, which they both engaged, hauled out of the line heeling over and on fire. The mist which now came down enveloped them, and 'Falmouth' reported they were last seen at 8.38 p.m. steaming to the Westward.

At 8.40 p.m. all our battle-cruisers felt a heavy shock as if struck by a mine or torpedo, or possibly sunken wreckage. As, however, examination of the bottoms reveals no sign of such an occurrence, it is assumed that it indicated the blowing up of a great vessel.

I continued on a south-westerly course with my light cruisers spread until 9.24 p.m. Nothing further being sighted, I assumed that the enemy were to the North-westward, and that we had established ourselves well between him and his base. 'Minotaur' (Captain Arthur C.S.H. D'Aeth) was at this time bearing North 5 miles, and I asked her the position of the leading Battle Squadron of the Battle Fleet. Her reply was that it was not in sight, but was last seen bearing N.N.E. I kept you informed of my position, course and speed, also of the bearing of the enemy.

In view of the gathering darkness, and of the fact that our strategical position was such as to make it appear certain that we should locate the enemy at daylight under most favourable circumstances, I did not consider it desirable or proper to close the enemy Battle Fleet during the dark hours. I therefore concluded that I should be carrying out your wishes by turning to the course of the Fleet, reporting to you that I had done so.

The 13th Flotilla, under the command of Captain James U. Farie, in 'Champion' took station astern of the Battle Fleet for the night. At 0.30 a.m. on Thursday,1st June, a large vessel crossed the rear of the flotilla at high speed. She passed close to 'Petard' and 'Turbulent,' switched on searchlights, and opened a heavy fire, which disabled 'Turbulent.' At 3.30 a.m. 'Champion' was engaged for a few minutes, with four enemy destroyers. 'Moresby' reports four ships of 'Deutschland' class sighted at 2.35 a.m., at whom she fired one torpedo. Two minutes later an explosion was felt by 'Moresby' and 'Obdurate.'

'Fearless'' and the 1st Flotilla were very usefully employed as a submarine screen during the earlier part of the 31st May. At 6.10 p.m., when joining the Battle Fleet, 'Fearless' was unable to follow the battle cruisers without fouling the battleships, and therefore took station at the rear of the line. She sighted during the night a battleship of the 'Kaiser' class steaming fast and entirely alone. She was not able to engage her, but believes she was attacked by destroyers further astern. A heavy explosion was observed astern not long after.

The 1st and 3rd Light Cruiser Squadrons were almost continuously in touch with the battle cruisers, one or both squadrons being usually ahead. In this position they were of great value. They very effectively protected the head of our line from torpedo attack by light cruisers or destroyers, and were prompt in helping to regain touch when the enemy's line was temporarily lost sight of. The 2nd Light Cruiser Squadron was at the rear of our battle line during the night, and at 9 p.m. assisted to repel a destroyer attack on the 5th Battle Squadron. They were also heavily engaged at 10.20 p.m. with five enemy cruisers or light cruisers, 'Southampton' and 'Dublin' (Captain Albert C. Scott) suffering severe casualties during an action lasting about 15 minutes. 'Birmingham' (Captain Arthur A.M. Duff), at 11.30 p.m., sighted two or more heavy ships steering South. A report of this was received by me at 11.40 p.m. as steering W.S.W. They were thought at the time to be battle cruisers, but it is since considered that they were probably battleships.

The work of 'Engadine' appears to have been most praiseworthy throughout, and of great value. Lieutenant-Commander C.G. Robinson deserves great credit for the skilful and seamanlike manner in which he handled his ship. He actually towed 'Warrior' for 75 miles between 8.40 p.m., 31st May, and 7.15 a.m., 1st June, and was instrumental in saving the lives of her ship's company.

It is impossible to give a definite statement of the losses inflicted on the enemy. The visibility was for the most part low and fluctuating, and caution forbade me to close the range too much with my inferior force.

A review of all the reports which I have received leads me to conclude that the enemy's losses were considerably greater than those which we had sustained, in spite of their superiority, and included battleships, battle-cruisers, light cruisers, and destroyers.

This is eloquent testimony to the very high standard of gunnery and torpedo efficiency of His Majesty's Ships. The control and drill remained undisturbed throughout, in many cases despite heavy damage to material and personnel. Our superiority over the enemy in this respect was very marked, their efficiency becoming rapidly reduced under punishment, while ours was maintained throughout.

As was to be expected, the behaviour of the ships' companies under the terrible conditions of a modern sea battle was magnificent without exception. The strain on their morale was a severe test of discipline and training. Officers and men were imbued with one thought, the desire to defeat the enemy. The fortitude of the wounded was admirable. A report from the Commanding Officer of 'Chester' gives a splendid instance of devotion to duty. Boy (1st class) John Travers Cornwell, of 'Chester,' was mortally wounded early in the action. He nevertheless remained standing alone at a most exposed post, quietly awaiting orders till the end of the action, with the gun's crew dead and wounded all round him. His age was under 16½ years. I regret that he has since died, but I recommend his case for special recognition in justice to his memory, and as an acknowledgment of the high example set by him.

In such a conflict as raged continuously for five hours it was inevitable that we should suffer severe losses. It was necessary to maintain touch with greatly superior forces in fluctuating visibility, often very low. We lost 'Invincible,' 'Indefatigable' and 'Queen Mary,' from which ships there were few survivors. The casualties in other ships were heavy, and I wish to express my deepest regret at the loss of so many gallant comrades, officers and men. They died gloriously.

Exceptional skill was displayed by the Medical Officers of the Fleet. They performed operations and tended the wounded under conditions of extreme difficulty. In some cases their staff was seriously depleted by casualties, and the inevitable lack of such essentials as adequate light, hot water, &c., in ships damaged by shell fire, tried their skill, resource and physical endurance to the utmost.

As usual, the Engine Boom Departments of all ships displayed the highest qualities of technical skill, discipline and endurance. High speed is a primary factor in the tactics of the squadrons under my command, and the Engine Room Departments never fail.

I have already made mention of the brilliant support afforded me by Rear-Admiral H. Evan-Thomas, M.V.O., and the 5th Battle Squadron, and of the magnificent manner in which Rear-Admiral Hon. H.L.A. Hood, C.B., M.V.O., D.S.O., brought his squadron into action. I desire to record my great regret at his loss, which is a national misfortune. I would now bring to your notice the able support rendered to me by Rear-Admiral W.C. Pakenham, C.B., and Rear-Admiral O. de B. Brock, C.B. In the course of my report I have expressed my appreciation of the good work performed by the Light Cruiser Squadrons under the command respectively of Rear-Admiral T.D.W. Napier, M.V.O., Commodore W.E. Goodenough, M.V.O., and Commodore E.S. Alexander-Sinclair, M.V.O. On every occasion these officers anticipated my wishes, and used their forces to the best possible effect.

I desire also to bring to your notice the skill with which their respective ships were handled by the Commanding Officers. With such Flag Officers, Commodores and Captains to support me my task was lightened.

The destroyers of the 1st and 13th Flotillas were handled by their respective

Commanding Officers with skill, dash and courage. I desire to record my very great regret at the loss of Captains C.F. Sowerby ('Indefatigable'), C.I. Prowse ('Queen Mary'), and A.L. Cay ('Invincible'), all officers of the highest attainments, who can be ill spared at this time of stress.

I wish to endorse the report of the Rear-Admiral Commanding the 5th Battle Squadron as to the ability displayed by the Commanding Officers of his squadron.

In conclusion, I desire to record and bring to your notice the great assistance that I received on a day of great anxiety and strain from my Chief of the Staff, Captain R.W. Bentinck, whose good judgment was of the greatest help. He was a tower of strength. My Flag Commander, Hon. R.A.R. Plunkett, was most valuable in observing the effect of our fire, thereby enabling me to take advantage of the enemy's discomfiture; my Secretary, F.T. Spickernell, who made accurate notes of events as they occurred, which proved of the utmost value in keeping the situation clearly before me; my Flag Lieutenant, Commander R.F. Seymour, who maintained efficient communications under the most difficult circumstances, despite the fact that his signalling appliances were continually shot away. All these Officers carried out their duties with great coolness on the manoeuvring platform, where they were fully exposed to the enemy's fire.

In accordance with your wishes, I am forwarding in a separate letter a full list of Officers and Men whom I wish to recommend to your notice.

I have the honour to be, Sir,
Your obedient Servant,
David Beatty,
Vice-Admiral.
The Commander-in-Chief,
Grand Fleet.

Footnotes:
All times given in this report are Greenwich mean time.
†*NOTE. – The list of ships and commanding officers which took part in the action has been withheld from publication for the present in accordance with practice.*

13

OPERATIONS AGAINST GERMAN EAST AFRICA, 1916-1917

FRIDAY, 15 JUNE, 1917.

Admiralty,
15th June, 1917.

The following despatch has been received from the Commander-in-Chief, Cape of Good Hope Station, describing the later coastal operations by H.M. ships against German East Africa:-

H.M.S. "Hyacinth,"
28th January, 1917.

SIR, – Be pleased to lay before their Lordships the following report of the later coastal operations against German East Africa by H.M. ships under my orders.

These operations may be said to have commenced with the occupation, on the 1st August, 1916, of the town of Saadani by naval forces, assisted by a detachment of the Zanzibar African Rifles. The capture of this coast town was undertaken at the request of General Smuts, and was well and effectively carried out under the immediate supervision of Captain A.H. Williamson, M.V.O., of "Vengeance" (flying my flag) for the outer squadron, and of Captain E.J.A. Fullerton, D.S.O., of "Severn" for the inshore squadron; Commander R.J.N. Watson of "Vengeance" being in command of the landing party.

The force was landed in boats from "Vengeance," "Talbot" (R.C. Kemble Lambert, D.S.O.), "Severn," and "Mersey" (Commander R.A. Wilson, D.S.O.) about one mile to the north of the town at 6 a.m., "Severn" and "Mersey" covering the landing with their guns. But slight opposition was experienced, only three casualties being sustained. The fort was enclosed in a "boma," which had been constructed originally to keep out leopards and savages, and was surrounded by the native village and dense bush, which had to be cleared.

During the period of naval occupation a few encounters took place between our advanced patrols and those of the enemy, but no attack in force was made and our energies were confined to consolidating the position.

On the 5th August the whole of the naval forces, except the Marines and a few special details, re-embarked on military forces being landed to relieve them.

On the 13th August I received a wireless message from the military officer in command at Saadani, giving the enemy force at Bagamoyo at about ten whites and forty Askaris, and asking if the Navy would take the town, as its earliest occupation was essential. I replied that this would be done and issued orders accordingly.

Although the information given me indicated that the enemy force was small, I knew that it would be strongly entrenched and would have Maxims, and I therefore decided to land what force I could raise from the ships immediately available, together with all machine guns, and to have a strong covering force of light-draught ships inshore with heavy-draught ships outside.

As it turned out the intelligence was very much at fault, the enemy having one 4.1-in. gun, one five-barrelled pom-pom, and two Maxims, their total force being more numerous than the landing party.

At 5.0 p.m. on the 14th August, "Vengeance" (Flag), with "Challenger" (Captain A.C. Sykes) and "Manica" (Commander W.E. Whittingham, R.N.R.) in company, left Zanzibar, anchoring at 3.24 a.m. on the 15th off Bagamoyo, the landing party leaving "Vengeance" at 4.40 a.m., under the command of Commander R.J.N. Watson.

There was a slight swell, little wind, and a bright moon, so that a complete surprise was not to be expected; but the landing turned out to be as near a surprise as was possible in the circumstances, and it is believed that the boats were not seen until they had left the monitors at 5.30 a.m.

Owing to the skill with which the advance was conducted by Commander Watson and Commander (acting) W.B. Wilkinson, and an alteration of course when some little way from the shore, the enemy were completely deceived as to the point of landing, and found themselves under a heavy fire from the monitors and motor boats, which effectually prevented them from firing on the landing party.

The latter proceeded and landed close under the 4.1-in. gun position to the left of the town, at a point where the gun, owing to its position some 30 feet back from the ridge on which it was sited, could not be sufficiently depressed to bear on them.

On the other hand this gun came under the enfilading fire of the 3-pounders, one each in my steam barge, "Vengeance's" picket boat, and the tug "Helmuth." This fire, at from 800 to 500 yards, so seriously discomposed the enemy that they abandoned the gun as soon as attacked by the shore party. This gun had come from Tanga in tow of 500 coolies, and had arrived at the position in which it was taken on the 9th August. Its capture was, in my opinion, a most remarkable piece of work, reflecting the greatest credit on the boats and the attacking section.

Meanwhile the "Manica" had got up her kite balloon and was spotting, but her seaplane had engine trouble and was forced to come down in the breakers at the mouth of the Kingani River, returning undamaged. I accordingly called on

"Himalaya" (Captain Colin Mackenzie, D.S.O.), which was just leaving Zanzibar, and at 6.0 a.m. her seaplane flew across from Zanzibar, and at once dropped bombs on the enemy in trenches, afterwards spotting. "Himalaya" herself followed and took a useful part in the subsequent bombardment.

At 6.30 a.m. it was reported from three sources – kite balloon, portable W./T. set ashore, and W./T. from seaplane – that the enemy were retiring between the French Mission and the sea, and were around the Mission.

The cause of this retreat was the endeavour of Captain von Bok to rush his troops round to the opposite side of the town to oppose our landing. About this time the pom-pom gun was hit by a 6-in. shell from "Severn" (Commander (acting) W.B.C. Jones) and nearly pulverised, Captain von Boedecke being killed. Shortly after Captain von Bok was also killed, and with both leaders gone all initiative on the part of the enemy was lost, and our men were able to firmly establish themselves in a small but important quarter of the town, from which they subsequently spread and gathered in all the Arabs, Indians, and natives. Beyond slight damage from shell fire and a fire in the native village – where an occasional fire is beneficial – the town is intact.

The importance of the capture of this town on the native mind was very great, as it is the old capital of the slave trade and the starting place of the great caravan routes into the interior.

The result from a military point of view was immediately apparent in the demoralisation of the enemy forces, particularly the native portion, and in the evacuation of the Mtoni Ferry, a strategic and strongly defended position about six miles above the town over the Kingani River, thereby giving our troops moving south from Saadani and Mandera an open road.

It is with deep regret that I record the death of Captain Francis H. Thomas, D.S.C., Royal Marine Light Infantry, whilst gallantly leading his men. He had taken part in all recent operations and was a most promising officer. Our other casualties were two seamen and two marines wounded, while the Zanzibar African Rifles had one sergeant and one Askari killed and one Askari wounded. Two native porters were also wounded.

The enemy casualties were estimated at two officers, one white soldier, and eight Askaris killed, three white and eight Askaris wounded, and four white and fifteen Askaris taken prisoner.

On the 20th August the naval forces were relieved by the military and re-embarked in their ships.

On the 21st August, in continuance of the policy of harassing Dar-es-Salaam, "Vengeance" and "Challenger" bombarded various gun positions; and during that night "Challenger" carried out a further bombardment, firing 50 rounds of 6-in. over the town into the railway station. On the 23rd, 26th, 28th, 30th and 31st August, and on the 1st September, other limited bombardments took place, and on the 3rd September the whalers "Pickle" (Lieutenant H.C. Davis, D.S.C., R.D., R.N.R.), "Fly" (Lieutenant D.H.H. Whitburn, R.N.R.), "Childers" (Lieutenant V.C. Large, R.N.R.), and "Echo" (Lieutenant C.J. Charlewood, D.S.C., R.N.R.), under Flag Commander the Hon. R.O.B. Bridgeman, D.S.O., simulated a landing at Upanga and attacked the front at short range from West Ferry Point to Ras Upanga. They were received with shrapnel fire from a field battery, but escaped injury.

Meanwhile preparations for the advance on Dar-es-Salaam were in full swing, and on the 31st August the military advance started from Bagamoyo, the main body marching south and being strongly reinforced at Konduchi on the 2nd September, for which landing they themselves formed the covering party. The plan succeeded admirably, the enemy retiring and making little attempt to oppose the advance, so that in the end the final reinforcements actually landed in face of the very formidable entrenchments at Mssassani Bay.

With the military column went six naval maxims, six Lewis guns, one 3-pounder Hotchkiss on field mounting, and a medical section, the party being under the command of Commander H.D. Bridges, D.S.O., of "Hyacinth."

Communication between the main column and the small craft inshore was maintained by a naval wireless party.

The march of 36 miles proved exceedingly arduous, the road turning into little better than a sandy track through a waterless district. Porters were short and speedily dropped behind with provisions, to add to which the first regiment of African descent which arrived at Mssassani consumed the 12,000 gallons of water and three days' provisions for the whole force.

On the 3rd September, following on the simulated landing from the whalers, a brisk bombardment of gun positions to the northward of the town, and in advance of our troops, was carried out for half an hour until 7.0 a.m., when firing ceased and our troops continued their advance to the outskirts of the town.

As matters now appeared ripe to demand the surrender of the town, on the morning of the 4th September, "Challenger," flying a white flag, proceeded to Makatumbe with a written demand, signed by me and by the Officer commanding troops. This was transferred to the "Echo," which took it as far as the boom and then sent it ashore in her boat.

About 8.0 a.m., the deputy burgomaster, the bank manager, and an interpreter came off in the "Echo" and agreed to the conditions of the demand, giving all the required guarantees. Our troops were at once told by wireless to advance into the town. All ships entered Dar-es-Salaam Bay, and during the afternoon the monitors entered the harbour after destroying the hawsers of the boom across the entrance.

I landed with my staff at 2.30 p.m., and at 3.0 o'clock the Union Jack was hoisted over the Magistracy with full honours.

Following on the occupation of Dar-es-Salaam it became necessary to seize other coast towns further south, and thus prevent the enemy from retreating by the coast to Lindi and the southern ports.

In consequence, on the 7th September, a simultaneous attack was made on the two Kilwas (Kivinje and Kisiwani), with the object of getting possession of these towns and holding the two hills, Singino Hill and Mpara Hill, which command Kilwa Kivinje and Port Beaver respectively. After four 12-in. shrapnel had been placed on the top of Singino Hill by "Vengeance," a white man was seen endeavouring to haul down the German colours at Kivinje and to hoist his boy's white "kanzu" in their place. This was observed just in time to prevent fire being opened from "Vengeance" with 6-in. guns on the trenches along the beach. A flag of truce was sent in, the town surrendered unconditionally, and a force was landed and occupied the town and the hill. Meanwhile, Kilwa Kisiwani had surrendered unconditionally to "Talbot," who landed a party and occupied Mpara Hill.

Operations against the three Southern Ports of Mikindani, Sudi and Lindi commenced on the 13th September, when 200 Marines, 700 Indian troops, 200 Zanzibar and Mafia African Rifles, 12 naval machine guns, 2 hotchkiss guns and 950 porters were landed at Mikindani in boats from "Vengeance," "Talbot," "Himalaya," and "Princess" (Captain C. La P. Lewin), assisted by the gunboats "Thistle" (Commander Hector Boyes) and "Rinaldo" (Lieutenant-Commander H.M. Garrett), and the kite balloon ship "Manica" and the transport "Barjora." There was no opposition, and the town was occupied by 9.0 a.m.

On the 14th September our troops commenced their advance towards Sudi, while "Vengeance," "Hyacinth," "Talbot" and "Himalaya," with "Barjora," proceeded round to the anchorage outside there. Whalers entered the inner harbour at daylight on the 16th, experiencing no resistance.

The whole force, having left a garrison of 100 men at Mikindani, marched to Sudi, arriving there at noon, when the marines, naval guns and African Rifles were embarked, the intention being to land these as a covering party outside Lindi under the guns of the squadron, while the main force marched from Sudi to Lindi, where, if any resistance was put up, they would have held a commanding position on the south side of the river.

Early on the 16th the ships proceeded to Lindi Bay and the Naval Brigade was landed after a short bombardment of the selected beach with 6-in. guns. An attempt to send in a flag of truce was made, but no answer could be obtained, and from seaplane observations the town appeared to be deserted. Supported by "Thistle," the force advanced along the beach and occupied the town.

The troops – who were thus saved a long and arduous march from Sudi to Lindi – were re-embarked at Sudi on the evening of the 16th, leaving a garrison of 100 men there. They arrived at Lindi on the 17th, and relieved the Naval Brigade and African Rifles, who were re-embarked.

The same evening "Talbot," "Thistle," and "Barjora," with a detachment of Indian troops on board, left Lindi, and by 8.0 a.m. on the 18th Kiswere was occupied without any opposition, the troops remaining as a garrison.

This was the last town of any importance on the coast of German East Africa, and the whole coast line is now occupied with the exception of the Rufiji Delta.

In connection with the operations covered by this despatch I append a list of officers and men whom I specially desire to bring to the notice of their Lordships for meritorious services.

I have the honour to be, Sir,
Your obedient servant,
(Signed) E. CHARLTON,
Rear Admiral,
Commander in Chief.

14

OPERATIONS IN MESOPOTAMIA, DECEMBER 1916 - MARCH 1917

FRIDAY, 21 SEPTEMBER, 1917.

Admiralty, 21st September, 1917.

The following despatch has been received from Vice-Admiral Sir Rosslyn E. Wemyss, K.C.B., C.M.G., M.V.O., late Commander-in-Chief, East Indies Station, covering a report by Captain Wilfrid Nunn, C.M.G., D.S.O., R.N., on the operations of H.M. Gunboats in Mesopotamia from December, 1916, to March, 1917:-

7th May, 1917.

SIR,-

Be pleased to submit to the Lords Commissioners of the Admiralty the enclosed report on the recent operations in Mesopotamia rendered to me by Captain Wilfrid Nunn. C.M.G., D.S.O., R.N.

2. I take this opportunity of specially bringing to Their Lordships' notice the excellent conduct of Captain Nunn during the whole period that he has commanded the Flotilla on the Tigris. Through force of circumstances this command devolved upon an officer of less standing than might have been otherwise expected, and he has shown himself under all circumstances not only to have been worthy of his

responsible position, but to have carried out his duties with a zeal and dash worthy of the best traditions and to have shown a very remarkable capacity for command.

I am, Sir,

Your obedient Servant,

R.E. Wemyss,

Vice-Admiral,

Commander-in-Chief.

H.M.S. "Mantis,"

21st March, 1917.

SIR, – I have the honour to submit the following report on the operations on the Tigris during the months of December, 1916, and January, February, and March, 1917, which led to the capture and occupation of Baghdad by our forces on 11th March, 1917.

2. Our advance on the right bank of the Tigris began on 13th December, 1916, when our troops established themselves on the Shatt al Hai.

The general situation early in January was as follows:-

On the left bank our forces were held up by the Turks in the extremely strong Sannaiyat position, while on the right bank we had advanced much further up the river. The Turks opposed to us were commanded by Khalil Pasha. They were well dug in in strong positions. Very large improvements have been effected in the Transport department, railways have been constructed, and a large number of river craft arrived.

A number of these, and also barges, were put together at Abadan and Basra, and the facilities for repairs much increased, and wharves constructed.

3. The gunboats at the Tigris front have co-operated with the Army in many intermittent bombardments of the enemy positions, and some very good results have been obtained, besides frequently engaging enemy aircraft.

We have at all times received great help from the Army, the Artillery officers and Staff being indefatigable in rendering the Navy every assistance.

The 14th Kite Balloon Section, R.N.A.S., commanded by Commander Francis R. Wrottesley, R.N., marked for us on many occasions, besides the useful work it has done keeping look-out for the Army.

Aeroplanes have also been frequently put at the disposal of the Royal Navy for spotting.

While keeping some gunboats at the Tigris front, I have also always, at the request of the military authorities, stationed others at various points on the line of communication, and two have been stationed in the Euphrates, in touch with the troops at Nasiriyah.

The following of H.M. Ships have been engaged in the operations at various times:-

H.M.S. "Tarantula," Commander Henry G. Sherbrooke.

H.M.S. "Mantis," Commander Bernard Buxton.

H.M.S. "Moth," Lieutenant-Commander C.H.A. Cartwright.

H.M.S. "Gnat," Lieutenant-Commander E.H.B.L. Scrivener.

H.M.S. "Butterfly," Lieutenant-Commander G.A. Wilson.

H.M.S. "Sawfly," Commander G.F.A. Mulock, D.S.O.

H.M.S. "Snakefly," Lieutenant R.P.D. Webster.

H.M.S. "Greenfly," Lieutenant-Commander A.G. Seymour, D.S.O.

H.M.S. "Gadfly," Commander E.K. Arbuthnot.

H.M.S. "Grayfly," Lieutenant C.H. Heath-Caldwell, D.S.C.

H.M.S. "Stonefly," Lieutenant M. Singleton, D.S.O.

H.M.S. "Mayfly," Lieutenant R.H. Lilley, D.S.C.

H.M.S. "Waterfly," Act. Commander Charles T. Gervers.

H.M.S. "Firefly," Lieutenant-Commander C.J.F. Eddis.

H.M.S. "Flycatcher," Lieutenant Hugh Lincoln, R.N.R.

H.M.S. "Scotstoun," Lieutenant S.E. Nicolle.

4. Operations proceeded in a most satisfactory manner, and early in February our forces were in possession of the right bank as far as to the westward of Kut el Amara, with bridges over the Hai, large numbers of prisoners having been taken, guns captured, and heavy loss inflicted on the enemy.

After intense bombardment, in which the gunboats co-operated, a successful assault of the Sannaiyat position was made on 22nd February, and a footing obtained in the Sannaiyat position. During the night of the 22nd-23rd dummy attempts were made to cross the river in various places above Sannaiyat, and just before daybreak of the 23rd covering parties were rowed across the Tigris near Shumran in pontoons, a surprise landing effected, and a bridge thrown across.

By evening the infantry of one division had crossed, and another followed, the enemy trying ineffectually to stem the British advance on the Shumran peninsula.

Meanwhile our troops were pushing forward boldly through the Sannaiyat position. The whole Turkish position was manifestly becoming untenable, and they commenced a general retreat, which developed later into a rout.

5. I was present at the operations on board H.M.S. "Tarantula," and later on on board H.M.S. "Mantis," other of H.M. Ships present being "Moth," "Butterfly," "Greenfly," "Gadfly," "Snakefly," "Waterfly" "Flycatcher," and "Scotstoun" were also present at the front from time to time, and H.M.S. "Gnat" rejoined me on 4th March.

6. On the forenoon of 24th February I moved up river with "Tarantula," "Moth," "Mantis," "Butterfly," "Gadfly," and arrived at Kut el Amara at 9.30 p.m., where I landed and hoisted the Union Jack.

The town was deserted and in ruins. Early on the morning of the 25th I moved on up river and communicated with our troops near Shumran.

Floating mines had been seen in the river, but were easily avoided.

7. During the morning I received a message from the Army Commander asking me to co-operate in pursuing the retreating Turkish Army, and I pressed on up river.

HMS *Dreadnought* pictured before the outbreak of the First World War. *Dreadnought*'s entry into service in 1906 represented such a marked advance in naval technology that her name came to be associated with an entire generation of battleships, the "dreadnoughts", as well as the class of ships named after her, while the generation of ships she made obsolete became known as "pre-dreadnoughts". She was the sixth ship of that name in the Royal Navy.

Two of HMS *Dreadnought*'s BL 12-inch Mk X naval guns. A pair of QF 12-pounder anti-torpedo boat guns are mounted on the turret roof. *Dreadnought* did not participate in any of the First World War naval battles; she was being refitted at the time of the Battle of Jutland. However, *Dreadnought* became the only battleship ever to sink a submarine when she rammed *U-29* when it unexpectedly broke the surface after firing a torpedo at another dreadnought in 1915. (US Library of Congress)

On 30 October 1914, the Royal Navy seaplane carrier HMS *Hermes* docked at Dunkirk with a cargo of seaplanes having sailed from Portsmouth earlier the same day. Early the next morning she set out on the return journey. However, *Hermes* had barely left harbour when it was sighted by *U-29*, which then fired two torpedoes. Both struck the former cruiser with devastating effect. Despite remaining afloat for nearly two hours, HMS *Hermes* eventually slipped beneath the waves. Twenty-two of the ship's crew (including four members of the Royal Marine Light Infantry) were lost; all but two have no known grave. (HMP)

An artist's depiction of either *Scharnhorst* or *Gneisenau* sinking during the Battle of the Falkland Islands. Casualties and damage during the engagement were extremely disproportionate; the British suffered only very lightly. German survivors, on the otherhand, amounted to just 215 men. (HMP)

Taken from HMS *Invincible*, this photograph shows HMS *Inflexible* standing by to pick up survivors from SMS *Gneisenau* on 8 December 1914, during the Battle of the Falklands Islands. Such was the decisive nature of this British victory, German commerce raiding on the high seas by regular warships of the Imperial German Navy was brought to an end. (HMP)

A view of the King George V-class battleship HMS *Audacious* slowly settling in the water after hitting a mine off the north coast of Ireland on 27 October 1914. HMS *Audacious* was the first principal naval casualty of the First World War, a victim of a mine laid by the converted German Norddeutscher Lloyd liner SS *Berlin*. The mine exploded on her port side just forward of her aft engine room bulkhead. After laying the mines *Berlin* attempted to return to Germany, but in the end was forced to put in to Trondheim where the ship was interned for the duration of the war. (HMP)

Passengers on the RMS *Olympic*, on the far right, watch the attempts to recover the sinking HMS *Audacious*. Despite the presence of these witnesses, the decision was taken by the Admiralty to maintain a veil of secrecy of the loss of the battleship. This situation was maintained until 14 November 1918, when the following notice was published in *The Times*: "The Secretary of the Admiralty makes the following announcement: HMS *Audacious* sank after striking a mine off the North Irish coast on October 27, 1914. This was kept secret at the urgent request of the Commander-in-Chief, Grand Fleet, and the Press loyally refrained from giving it any publicity." (HMP)

HMS *Pegasus* encountered the German heavy cruiser *Königsberg* on 20 September 1914 off the east coast of Africa. The original captain states: "During the action the flag of the *Pegasus* was shot away from its staff. A Marine at once ran forward, picked it up, and waved it aloft. He was struck down while standing on the deck exposed to the enemy's fire, but another came forward to take his place. Until the end the flag was kept flying." This illustration was one of a number produced during the First World War in an attempt to obscure the fact that *Pegasus* had actually struck the colours. (HMP)

The Formidable-class pre-dreadnought battleship HMS *Irresistible* listing and sinking in the Dardanelles, 18 March 1915 – an image taken from the battleship HMS *Lord Nelson*. Having struck a mine at 16.16 hours, the badly-damaged *Irresistible* was left without power, causing her to drift within range of Turkish guns which laid down a heavy barrage on her. HMS *Irresistible* finally sank at about 19.30 hours, her crew suffering about 150 casualties. (HMP)

It was at about 18.30 hours that the German battlecruisers *Lützow* and *Derfflinger* then fired three salvoes each at HMS *Invincible* during the Battle of Jutland. At least one 12-inch shell from the third German salvo is believed to have penetrated HMS *Invincible*'s midships 'Q' turret, which blew off its roof and detonated the midships magazines. This photograph itself was taken from the deck of HMS *Inflexible*, the next ship astern. (HMP)

The original caption to this image states that it shows the damage caused to a British light cruiser during the Battle of Jutland. Unfortunately, it is not known which of the light cruisers this is. Two, HMS *Black Prince* and HMS *Tipperary*, were sunk, whilst HMS *Southampton* was the light cruiser hit the most times – with eighteen shells striking her. (HMP)

The funeral pyre of HMS *Queen Mary* during the Battle of Jutland. After a German salvo had hit this battlecruiser amidships, her bows plunged down and her stern rose high in the air. A few moments later witnesses reported that her propellers were still slowly turning. A few minutes later there was nothing to be seen but this pillar of smoke rising hundreds of feet into the air. All but nine of her 1,266 crew were lost - two of the survivors were picked up by German ships. Her wreck was discovered in 1991 and rests partly upside-down, on sand, sixty metres down. Much of her equipment is reported to be scattered about the wreck. (HMP)

British and German sailors buried side by side in Frederikshavn Cemetery. Pictured here during the 1920s, the British memorial is on the left; the German one nearest the camera. Frederikshavn is a port in northern Jutland, about twenty-five miles from the northernmost point of Denmark. Buried here are four First World War casualties, all naval ratings killed in the Battle of Jutland. They include Officer's Cook 1st Class A. Gray, HMS *Tipperary*; Petty Officer W.E. Johnson, HMS *Turbulent*; and Officer's Steward 2nd Class W. Ellis, HMS *Ardent*. (HMP)

A surprising relic from Jutland – the last surviving warship that participated in the battle that is afloat today. Until recently, HMS *Caroline*, a C-class light cruiser, was the second-oldest ship in Royal Navy service after HMS *Victory*. Built by Cammell Laird at Birkenhead, and launched in December 1914, she served throughout the war in the North Sea – predominantly with the Fourth Light Cruiser Squadron, in which she fought at Jutland. HMS *Caroline* and her squadron formed part of the anti-submarine screen for the battleships as they rushed south towards the battlecruisers. During the main battle she took part in the destroyer clash between the main fleets between 19.15 and 19.30 hours. Towards the end of this main action, her squadron caught sight of a group of German capital ships, believed to be their battlecruisers and pre-dreadnaught battleships, and fired two torpedoes at them. (Courtesy of NI Science Park)

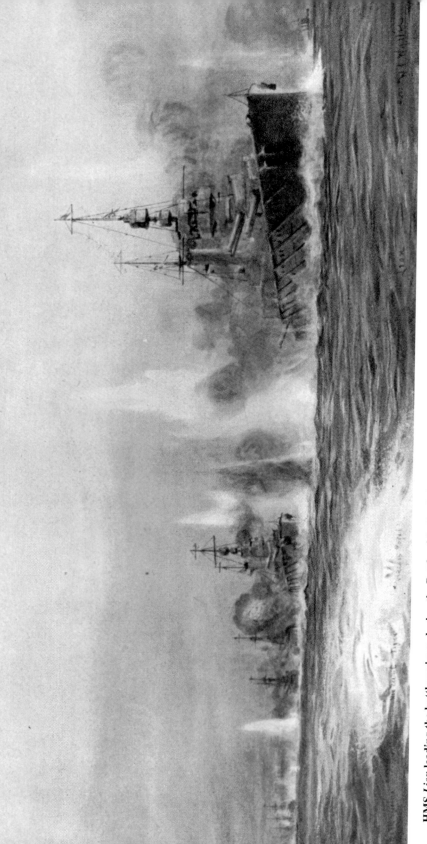

HMS *Lion* leading the battlecruisers during the Battle of Jutland. At one point in the battle, a heavy shell struck HMS *Lion*'s Q-turret, entered the gun-house, burst over the left gun, and killed nearly the whole of the guns' crews. It was only the presence of mind and devotion of the officer of the turret, Major F.J.W. Harvey, RMLI that saved the flagship from sudden destruction; in spite of both his legs being shot off he was able to pass the word down to close the magazine doors and flood the magazines. Harvey thus prevented the fire which started from reaching the ammunition, and so saved the ship, an action for which he was awarded the Victoria Cross after death. By the end of the battle, HMS *Lion* had been hit a total of fourteen times and suffered ninety-nine dead and fifty-one wounded during the battle. She fired 326 rounds from her main guns, but can only be credited with four hits on *Lützow* and one on *Derfflinger*. She also fired seven torpedoes, four at the German battleships, two at *Derfflinger* and one at the light cruiser *Wiesbaden* without success. (HMP)

By the latter half of the First World War the German surface fleet was limited to hit and run raids across the Channel and in response British destroyers were deployed to guard the Dover Strait. One night in April 1917 the opposing forces met. The British ships were outnumbered, but the German ships were outfought. This contemporary artist's depiction was "based on the accounts of eyewitnesses" and depicts the hand-to-hand fighting on board the Faulknor-class destroyer HMS *Broke* following the ramming of the German destroyer G.42 on 20 April 1917. (HMP)

Launched on 9 December 1897, and completed in 1899, the *Arrogant*-class protected cruiser HMS *Vindictive* is best remembered for its part in the Zeebrugge Raid in April 1918. In preparation for the attack, most of *Vindictive*'s guns were removed and replaced by howitzers, flamethrowers and mortars. On 23 April 1918 she was involved in the fierce action at Zeebrugge when she went alongside the Mole, and her upperworks were badly damaged by gunfire. The battered and badly-damaged HMS *Vindictive* is seen here after the attack at Dover. (HMP)

Some of the crew of HMS *Vindictive* inspecting equipment and souvenirs from the raid upon their return to Dover. The sailor on the far right is holding a lump of concrete from the Mole. Sir Roger Keyes once wrote that "over a hundredweight of concrete fell on the deck of the *Vindictive* while she was alongside the Mole … Pieces of it were carried away as souvenirs by many of the crew after the ship returned". (HMP)

An unusual relic of the attacks on Zeebrugge and Ostend in 1918 – the bow section of HMS *Vindictive*, which was sunk as a blockship at Ostend on 10 May 1918. The wreck was raised on 16 August 1920 and subsequently broken up. The bow section was preserved as a memorial and can be seen today near the bridge at the end of the De Smet-De Naeyer Avenue in Ostend. One of the protected cruiser's 7.5-inch howitzers was also saved, and is now in the care of the Imperial War Museum. (With the kind permission of Peter De Rycke)

One of those awarded the Victoria Cross for his participation in the attack on Zeebrugge – in this case decided by a ballot of Royal Navy officers – was Captain Alfred Carpenter RN, the commander of HMS *Vindictive*. The announcement of his award included the following: "He set a magnificent example to all those under his command by his calm composure when navigating mined waters, bringing his ship alongside the mole in darkness. When 'Vindictive' was within a few yards of the mole the enemy started and maintained a heavy fire from batteries, machine guns and rifles on to the bridge. He showed most conspicuous bravery …" Carpenter is pictured here being received by King George V and Queen Mary at a garden party for holders of the VC held at Buckingham Palace, July 1920. (HMP)

Warships from the German High Seas Fleet are pictured whilst en route to captivity on 21 November 1918. According to the terms of the Armistice, Germany was obliged to hand over and surrender all her U-boats and about seventy-four surface warships. On 19 November 1918 the German naval force set sail for the Firth of Forth, where they arrived on the morning of 21 November 1918. The German fleet was met by an Allied force of about 250 ships. From 22 November the German ships were moved in groups to Scapa Flow. (HMP)

The scuttling of the German Fleet underway in Scapa Flow on 21 June 1919. By the culmination of what were, in terms of maritime history, an almost unique series of events, over 400,000 tons of some of the finest warships then in existence, seventy-two vessels of which fifty-two actually went to the bottom, had been scuttled. This is the battlecruiser *Hindenburg* pictured late on the afternoon of 21 June 1919. This was the largest (but not the heaviest) warship scuttled at Scapa Flow. She sank slowly on an even keel, and her upper works, seen here, remained a part of the Orkney scenery for some eleven years before the warship was finally salvaged in 1930. (HMP)

We were abreast of our leading Infantry at about 9.30 a.m. and in sight of the Turkish rearguard, on which we at once opened with rapid fire, inflicting heavy casualties. This the enemy soon returned, opening an accurate fire on us with field batteries, and several 5.9 howitzers from a prepared position among the sand hills in the neighbourhood of Imam Mahdi. Our troops were advancing, and some of our field artillery considerably relieved the situation by the rapidity with which they came into action.

The battle continued, during the day – all ships being hit by splinters of shell, but luckily no serious damage was done.

Lieutenant John H. Murdock, R.N.R., of H.M.S. "Mantis," was somewhat severely wounded in the afternoon.

8. The enemy evacuated their position during the night, and we pushed on with the Army in pursuit on the morning of 26th February.

It soon became evident that the Turkish Army was much demoralised, and I received a message by W/T from General Sir F.S. Maude during the forenoon to push on and inflict as much damage as possible.

We proceeded at full speed in "Tarantula," leading "Mantis" and "Moth," H.M. ships "Gadfly" and "Butterfly" following at their utmost speed.

My flotilla passed the small town of Bghailah at 2 p.m. White flags were flying over the town, and later on Commander Ernest K. Arbuthnot, of "Gadfly" hoisted the Union Jack over the town, bringing in also about 200 prisoners and some trench mortars.

9. Just above Bghailah we now began to come up to numbers of Turkish stragglers on the left bank of the Tigris, and some guns partially submerged in the river, where they had been abandoned. We opened fire on all who did not surrender.

The smoke of steamers had been seen ahead, and we were soon able to distinguish several steamers, including H.M.S. "Firefly," which we had to abandon on 1st December, 1915, when her boiler was disabled by a shell during the retreat from Ctesiphon and we were surrounded by the Turkish Army.

We shortly afterwards got into gun range of the small shipping and opened a heavy fire, particularly on "Firefly" and the armed enemy ship "Pioneer," who both replied. The "Firefly" made some good shooting at us with her 4-inch gun.

10. The Turks retreating on the left bank were becoming more numerous; they now had our cavalry division in pursuit of them on their right flank and the gunboats on their left.

The enemy were firing at us from three directions, and on approaching Nahr Kellak bend I observed a large body of enemy on the left bank at the head of the loop in the river, and gave orders for all guns to be fired on them.

They proved to be a strong rearguard, and opened on us with field and machine guns and heavy rifle fire. At this close range there were casualties in all ships, who were all hit many times, but our guns must have caused immense damage to the enemy, as we were at one time firing six-inch guns into them at about 400 to 500 yards.

Besides the Turkish Artillery there were a large number of enemy with rifles and machine guns behind the bend at a range of about 100 yards from the ships.

In the act of turning round the bend shot came from all directions, and casualties of "Moth," which came last in the line, were particularly severe.

There were casualties in all three ships, "Moth," which was magnificently handled by Lieutenant Commander Charles H.A. Cartwright, who was himself wounded, had three officers wounded – all severely – out of four, and two men killed and eighteen wounded, which is about 50 per cent. of her complement.

She was hit eight times by shell – one from ahead hit the fore side of stokehold casing, burst, and pierced the port boiler, both front and back, but luckily missed the boiler tubes. The after compartment was holed below the water line, and the upper deck and funnels of all ships riddled with bullets.

The quartermaster and pilot in the conning tower of H.M.S. "Mantis" were killed, but the prompt action of her Captain saved her from running ashore. I consider that the excellent spirit of the men and skilful handling of the ships by their Captains in a difficult and unknown shallow river were most praiseworthy.

11. We thus passed the enemy rearguard, and large numbers of the retreating Turkish Army were on our starboard beam. I opened rapid fire from all guns that would bear (this included heavy and light guns, pom-poms, maxims, and rifles), and at this short range we did enormous execution, the enemy being too demoralised to reply, except in a very few cases.

We were also able to shoot down some of their gun teams, which they deserted, and several guns thus fell into the hands of our forces when going over this ground.

12. The vessels ahead were now in easy range, and several small craft stopped and surrendered, including the armed tug "Sumana," which we had left at Kut during the siege, and had been captured at the fall of that place.

About 5.20 p.m. the large Turkish steamer "Basra" stopped and surrendered when brought to by a shell from H.M.S. "Tarantula," which had, I was afterwards informed, killed and wounded some German machine gunners. The "Firefly" kept up a heavy fire from her 4-inch gun, but our reply began to tell on her, and having been hit several times she ran into the bank and fell into our hands about 6.15p.m. in the north-west part of the Zaljah reach, to westward of Umm al Tubul.

The "Pioneer" having been badly hit by "Mantis," was in flames near her, and some barges laden with munitions in the vicinity.

The Turks had endeavoured to set fire to the "Firefly's" magazine, but we were able to put it out and took possession of her at once, and I put a prize crew on board and hoisted the White Ensign.

Darkness now came on, and I considered it inadvisable to go on further, as we were far ahead of our troops.

I placed Lieutenant John P. Bradley, R.N.R. (of H.M.S. "Proserpine") in temporary command of H.M.S. "Firefly," with a small crew, and we moved out of the way of the burning "Pioneer," anchored for the night, and buried our men who had been killed.

13. We remained in the vicinity the following day, and I sent the "Moth" back to

Basra for repairs, and the prizes down river. The advance, of our Army continued, and we reached Aziziyah on 1st March. Here the Turks had abandoned more guns and again retreated. I was joined here by H.M.S. "Waterfly."

The pursuit was continued on 5th March, and our cavalry again engaged the enemy rearguard near Lajj, but we were unable to distinguish anything owing to a dense sandstorm.

14. We arrived at Ctesiphon on the 6th, finding the strong position there deserted, and next day arrived in gun-range of the enemy position on the north bank of the Dialah River, which joins the Tigris on the left bank about eight miles below Baghdad.

In attacking this position we again came under heavy fire from the Turkish guns, to which we briskly replied. During the night of the 10th-11th the enemy evacuated the position, as some of our troops had crossed the Dialah, and others were carrying out a wide flanking movement on the right bank to the south-west and west of Baghdad.

An attempt had also been made to send two motor lighters full of troops to land them on the left bank above the Dialah on the night of 10th March. One of them, however, grounded in the shallow river in gun range of the enemy. I sent H.M. Ships "Tarantula" and "Snakefly" to assist, and "Tarantula" rendered valuable assistance by extricating the motor lighter from her dangerous position before daylight.

15. The Baghdad railway was seized early on the 11th March.

I proceeded up river with the gunboat flotilla, which included H.M.S. "Firefly," Lieutenant-Commander C.J.F. Eddis in command, during the day, with minesweepers ahead, and arrived at the Citadel at Baghdad in H.M.S. "Mantis" at 3.40 p.m., on Sunday, 11th March. Paddle Steamer No. 53, having on board Sir F.S. Maude and Staff, being in company with the Flotilla.

The pursuit of the enemy was continued up river, and two iron barges captured.

16. I have much pleasure in bringing to your notice the excellent behaviour and spirit of the Captains, Officers, and men under my command during these operations, which were, in my opinion, worthy of the great traditions of His Majesty's Service.

In conclusion, I desire to express how greatly the Naval Forces serving in Mesopotamia have always been indebted to the Military and Political services for never-failing help and assistance on all occasions.

I have the honour to be,

Sir,

Your obedient Servant,

Wilfrid Nunn,

Captain and S.N O., Mesopotamia.

I have the honour to submit the following for special mention, promotion, honours or awards:-

OFFICERS

H.M.S. "Tarantula."

Commander Henry G. Sherbrooke, R.N.
For skilful handling of his ship, and especially on 26th February, when he contributed largely to the success of the operations.

Lieutenant J.P. Bradley, R.N.R.
For coolness under fire on all occasions.
Lieutenant Bradley did very good work by personally taking the captured Turkish steamer "Basra" down the river laden with enemy wounded.

Sub-Lieutenant G.A. Feilman, R.N.V.R.
For coolness and resource under very heavy fire, in firing with machine guns on the Turkish infantry and machine guns, when all other men were employed in working the main armament of 6-in., 12-pdr. and pompoms.

Surgeon J.C. Kelly, R.N.
Attended to wounded whilst fire was at its hottest in an exposed position.

H.M.S. "Mantis."

Commander Bernard Buxton, R.N.
For good work done on all occasions. His prompt action under heavy fire on 26th March saved H.M.S. "Mantis" from running aground in a critical position.

Surgeon James P. Shorten, R.N.
Continued to dress and attend to the wounded in the open while under very heavy fire.

Sub-Lieutenant E.C.W. Vane Tempest, R.N.V.R.
Was in charge of the gunnery of the ship, and while under hot fire he did his duty with coolness. At one time he personally worked a maxim though wounded.

H.M.S. "Moth."

Lieutenant-Commander Charles H.A. Cartwright, R.N.
For excellent handling of his ship and gallant conduct on all occasions under fire, and particularly on 26th February, 1917. I submit that this officer is fully worthy of special promotion.

Surgeon Frederick G.E. Hill, R.N.
Who, finding a man wounded on the battery deck, gallantly, under heavy fire, carried him into the sick bay to dress his wounds. Whilst doing this, the man received another wound through his throat, and Surgeon Hill himself received a nasty wound in his forearm. Nevertheless, although in considerable pain, and until his arm became too stiff to use it, he proceeded to dress and attend to all the wounded on board.

Lieutenant John H.A. Wood, M.C., R.N.V.R.
Who was severely wounded while firing a machine gun in a totally exposed position.

H.M.S. "Snakefly."

Lieutenant R.P.D. Webster, R.N.
Has shown judgment and resource on many occasions under fire.

H.M.S. "Flycatcher."

Lieutenant Hugh Lincoln, R.N.R.
For good work while in command of H.M. ships "Comet" and "Flycatcher," and he has carried out the duty of forward observing Officer under fire in a very satisfactory manner.

H.M.S. "Gadfly."

Commander Ernest K. Arbuthnot, R.N.
During the recent advance to Baghdad I have found this officer's knowledge and experience of great benefit, and he has shown great coolness under fire on all occasions.

Temporary Surgeon Robert G. Elwell, R.N.
Has rendered valuable service under fire on many occasions.

H.M.S. "Proserpine."

Lieutenant Cecil G. Hallett, R.I.M.
Has given me most valuable help throughout the campaign, and has carried out the gunnery duties for the Squadron. His experience, particularly of spotting the enemy gun positions, is of great value, and he has frequently done this under fire.

MEN.

H.M.S. "Tarantula."

Chief Petty Officer W.B. Ayre, O.N. 171045 (Ch.).
Chief Engine Room Artificer H. Lovell, O.N. 268831 (Ch.).
Leading Seaman H.M.J. Thompson, O.N. 236295 (Ch.).
Able Seaman W. Stephenson, O.N. 234863 (Ch.).

H.M.S. "Mantis."

Chief Engine Room Artificer, 2nd Class, Alexander Greig, O.N. M.17441 (Ch.).
Petty Officer James Revell, O.N. 208740 (Ch.).

Petty Officer William H. Saunders, O.N. J5200 (Ch.).
Stoker Petty Officer Edward S. Crossman, O.N. 287047 (Ch.).
Leading Telegraphist Sydney W. Boulter, J15349 (Ch.).

H.M.S. "Moth."

Acting Chief Engine Room Artificer, 4th Class, William J. Hollies, O.N. M.12130 (Ch.).
Stoker Petty Officer George T. Hasler, O.N. K1366 (Ch.).
Signalman Charles Poulter, R.N.V.R., O.N. London Z/3247 (Ch.).
Telegraphist Herbert W. Prior, O.N. J.32080 (Ch.).
Able Seaman Alfred E. Lucas, O.N. J.15975 (Ch.).
Able Seaman Percy W. Dean, R.F.R., Chatham B.3950 O.N. 209195 (Ch.).
Stoker John Farrell, R.N.R., O.N. S.8533.

H.M.S. "Snakefly."

Stoker Petty Officer John W. Mallinson, O.N. 303741 (Dev.).
Leading Telegraphist Martin L. Elliott, O.N. J.29215 (Dev.).

H.M.S. "Gadfly."

Petty Officer, 1st Class, Ronald Godfrey Robinson, O.N. 198809 (Po.).
Engineroom Artificer, 2nd Class, Leonard Ernest Brown, O.N. 271864 (Po.).

The following are recommended for good services at the base, which contributed largely to the successful operations:-

Captain Cathcart B. Wason, C.M.G., R.N.
Staff Surgeon Thomas W. Jeffery, R.N., H.M.S. "Proserpine."
Staff Surgeon George G. Vickery, R.N., H.M.S. "Dalhousie."
Engineer Lieutenant-Commander Stanley W. Cooke, lately of H.M.S. "Proserpine."
Paymaster Herbert G. Cavanagh, R.N , H.M.S. "Dalhousie."
Lieutenant A.H.B. Gray, R.I.M., H.M.S. "Dalhousie."
Chief Gunner Patrick J. O'Connor, R.N., H.M.S. "Dalhousie."
Carpenter William Brown, R.N., H.M.S. "Proserpine."

(Sgd.) W. NUNN,
Captain and S.N.O., Mesopotamia.

15

SINKING OF SMS *LEOPARD*, 16 MARCH 1917

FRIDAY, 18 APRIL, 1919.

Admiralty,
18th April, 1919.

The following, despatches describe the sinking of an enemy raider by H.M. Ships "Achilles" and "Dundee" in March, 1917. This raider was, it is now known, commissioned as the German auxiliary cruiser "Leopard," being in fact no other than the British steamer "Yarrowdale," captured by the raider "Moewe" in December, 1916, and fitted out in Germany for service as a raider:-

From Commander-in-Chief, Grand Fleet, to Admiralty.

"Queen Elizabeth,"
21st March, 1917.

Sir,

I have the honour to transmit, herewith, for the information of their Lordships, reports from the Commanding Officers of "Achilles" and "Dundee," on the action between those ships and an enemy raider on 16th March, 1917, in latitude 64° 54' N., longitude 0° 22' E., resulting in the sinking of the raider with all hands.

The raider appears to have had a heavy torpedo armament, and evidently hoped, by manoeuvring during chase and boarding, to torpedo both "Achilles" and "Dundee." This was prevented by the skilful handling of both ships. The Commanding Officer of "Dundee" displayed excellent judgment in manoeuvring his ship in such a way that he was able to pour in a hot fire for five or six minutes at a range of 1,000 yards before the raider could bring a gun to bear.

After weighing the evidence, I am satisfied that no submarine was present. The object reported by "Achilles" as a mine, and by "Dundee" as a submarine, was probably a cask, possibly containing oil, leakage of which would have given the appearance of the wake noted by "Dundee."

I very much regret the loss of Lieutenant Frederick H. Lawson, R.N.R., and his gallant boat's crew of volunteers, who undoubtedly perished with the raider. The boarding parties from the patrol squadrons have, throughout the war, displayed the greatest skill and fearlessness in carrying out their hazardous work in all weathers.

That the raider was intercepted and brought to action is the result of much patient work under trying conditions. Much credit is due to Rear-Admiral Sydney R. Fremantle, M.V.O., for his conduct of the Second Cruiser Squadron patrol.

I submit, for the favourable notice of their Lordships, the ability and sound judgment displayed by Captain Francis M. Leake, R.N., of "Achilles," and Commander Selwyn M. Day, R.D., R.N.R., of "Dundee," in rounding up and destroying the vessel which was capable of doing such damage to our commerce.

The Rear-Admiral Commanding, Second Cruiser Squadron, is being furnished with a copy of this letter, and will submit, in due course, a list of recommendations of other Officers and Men whose services he considers special noteworthy.

I am, Sir,
Your obedient servant,
David Beatty,
Admiral.
The Secretary
of the Admiralty.

H.M.S. "Achilles,"
17th March, 1917.

Sir, – I have the honour to report that on the 16th March, when patrolling in accordance with orders from the Rear-Admiral Commanding Second Cruiser Squadron, in latitude 64.42 north, longitude 0.56 west, at 11.45 a.m., a steamer was sighted steering 66°, bearing N. 84 E, distance about nine miles. Weather at the time being: Wind south-easterly, force 4 to 5, snow and rain squalls, sea moderate. "Achilles" was steering N. 15 W., and altered course N. 84 E., to close steamer, and directed "Dundee" to conform. Speed of advance 15 knots.

At 1.00 p.m., finding a very small gain, "Achilles" increased speed to 18 knots, and at 1.45 p.m. course was altered to S. 87 E., to avoid following directly astern.

At 2.00 p.m. steamer was overhauled and directed to stop, which signal she obeyed. She was then directed to steer W. by S., and at 2.35 p.m. was again stopped for "Dundee" to examine her. "Achilles" manoeuvring at a distance of two and a half to three miles.

At 3.45 p.m. "Dundee" and raider commenced an action simultaneously. "Achilles" at once joined in, at a range of 5,300 yards, raider firing at her, but with more intensity at "Dundee," whose safety was due to the prompt manner in which Commander Selwyn Mitchell Day, R.N.R., answered the raider's first hostile act, and the initial success she gained in getting raking hits; hers was the dangerous position, and she extracted herself with the utmost credit.

On opening fire the raider at once enveloped herself in smoke of a light colour. At 3.55 p.m. she fired a torpedo at "Achilles," which broke surface off the port quarter. A submarine was reported at the same time in this direction, and speed was increased from 16 to 20 knots. Hits were now being obtained, and the raider was on fire forward. About this time she was hit in the bow (on the gripe) by a torpedo from "Achilles."

About 4.00 p.m. fire was checked, the raider being well on fire, with occasional explosions forward. Soon after this, "Dundee" took station astern of "Achilles," and was then ordered to steer west. At 4.23 p.m. she reported a submarine between herself and the raider. Consequently, fire was again opened on the raider and continued until, at 4.33 p.m., she listed to port and sank, more or less horizontally, a mass of flames, and red hot forward, leaving no visible survivors.

The position of this action was latitude 64.54 north, longitude 0.22 east. The weather during the time was: Wind south-easterly, force three to four, with continuous rain and moderate sea.

The loss of the "Dundee" boarding party is greatly regretted. The actual movements of this boat could not be seen from "Achilles," but she was apparently alongside the raider when the action commenced. An overturned boat was sighted from "Achilles." Excepting this, at no time was anything resembling a boat seen.

List of "Dundee" boarding party attached.

I have the honour to be,
Sir,
Your obedient Servant,
F.M. Leake,
Captain.

H.M.S. "DUNDEE" BOARDING PARTY.

Lawson, Frederick Herman, Lieutenant, R.N.R.
Anderson, Henry, Seaman, R.N.R., 2845 A.
Anderson, Henry James, Seaman, R.N.R., 4911 B.
Anderson, Magnus John, Seaman, R.N.R., 3936 B.
Anderson, Robert John, Seaman, R.N.R., 3717 C.
Birchall, Alfred, Able Seaman, R.N.V.R., Mersey, 1/150.

H.M.S. "Dundee,"
11th March, 1917.

Sir,

Re Action with German twin-screw Armed Merchantman, approximately 7,000 tons – Seven or eight guns – Complement unknown – Flying Norwegian colours – With "Rena," Norge, painted on each side – in 64.50 N., 0.32 E., on Friday, March 16th, 1917.

I have the honour to report that whilst patrolling with H.M.S. "Achilles" on Friday, March 16th, p.m., I proceeded to the examination of the above steamer bound East (Mag.), which had been overhauled and stopped by "Achilles" for that purpose.

At 2.42 p.m. "Dundee" lowered a boat with Lieut. F.H. Lawson, R.N.R., and five R.N.R. Seamen forming the boarding and boat party. The boat was towed towards the intercepted vessel, at that time about two miles distant and steaming slowly towards us.

The following signals were then exchanged:-

	"Dundee"	*"Rena"*
2.40.	"What ship is that?"	No Reply.
2.45.	"Stop instantly."	Answered by A.P.
2.50.	"Pay attention to my signals."	No reply.
Blank round fired.		
2.59.	"What is your cargo?"	"General."
3.10.	"Where are you from?"	"Mobile."
3.30.	"When did you leave?"	No reply.

Her size, manoeuvres, and the information in confidential books supplied convinced me eventually she was a raider, and it was obvious he was trying to defeat my object of maintaining a position (for attack) close up to the weather quarter and heading across his stern, and he constantly moved the propellers, slewing to port or starboard. Keeping station thus we awaited some sign from the boarding Officer or the boat, which was, of course, on the lee side, and could not be seen by us.

At 3.40 I heard the noise of the large Norwegian flag painted on her port quarter fall outboard, being hinged on the lower side, and I gave the orders "Fire" and "Half speed ahead" to keep station, the raider now slewing rapidly to port with slight, if any, headway. Two torpedoes followed from her in quick succession, passing from 20 to 50 feet astern. The Norwegian flag remained hoisted on the ensign staff throughout and no other flag was seen. Our guns were already firing, and every shot was a hit. The first (from our aft 4″) raked her port battery deck, causing an explosion and volumes of smoke. The fore gun fired through the deck into her engine-room, and volumes of steam spread with intense smoke and flames, caused by further hits, so as to completely hide the ship from us from bridge to stern. The 3-pdr. gun fired at her bridge.

Forty-four 4″, and twenty-five 3-pdr. rounds were fired at about 1,000 yards' range before the raider fired her first gun. "Dundee" was then in the smoke (wind south-easterly, force 4 to 5) to leeward, and both ships practically obscured from each other in consequence.

Observing "Achilles" on almost opposite bearing, I turned, and went full speed and down the lane of smoke so as to clear the range for the cruiser. On turning, one torpedo was fired at us, and also three salvoes, two short and one over of three or four guns by her port broadside. Then followed some very wild single shots, including shrapnel, fragments of the latter only hitting ship. The aft gun was bearing the whole time, and made consistently excellent hitting on any visible part of the enemy. Ignited oil was observed streaming from her port beam.

At 4.10, when out of torpedo range, we again engaged enemy in company with "Achilles" already firing, and ceased fire at 4.15, having no more ammunition. The raider was a mass of flame, and obviously a doomed ship, although she continued to fight with apparently but one gun. Enemy sank whilst under fire of "Achilles," 4.35p.m.

We saw a submarine about half a mile from the raider, of which fact I immediately advised "Achilles."

I desire to submit the names of the following Gunlayers:-

W. Lee, P.O.1, R.F.R., Off. number, Po. 129854;

J.M. Cullen, A.B., R.N.V.R., Off. number, Mersey 35, 1/30;

J.L. Arthurson, Ldg. Sea., R.N.R., Off. number, B.3673;

J.G. Anderson, Sea., R.N.R., Off. number, C. 2485;

for favourable consideration, because with no Officers of Quarters available (two were absent on duty), they calmly and skilfully controlled the guns' crews and their own firing, doing their own spotting and judging point of aim to the most vital places about the raider's decks and hull, so that the enemy, who was approximately three times our size, complement and armament, was made by their marksmanship incapable of inflicting the smallest damage to us within the same period. In fact, the enemy ship at this time was stopped, disabled, and in time would have been entirely consumed by the fire then raging.

With the utmost regret I have to report that Lieut. Lawson, R.N.R., and the boat's crew who volunteered to accept the extreme risk entailed by a boarding operation under such conditions, are missing, having undoubtedly been forced into the raider and lost with her. The boat was observed empty at the commencement of the action as we followed round the stern of the enemy. Other than the boarding party, we suffered no casualties nor any damage to the ship.

I have the honour to be,
Sir,
Your obedient servant,
Selwyn M. Day,
Commander, R.N.R.
The Rear-Admiral Commanding
Second Cruiser Squadron,
H.M.S. "Minotaur."
Copy to Commanding Officer,
H.M.S. "Achilles."

16

OSTEND RAID, 9 MAY 1918

WEDNESDAY, 28 AUGUST, 1918.

Admiralty, 28th August, 1918.

The following despatch has been received from Vice-Admiral Sir Roger J.B. Keyes, K.C.B., C.M.G., C.V.O., D.S.O., Commanding the Dover Patrol:-

Fleet House,
Dover,
24th July, 1918.

SIR,

With reference to my despatch No. 2305/003 of 15th June, 1918*, I have the honour to bring to the notice of the Lords Commissioners of the Admiralty the names of the following Officers and Men who performed distinguished service in the second blocking operation against Ostend on the night of 9th/10th May, 1918.

2. – Aerial photographs taken prior to the operation clearly showed that the enemy had made special preparations in anticipation of a renewed attack.

3. – The operation was carried out in mined waters in the face of a tremendous fire, and the greatest credit is due to those who so readily volunteered for hazardous service in the "Vindictive" and in motor launches detailed for rescue work, and to the crews of the numerous craft which covered and screened the approach of the "Vindictive," led her to her objective, and rescued the survivors of her crew after she had been blown up between the piers of Ostend harbour.

The following Officers, Petty Officers and Men performed specially distinguished service in action on the night of 9th/10th May, 1918:-

Capt. Hubert Lynes, C.B., C.M.G., R.N. (Cdre., 2nd Cl.).
Commodore Lynes at Dunkirk having so ably carried out the direction of the former attempt to block Ostend as part of the Zeebrugge and Ostend scheme on the night of 22nd/23rd April, I entrusted the conduct of the operation again to him. He directed it in a most able manner, proceeding himself in H.M.S. "Faulknor," and supporting the "Vindictive" from an inshore position.

Cdr. Alfred E. Godsal, D.S.O., R.N.
This officer led the previous attempt to block Ostend in the "Brilliant," and on his return at once begged to be allowed to try again. On being appointed to the "Vindictive" he worked with the greatest energy to get her ready for further service at the earliest possible moment. On the night of 9th/10th May, having placed his vessel between the piers of Ostend harbour, he left the shelter of the conning tower for the forecastle in order to get a better view for manoeuvring her into the required position. He was almost immediately killed, and the Service lost in him a very gallant and valuable officer.

Lieut. Angus H. Maclachlan, R.N.
Lieutenant MacLachlan was in the "Brilliant" in the previous attempt to block Ostend, and at once volunteered for the second operation. This gallant young officer was in charge of the "Vindictive's" after control on the night of the 9th/10th May, and was killed at his post.

Lieut. Geoffrey H. Drummond, R.N.V.R.
Volunteered for rescue work in command of M.L. 254. Following "Vindictive" to Ostend, when off the piers a shell burst on board, killing Lieutenant Gordon Ross and Deckhand J. Thomas, wounding the coxswain, and also severely wounding Lieutenant Drummond in three places. Notwithstanding his wounds he remained on the bridge, navigated his vessel, which was already seriously damaged by shell fire, into Ostend harbour, placed her alongside "Vindictive," and took off two officers and thirty-eight men – some of whom were killed and many wounded while embarking. When informed that there was no one alive left on board he backed his vessel out clear of the piers before sinking exhausted from his wounds. When H.M.S. "Warwick" fell in with M.L. 254 off Ostend half an hour later the latter was in a sinking condition. It was due to the indomitable courage of this very gallant officer that the majority of the crew of the "Vindictive" were rescued.

Lieut. Roland Bourke, D.S.O., R.N.V.R.

Volunteered for rescue work in command of M.L. 276, and followed "Vindictive" into Ostend, engaging the enemy's machine guns on both piers with Lewis guns. After M.L. 254 had backed out Lieutenant Bourke laid his vessel alongside "Vindictive" to make further search. Finding no one he withdrew, but hearing cries in the water he again entered the harbour, and after a prolonged search eventually found Lieutenant Sir John Alleyne and two ratings, all badly wounded, in the water, clinging to an upended skiff, and rescued them. During all this time the motor launch was under a very heavy fire at close range, being hit in fifty-five places, once by a 6 in. shell – two of her small crew being killed and others wounded. The vessel was seriously damaged and speed greatly reduced. Lieutenant Bourke, however, managed to bring her out and carry on until he fell in with a Monitor, which took him in tow. This episode displayed daring and skill of a very high order, and Lieutenant Bourke's bravery and perseverance undoubtedly saved the lives of Lieutenant Alleyne and two of the "Vindictive's" crew.

Lieut. Victor A.C. Crutchley, D.S.C., R.N.
This officer was in "Brilliant" in the unsuccessful attempt to block Ostend on the night of 22nd/23rd April, and at once volunteered for a further effort. He acted as 1st Lieut, of "Vindictive," and worked with untiring energy fitting out that ship for further service. On the night of 9th/10th May, after his commanding officer had been killed and the second in command severely wounded, Lieut. Crutchley took command of "Vindictive" and did his utmost by manoeuvring the engines to place that ship in an effective position. He displayed great bravery both in the "Vindictive" and in M.L. 254, which rescued the crew after the charges had been blown and the former vessel sunk between the piers of Ostend harbour, and did not himself leave the "Vindictive" until he had made a thorough search with an electric torch for survivors under a very heavy fire. Lieut. Crutchley took command of M.L. 254 when the commanding officer sank exhausted from his wounds, the second in command having been killed. The vessel was full of wounded and very seriously damaged by shell fire, the fore part being flooded. With indomitable energy and by dint of baling with buckets and shifting weight aft, Lieut. Crutchley and the unwounded kept her afloat, but the leaks could not be kept under, and she was in a sinking condition, with her forecastle nearly awash when picked up by H.M.S. "Warwick." The bearing of this very gallant officer and fine seaman throughout these operations off the Belgian coast was altogether admirable and an inspiring example to all thrown in contact with him.

Lieut. Sir John M. Alleyne, Bart., D.S.C., R.N.
Volunteered from a Monitor of the Dover Patrol for service in the "Vindictive." He rendered valuable service in refitting navigational arrangements which were destroyed in "Vindictive" on 23rd April, and on the actual night of the operation was invaluable on account of his local knowledge. He showed great coolness under a very heavy fire, and most skilfully navigated the "Vindictive" to the entrance to Ostend harbour. He

was severely wounded and rendered unconscious when his Captain was killed.

Eng. Cdr. William A. Bury, R.N.
This gallant officer greatly distinguished himself in "Vindictive" on 23rd April, and as soon as he knew another operation was contemplated, volunteered, begging to be allowed to remain in charge of the engine room department of that vessel. He worked most energetically to fit her out for further service, and on the night of 9th/10th May he again rendered invaluable service, setting a fine example to his men. He remained in the engine room until the last possible moment, and when everyone was clear he blew the bottom out of the ship by firing the main and auxiliary after charges. He was very severely wounded.

Cdr. (act. Capt.) Ion Hamilton Benn, D.S.O., M.P., R.N.V.R.
This officer led the motor launches in M.L. 105 with conspicuous ability and success. This is the third occasion Capt. Benn has led the inshore motor launch division off Ostend under a very heavy fire. Capt. Benn has set a very fine example of bravery and devotion to duty to the officers and men of the motor launches of the Dover Patrol, which he has commanded for nearly three years, and has thus contributed greatly to the success which has attended the gallant efforts of these small craft in carrying out the dangerous duties assigned to them during these operations off the Belgian coast.

Cdr. Reginald St. P. Parry, R.N.
Commander Parry commanded a Destroyer, and handled his vessel with skill and decision, performing a most valuable service under difficult conditions.

Capt. Ernest Wigram, D.S.O., R.N.
This officer was in command of H.M. Monitor "Prince Eugene." He led his division well inside the allotted range in order to bring the secondary armament of the vessel into action. This brought the ships under a heavy fire from the shore batteries, and undoubtedly contributed considerably to the success of the operations.

Lieut. Arthur E.P. Welman, D.S.O., D.S.C., R.N.
The part played by the Coastal Motor Boats during the operation was all-important. Lieut. Welman organised and led them in a coastal motor boat in a most spirited manner. He encountered an enemy torpedo boat near the entrance to Ostend, which switched on searchlights and opened fire. He at once closed with her, and engaged her with Lewis guns to such good effect that she withdrew and left the channel clear for the approach of the blockships.

Lieut. (act. Lieut.-Cdr.) Keith R. Hoare, D.S.O., D.S.C., A.M., R.N.V.R.
Volunteered for rescue work at Ostend in command of M.L. 283. He was
ordered to follow astern and assist two other motor launches which were
detailed for rescue work. He remained at the Stroom Bank Buoy position
until "Vindictive" had passed and then followed her, patrolling east and
west within a quarter of a mile of the shore under heavy pom-pom and
machine-gun fire, searching for survivors until 3.20 a.m., when all hope of
finding anyone had passed.

Cdr. William W. Watson, R.N.V.R.
Was in command of M.L. 105, and was of the greatest assistance to Capt.
Benn in arranging and supervising the smoke screen. This involved going
from end to end of the line and taking his vessel close inshore several
times, when he came under heavy barrage fire. He showed great courage
and coolness throughout the operation.

Lieut.-Cdr. Raphael Saunders, R.N.V.R.
This officer volunteered for rescue work at Ostend in command of M.L.
128. In company with M.L. 283 he went in after "Vindictive" to look for
survivors. When near the shore he came under heavy fire – his signalman
was killed and Lieut. Brayfield and one of the crew wounded. This officer
showed great coolness, setting a fine example to his men throughout, and
was of the greatest assistance in organising the smoke screen.

Lieut. Russell H. McBean, R.N.
In command of a coastal motor boat. He escorted "Vindictive" close up to
the entrance at Ostend, covering her with smoke screen and then assisting
her with guiding lights. He torpedoed the eastern and western piers, and
finally engaged the machine guns there with his own machine guns at
point-blank range with apparently good effect. He most skilfully handled
his vessel under a heavy fire until he was wounded.

Sub-Lieut. George R. Shaw, R.N.R.
Second in command of a coastal motor boat which escorted "Vindictive"
with smoke screen close up to the entrance of Ostend Harbour, assisting
her with guiding lights. His vessel then torpedoed the eastern and western
piers, and finally engaged the machine guns at point-blank range. During
this engagement the commanding officer was wounded and the chief
motor mechanic killed. Having seen "Vindictive" inside the piers, and the
work of his vessel completed, Sub-Lieut. Shaw brought her safely back to
harbour.

Lieut. William H. Bremner, R.N.
Was in command of a coastal motor boat. When carrying out his smoke
screening of the enemy shore batteries, he encountered close inshore an
enemy torpedo boat, which switched on her searchlight and opened fire.
Lieut. Bremner had no better weapons than Lewis guns, but with these he

attacked and peppered the torpedo boat to such good effect as to drive her away from the harbour entrance and prevent her interfering with the blocking operation.

Lieut. The Hon. Cecil E.R. Spencer, D.S.C., R.N.
This officer was in command of a coastal motor boat and escorted "Vindictive" close inshore and kept touch with her until she gave the "last resort" signal, on which he laid and lit the flare, which greatly assisted the operation, drawing heavy fire previously directed at the "Vindictive" on to himself.

Lieut. Rawsthorne Procter, R.N.V.R.
This officer was in charge of a section of motor launches screening Monitors during the bombardment of the Ostend shore batteries. He exhibited conspicuous ability and initiative under heavy fire, and materially contributed to the success of the operation.

Lieut. Archibald Dayrell-Reed, D.S.O., R.N.R.
Was in command of a coastal motor boat, and carried out a successful attack on the pier ends, afterwards laying and maintaining good smoke screens close inshore throughout the remainder of the operation under a heavy fire.

Lieut.-Cdr. Jean S. Miéville, R.N.V.R.
Was in command of M.L.280 and leader of a smoke-screen unit. He led his unit with skill and judgment in a very exposed position, and it was largely due to him that he screen was so extremely successful in his section.

Sub-Lieut. James Petrie, R.N.V.R.
This officer volunteered for rescue work in M.L.276. When the coxswain was killed near the Ostend piers, he jumped to the wheel and steered the launch into the harbour. When fired on by machine guns from the piers, he manned the Lewis gun and returned the fire on both pier-heads. Later, when three wounded men were discovered in the water, he personally assisted them into the launch, being exposed all the time to heavy fire.

Lieut. Cuthbert F.B. Bowlby, D.S.C., R.N.
In command of a coastal motor boat, and escorted "Vindictive" close up to the entrance, then ran ahead, and finding one of the piers, fired a torpedo at it. The water being shallow and the range short, the explosion shook the boat so severely as to damage her engines and open her seams. She commenced to sink, but by his presence of mind he got the leak stopped, engines going again, and brought his boat out of the fire zone, where he was taken in tow by H.M.S. "Broke."

Lieut. Albert L. Poland, R.N.
In command of a coastal motor boat, and carried out a successful torpedo attack on the pier ends, afterwards laying and maintaining good smoke

screens close inshore throughout the remainder of the operation under a
heavy fire.

Lieut. Anthony C. Mackie, R.N.V.R.
This officer was of great assistance in command of M.L.279. He pluckily
carried on his smoke-screen work under fire for one and a half hours after
breaking the starboard shaft, retiring with the rest of the flotilla, when
operations were completed, under one engine.

Lieut.-Cdr. Arthur G. Watts, R.N.V.R.
This officer was in command of M.L.239 and leader of a smoke screen
unit. He led his unit with skill and judgment in a very exposed position,
and it was largely due to him that the screen was so extremely successful
in his section.

Lieut. Felix F. Brayfield, R.N.V.R.

This officer volunteered for rescue work as second in command of M.L.
128. M.L. 128, in company with M.L. 283, went in after "Vindictive" to
look for survivors. When near the shore she came under heavy fire, the
signalman was killed and Lieut. Brayfield and one of the crew wounded.
Lieut. Brayfield showed great devotion to duty, remaining on the bridge
and carrying on with his duties until the operation was over, though
wounded in the leg.

Lieut. Allan L. Geddes, R.N.V.R.
This officer was in command of M.L. 553 and leader of an inshore smoke
screen unit. He led his unit with skill and judgment under fire, and it was
largely due to him that the smoke screen was so extremely successful in
his section.

Lieut. Gordon F. Ross, R.N.V.R. (Killed in action.)
Volunteered for rescue work in M.L. 254 – killed in the entrance to Ostend
harbour.

P.O. Joseph James Reed, D.S.M., O.N. 230360 (Ch.).
This Petty Officer was in "Brilliant" in the previous attempt to block
Ostend. He immediately volunteered to accompany his officers in a second
operation. On the night of 9th/10th May he steered the "Vindictive" into
Ostend harbour and, when the charges were fired and the ship abandoned,
he picked up Lieut. Sir John Alleyne, who was lying unconscious in the
conning tower, carried him to the gangway, and lowered him over the side.
This very gallant Petty Officer then assisted others to escape, and on board
M.L. 254 was of the greatest assistance in keeping that vessel afloat until
she was picked up.

Ldg. Dkhnd. David George Rees, R.N.R., O.N. 3146 S.D.
For his conspicuous gallantry as coxswain, of M.L. 254, remaining at the wheel after being wounded. He assisted Lieut.-Cdr. Drummond – also seriously wounded – to put the motor-launch alongside "Vindictive" in Ostend harbour and carried on until he was relieved by one of the rescued crew.

Not published.

17

ZEEBRUGGE & OSTEND RAIDS, APRIL & MAY 1918

WEDNESDAY, 19 FEBRUARY, 1919.

Admiralty, 19th February, 1919.

DESPATCHES FROM THE VICE-ADMIRAL, DOVER PATROL, ON ZEEBRUGGE AND OSTEND OPERATIONS, 22ND-23RD APRIL, 1918, AND OSTEND OPERATIONS, 10TH MAY, 1918.

REPORT OF VICE-ADMIRAL, DOVER PATROL, ON OPERATIONS, 22ND-23RD APRIL, 1918.

Fleet House, Dover,
*9th May, 1918.
(No. 1806/001.)

SIR,

Be pleased to submit for the information of the Lords Commissioners of the Admiralty the following Report on the Operations on the Belgian Coast on the night of the 22nd-23rd April, 1918.

I. – GENERAL SUMMARY.

2. To make the report clear, the different sections of the operations have been separated as much as possible. Fuller details than appear in this despatch will be found in the complete set of orders and reports forwarded herewith.

(NOTE. – These orders and reports are not published with this despatch.)

3. The main objects of the enterprise were (1) to block the Bruges ship-canal at its entrance into the harbour at Zeebrugge; (2) to block the entrance to Ostend harbour from the sea; and (3) to inflict as much damage as possible upon the ports of Zeebrugge and Ostend.

4. Zeebrugge harbour is connected by a ship-canal with the inland docks at Bruges, which communicate again by means of a system of smaller canals with Ostend harbour. The whole forms a triangle with two sea entrances. The eastern side, which is 8 miles long, is the ship-canal from Zeebrugge to Bruges; the southern side, which is 11 miles long, consists of smaller canals from Bruges to Ostend; the base, facing north-west, is the 12 miles of heavily fortified coast line between Ostend and Zeebrugge. This fortified line is prolonged 8½ miles to the westward, extending to the right flank of the German Army, facing Nieuport, and 7 miles to the eastward as far as the Dutch frontier. The defences include a number of batteries mounting over 225 guns, 136 of which are from 6-in. to 15-in. calibre, the latter ranging up to 42,000 yards.

5. This formidable system has been installed since the German occupation in 1914, and Bruges has recently provided a base for at least 35 enemy torpedo craft and about 30 submarines. By reason of its position and comparative security it has constituted a continual and ever-increasing menace to the sea communications of our Army and the seaborne trade and food supplies of the United Kingdom.

6. When the operations of the 22nd-23rd April were undertaken it was believed that, although the blocking of the Zeebrugge entrance to the Bruges ship-canal was the most important of all objects, it would be necessary also to block the entrance to the Ostend harbour in order to seal up the Bruges ship-canal and docks; for unless this were done the lighter craft would still be able to pass to and fro more or less freely through the smaller canals.

7. The attack upon the Zeebrugge Mole, as well as the bombardment of Zeebrugge by monitors and from the air, were designed to distract the attention of the enemy from the main operations. Without this diversion the attempt of the blocking ships to pass round the end of the Mole, to enter the harbour, and to reach the ship-canal entrance at the inner end must almost certainly have been discovered, with the result that the vessels would have been sunk by the shore batteries long before they reached their goal.

8. An important, though subordinate, object of the attack upon the Zeebrugge Mole was to inflict as much damage as was possible in the time upon the harbour works and defences. In order to prevent enemy reinforcements being brought from shore, while this work was in progress arrangements were made for blowing up the viaduct which connected the Mole with the land.

9. Similarly the bombardment of the Ostend defences by our shore batteries in Flanders, by the monitors and also from the air was designed to cover the attempt to block the entrance to that harbour.

10. It was anticipated that, in addition to the fire from the land batteries and harbour works, the attacking forces would have to face a counter-attack from the powerful destroyer flotilla which was known to be inside. One destroyer emerged from Zeebrugge harbour, and is reported to have been struck by a torpedo fired from C.M.B. No. 5. Other torpedo craft, which apparently had not steam up, remained alongside the Mole, and their crews assisted in its defence. The greater part of the flotilla had for some reason been previously withdrawn to the Bruges docks.

11. As will be seen from the subsequent narrative, our operations were completely successful in attaining their first and most important object. The entrance to the Bruges ship-canal was blocked. The second object – the blocking of the entrance to Ostend harbour – was not achieved, for reasons which will be explained subsequently. The attack on the Zeebrugge Mole was completely successful as a diversion to enable the blocking ships to enter the harbour, to proceed to their allotted stations, and, with the exception of the "Thetis," to be sunk in accordance with the plan. The blowing up of the viaduct was carried out without any hitch, and produced the desired results. Owing, however, to various reasons which will be more particularly dealt with later, the less important objective, the destruction of the defences on the Mole, was not so thorough as had been hoped.

12. The main results achieved have, however, proved greater than I expected when the fleet returned to port on the morning of the 23rd April. Aerial observation and photographs show clearly that even the lighter craft in the Bruges ship-canal and docks have so far been unable to find an exit through the smaller waterways to Ostend harbour. At least 23 torpedo craft have remained sealed up at Bruges ever since the operations on St. George's Day, and so far as can be seen not less than 12 submarines would likewise appear to be still imprisoned. As yet no effective steps seem to have been taken to clear the Zeebrugge entrance to the Bruges ship-canal, where the silt is shown to be collecting; and although doubtless in time the enemy will succeed in opening a way out, it seems likely that this important section of his raiding and commerce-destroying forces must inevitably be seriously hampered for a considerable period. In addition to suffering this substantial injury, the enemy has been obliged to bring down reinforcements from the Bight of Heligoland to Zeebrugge and Ostend.

13. The preparations and training for the attack extended over a long period, during the latter portion of which (*i.e.*, from the 22nd March) the Dover Patrol was subjected to an exceptional strain owing to the unprecedented transport of reinforcements to France.

14. Success would have been impossible without the eager and generous co-operation of the Grand Fleet, the neighbouring commands and dockyards, and the Harwich Force.

15. The concentration of the attacking fleet had to take place about 63 miles distant from Zeebrugge and Ostend. As the length of time needed for reaching these objectives after the forces had been assembled was seven hours, it was inevitable that

there should be a period of not less than four hours of daylight during which enemy observation by air and submarine might discover our movements. In order to guard against this, which would have meant the certain failure of the expedition, it was necessary for the patrols and air forces to show the utmost degree of vigilance and energy. There is every reason for believing that, as a result of their efforts, the enemy remained up to the last entirely unaware of our intentions.

16. In order not only that the attack might have a reasonable prospect of success, but that it might not end in disaster, various conditions were essential – (*a*) a certain state of the tide; (*b*) calm weather; (*c*) a more or less favourable direction of the wind; and (*d*) absence of fog, with, if possible, a moderate amount of haze. The first of these conditions (the state of the tide) fixed the dates between which it was practicable to make the attempt. The others it was not possible to reckon with in advance, owing to the uncertainty of the weather, more especially at that time of year, and also to the fact that all these conditions might be different on the Flanders coast from what they were off the Goodwins, or that they might change for the worse between the starting of the expedition from the point of concentration and its arrival at its destination seven hours later.

17. It was anticipated that minefields, which would endanger the heavier draught vessels, might be encountered in the enemy's waters, but this risk had to be faced, and special arrangements were made to save the crews and storming-parties in the event of vessels being sunk.

18. On two occasions previous to the 22nd April the concentration took place, but, owing to unfavourable weather conditions setting in, had to be dispersed. This fact, although it caused disappointment among the officers and men, and also contained a danger that the enemy might become aware of our designs, had a considerable practical value as a rehearsal of the preliminary stages of the undertaking. On this point I may say here that, although on this occasion the wind changed and served us badly at a moment when we were finally committed to the attack, better conditions had, not – since the preparations were completed – occurred before, nor have they recurred up to this date.

19. The main force started from the point of concentration at 4.53 o'clock on the afternoon of Monday, the 22nd April.

20. The bombardment of Zeebrugge by monitors began at 11.20 p.m., simultaneously with that of the Ostend defences by monitors, and by our shore batteries in Flanders. These bombardments had been carried out on several nights prior to the 22nd April to give the enemy no reason to anticipate further action on our part on this particular occasion.

21. The vessels charged with making a smoke screen began operations simultaneously off Zeebrugge and Ostend at 11.40 p.m.

22. According to time-table, the hour at which the "Vindictive" (Captain Alfred F.B. Carpenter) should have been laid alongside the Zeebrugge Mole was midnight. She reached her station one minute after midnight, closely followed by the "Daffodil" (Lieutenant Harold Campbell) and "Iris II" (Commander Valentine Gibbs). A few minutes later the landing of the storming and demolition parties began. By 1.10 a.m.

the "Vindictive" had taken off the survivors, who had meanwhile done their work upon the Mole, and by 1.15 a.m. she and her consorts were clear of the Mole.

23. At 12.15 a.m. Submarine C3 (Lieutenant Richard D. Sandford) had succeeded in ramming herself between the iron piers of the viaduct, and was thereupon abandoned by her crew after they had lit the fuses. Five minutes later the cargo of explosives blew up, completely destroying communication between the Mole and the shore.

24. The "Thetis" (Commander Ralph S. Sneyd, D.S.O.), the first of the blocking ships, passed the end of the Mole, according to arrangement, fifteen minutes after midnight. Making her way to the entrance of the ship-canal, she carried away the obstructing nets, and being then in a sinking condition from gunfire, with both her propellers fouled, was sunk by her crew close to the entrance of the canal. The "Intrepid" (Lieutenant Stuart S. Bonham-Carter), the second of the blocking ships, following a few minutes later, was sunk in the ship-canal itself; and the "Iphigenia," (Lieutenant Edward W. Billyard-Leake), the last of the three blocking ships, following close astern of the "Intrepid," was sunk with the most complete success across the narrowest part of the ship-canal at 12.45 a.m.

25. It was expected that the blocking ships "Brilliant" (Commander Alfred E. Godsal) and "Sirius" (Lieutenant-Commander Henry N.M. Hardy, D.S.O.) would have found the entrance to Ostend harbour by midnight. For the reason, however, which is explained in the next paragraph, they missed their objective, ran ashore, and had both to be sunk about 12.30 a.m.

26. The success of the Ostend enterprise was affected to some extent by two adverse factors: (1) at 12.15 a.m. the wind (N.N.E.), which so far had been favourable for purposes of the smoke screen, shifted into an unfavourable quarter (S.S.W.), thereby exposing the attacking forces to the fire of the enemy; (2) the buoy which marks the Channel to Ostend harbour had been moved very shortly before, unknown to us, to a position some 2,400 yards further east, so that when "Brilliant" and "Sirius" found it and put their helms to starboard they ran ashore.

27. The manner in which the survivors of the crews of the five blocking ships and of Submarine C3 were rescued and brought away by volunteer crews in motor launches and a picket boat was beyond praise. The various incidents are described in subsequent paragraphs.

28. In the course of the attack on St. George's Day our casualties to officers and men were as follows:- Killed, 176; wounded, 412; missing, 49; of the latter 35 are believed to have been killed. Although these casualties are light compared to those that the Army constantly suffers in similar enterprises, we have to mourn the loss of comrades selected from practically every unit of His Majesty's sea forces. Our losses in ships were as follows: H.M.S. "North Star" and motor launches Nos. 424 and 110, sunk. No other vessel was rendered unfit for further service.

29. I have already submitted to the Lords Commissioners of the Admiralty the list of naval officers whom I considered deserving of promotion, either immediately or as soon as they have the prescribed service. I propose to forward as soon as possible a supplementary despatch bringing to their Lordships' notice the names of other

officers and men who distinguished themselves, for they are naturally numerous. They came from many ships, and were scattered immediately the operations were over, so that it is difficult to obtain the details relating to them.

30. I cannot close this brief summary without reference to those gallant souls who did not live to see the success of their endeavours. It seems almost invidious to mention names when every officer and man who took part was animated by one spirit, ardently welcoming the opportunity of achieving a feat of arms against odds in order that honour and merit might be added to that which our Service has gained in the past. Amongst those who lost their lives were many who shared with me the secrets of the plan, and of those I cannot refrain from recalling Lieutenant-Colonel Elliot, Captain Halahan, Commander Valentine Gibbs, Majors Cordner and Eagles, Lieutenant-Commanders Harrison and Bradford, Lieutenants Hawkings and Chamberlain, and Wing-Commander Brock, who all worked for many weeks in the training of the personnel and the preparation of material. Their keen enthusiasm and absolute confidence that the enterprise would be carried to a successful issue were invaluable to me. During the anxious days of waiting in crowded ships in a secluded anchorage, and in spite of two disappointments, the patience and faith that our chance would came, which were displayed by all, owed much to the fine example of these officers.

NARRATIVE.
II. – COMPOSITION OF FORCES.

31. In order that all parts of the Naval Service might share in the expedition, representative bodies of men were drawn from the Grand Fleet, the three Home Depôts, the Royal Marine Artillery and Light Infantry. The ships and torpedo craft were furnished by the Dover Patrol, which was reinforced by vessels from the Harwich Force and the French Navy. The Royal Australian Navy and the Admiralty Experimental Stations at Stratford and Dover were also represented.

The details thus contributed, which finally composed the whole striking force, were as shown in the following table:-

| From | Ship | Besides those belonging to ships in preceding columns. | |
		Officers	Men
Grand Fleet (exclusive of Royal Marines)	-	27	365
Harwich Force:			
Covering Squardron	7 light cruiser, 2 leaders, 14 T.B.D.s		
For Operations	1 leader, 6 T.B.D.'s		
Dover Patrol	9 monitors, 1 light cruiser, 4 leaders, 17 T.B.D.s, 36 M.L's, 12 C.M.B.'s, 1 minesweeper		
Portsmouth	11 M.L.s, 12 C.M.B.'s, 1 parent ship, 1 blocking ship, 2 submarines, 1 boarding ship	9	41
The Nore	12 M.L.'s, 1 picket boat, 1 parent ship, 4 blocking ships, 2 boarding ships	7	469
Plymouth	-	2	8
Royal Australian Navy	-	1	10
French Navy	7 T.B.D.s, 4 M.L.'s		
Dover Experimental Base	-	4	87
Royal Marine Artillery	-	2	58
Royal Marine Light Infantry	-	30	660
Total		**82**	**1,698**

III. – TRAINING OF PERSONNEL, PREPARATION OF MATERIAL.

32. A force thus composed and its weapons obviously needed collective training and special preparation to adapt them to their purpose.

33. With these objects, the Blocking Ships and the Storming Forces were assembled towards the end of February and from the 4th April onwards in the West Swin Anchorage, where training specially adapted to the plan of operations was given, and where the organisation of the expedition was carried on. The material as it was prepared was used to make the training practical, and was itself tested thereby. Moreover, valuable practice was afforded by endeavours to carry out the project on two occasions on which the conditions of wind and weather compelled its postponement, and much was learnt from these temporary failures. The "Hindustan," at first at Chatham and later at the Swin, was the parent ship and training depôt, and it is due to Captain A.P. Davidson, D.S.O., who also did good work in fitting out the

various ships, that the accommodation of the assembling crews and their maintenance during the weeks of preparation and postponement was so ably organised as to reduce the discomforts inseparable from the situation to a minimum. After the second attempt, when it became apparent that there would be a long delay, the "Dominion" joined the "Hindustan," and the pressure on the available accommodation was relieved by the transfer of about 350 seamen and marines to her.

34. Two special craft, the Liverpool ferry-steamers "Iris" (renamed "Iris II.") and "Daffodil," were selected after a long search at many ports by Captain Herbert C.J. Grant (Retired) and a representative of the Director of Dockyards, on account of their power, large carrying capacity (1,500), and shallow draft, with a view in the first place to their pushing the "Vindictive" alongside the Mole (for which they were in the result most useful); to the possibility, should the "Vindictive" be sunk, of their bringing away all her crew and the landing parties; and to their ability to manoeuvre in shallow waters or clear of minefields or torpedoes. They proved to be admirably chosen, and rendered good service.

35. The blocking ships and "Vindictive" were specially prepared for their work in Chatham Dockyard, the "Iris II" and "Daffodil" at Portsmouth. I received the most zealous and able help from all officers and Departments concerned, who did their utmost to expedite the work in every way.

36. I was able to devote more personal attention and time to working out the plan of operations and the preparation of personnel and material than would otherwise have been possible, because Rear-Admiral Cecil F. Dampier, Admiral Superintendent and second in command of the Dover Flotilla, Commodore the Hon. Algernon Boyle, C.B., M.V.O., Chief of Staff, and Captain Wilfred Tomkinson, commanding the Sixth (Dover) Flotilla of Destroyers, practically relieved me of all the routine work of the Dover base and patrol. I am greatly indebted to Admiral Dampier for his loyal co-operation in connection with the operations. In order to bring together the number of destroyers requisite for the operation, while maintaining the work of the patrol, it was necessary to have the entire available force in running order. This called for high organisation on Captain Tomkinson's part, and was made especially difficult because the period of preparation coincided with that in which very heavy demands were suddenly made on the escort flotilla by the pressing needs of the army in France. The fact that the many additional services which the Dover Patrol was called on to carry out in addition to its routine, were performed without deranging its working, reflects the greatest credit on Commodore Boyle, whose exceptional powers of organisation have been invaluable to me.

37. Reference to Wing-Commander F.A. Brock's services during the operation will be made in connection with the attack on the Mole, but I cannot leave this part of the subject without recording my indebtedness to him for the indispensable share he had in the operation. When, as Vice-Admiral of the Dover Patrol, I first began to prepare for this operation, it became apparent that without an effective system of smoke-screening such an attack could hardly hope to succeed. The system of making smoke previously employed in the Dover Patrol was unsuitable for a night operation, as its production generated a fierce flame, and no other means of making an effective

smoke screen was available. Wing-Commander Brock and sixty ratings were lent to my command, a factory was established in the dockyard, and he worked with great energy to obtain materials, designing and organising the means and the plans, and eventually developing the resources with which we finally set out. These were of great value even in the adverse circumstances which befell us, and I greatly deplore the loss of a man so well qualified to carry experiments in this matter further. When on the Mole he was very keen to acquire knowledge of the range-finding apparatus which might be of use to the country, and his efforts to do this were made without any regard to his personal safety, and I fear cost this very brave and ingenious officer his life.

38. The fitting out of the motor launches and coastal motor boats with smoke apparatus, designed by Wing-Commander Brock, was carried out at Dover, under short notice and with untiring energy by my Flag Captain, Ralph Collins, ably assisted by Commander Hamilton Benn, Engineer Lieutenant-Commander M.G.A. Edwards, Lieutenant F.C. Archer, and Mr. G.D. Smart, of H.M. Dockyard, Dover.

39. Staff-Paymaster Walter C. Northcott, R.N.R., the Naval Supply Officer at Dover, was at all times most zealous and untiring in dealing with the vast quantities of stores and munitions which had to be checked and distributed, often at very short notice.

40. The first officer who became available for a command in the blockships was Lieutenant Ivan B. Franks ("Dolphin"). Although suffering from the severe effects of an accident on service, his confident enthusiasm fired all who came into touch with him. He was put in charge of the early preparations of all the blockships and commanded the "Iphigenia" in the two abandoned attempts, but to his great disappointment he was taken ill with appendicitis two days before the actual attack, and had to be sent to hospital to undergo an operation. I do not wish the good work he did, and the good example he set, to go unrecorded.

41. The flag officers of other commands who were in a position to assist me did so most generously. The Commander-in-Chief of the Grand Fleet sent me a selected body of officers and men truly representative of his command, for I understand that the whole of his command would have been equally glad to come. From the neighbouring commands at Portsmouth and the Nore, the Adjutant-General, Royal Marines, and the Depôt at Chatham, I received support and assistance, not only in ships and men, but in every possible way. The Rear-Admiral Commanding the Harwich Force spared me a flotilla leader and six destroyers, besides protecting the northern flank of the area in which I was operating.

Brigadier-General McEwan and his staff at Chatham supervised the training of the officers and men from the Grand Fleet as if for the Royal Naval Division, France. Their assistance was invaluable, and I much appreciate their whole-hearted co-operation.

42. I am much indebted to Brigadier-General Charles L. Lambe, C.M.G., D.S.O., commanding the 7th Brigade of the Royal Air Force, and Lieutenant-Colonel Frederick C. Halahan, M.V.O., D.S.O., in command of the Air Forces under my command, for the co-operation of the 61st and 65th Wings, under Lieutenant-

Colonels P.F.M. Fellowes, D.S.O., and James T. Cull, D.S.O., respectively, throughout the preparation and execution of the operations. The 65th Wing was lent for the purpose by the Field-Marshal Commander-in-Chief British Armies in France. For several weeks the 61st Wing was engaged in frequent reconnaissances, and took a large number of photographs in different conditions of tide, from which photographs plans and models were constructed. On the first occasion of attempting the operation, the 65th Wing was already committed to their attack when I was compelled by shift of wind to withdraw the sea attack. The air attack was delivered with the greatest gallantry at a low altitude, and against a tremendous anti-aircraft defence. To the intense disappointment of the 65th Wing, mist and rain made it impossible to co-operate by repeating the aerial bombardment on the night of the 22nd-23rd April, but the 61st Wing and aircraft from the Guston aerodrome at Dover escorted the main force across the North Sea.

IV. – PREPARATION AND DEFENCE OF ROUTE.

43. The preparation of the routes from the starting points of attack, by the removal of obstructions and the placing of navigational marks and those for the long-range bombardments was carried out by Captain Henry P. Douglas, borne for surveying duties on my staff, and Lieutenant-Commander Francis E.B. Haselfoot, his assistant. The completely successful manner in which this very important work was done, in circumstances of interference from the enemy and the elements, does great credit to these officers, both of whom I recommend to the favourable notice of the Lords Commissioners.

44. To afford protection at a certain point in the route, and to maintain the aids to navigation during the approach, and retirement of the expedition, a force consisting of the flotilla-leader "Scott" and the destroyers "Ulleswater," "Teazer," and "Stork," lent from the Harwich Force, and the light cruiser "Attentive," flying the broad pendant of Commodore the Hon. Algernon D.E.H. Boyle, my Chief of Staff, was stationed there. The duties of this force were not interrupted by the enemy, but it was instrumental in controlling and directing the movements of detached craft in both directions, and relieved me of all anxiety on that score.

V. – THE PASSAGE OF THE FORCES.

45. At the moment of starting, the forces were disposed thus:-

(a.) *In the Swin.*
For the attack on the Zeebrugge Mole:
"Vindictive," "Iris II.," and "Daffodil."
To block the Bruges Canal:
"Thetis," "Intrepid," and "Iphigenia."
To block the entrance to Ostend:

"Sirius" and "Brilliant."

(b.) *At Dover.*
   T.B.D. "Warwick" (flag of Vice-Admiral).
   Unit L, "Phoebe" and "North Star."
   Unit M, "Trident" and "Mansfield."
   Unit F, "Whirlwind" and "Myngs."
   Unit R, "Velox," "Morris," "Moorsom," and "Melpomene."
   Unit X, "Tempest" and "Tetrarch."
   To damage Zeebrugge viaduct: Submarines C.1 and C.3.
   A special picket boat to rescue crews of C.1 and C.3.
   Minesweeper "Lingfield" to take off surplus steaming parties of
      blockships, which had 100 miles to steam.
   Eighteen coastal motor boats, numbers 5, 7, 15, 16, 17, 21B, 22B, 23B,
      24A, 25BD, 26B, 27A, 28A, 29A, 30B, 32A, 34A, 35A.
   Thirty-three motor launches, numbers 79, 110, 121, 128, 223, 239, 241,
      257, 258, 262, 272, 280, 282, 308, 314, 345, 397, 416, 420, 422, 424,
      513, 525, 526, 533, 549, 552, 555, 557, 558, 560, 561, 562.
   To bombard vicinity of Zeebrugge: Monitors "Erebus" and "Terror."
   To attend on monitors, &c.: "Termagant," "Truculent," and "Manly."
   Outer Patrol off Zeebrugge: "Attentive," "Scott," "Ulleswater,"
      "Teazer," and "Stork."

(c.) *At Dunkirk.*
   Monitors for bombarding Ostend: "Marshal Soult," "Lord Clive,"
      "Prince Eugene," "General Craufurd," M.24, M.26.
   For operating off Ostend: "Swift," "Faulknor," "Matchless," "Mastiff,"
      and "Afridi."
   The British destroyers "Mentor," "Lightfoot," "Zubian," and French
      torpedo-boats "Lestin," "Capitaine Mehl," "Francis Garnier,"
      "Roux," and "Bouclier," to accompany the monitors.
   Eighteen British motor launches, numbers 11, 16, 17, 22, 23, 30, 60,
      105, 254, 274, 276, 279, 283, 429, 512, 532, 551, 556, engaged in
      smoke-screening duty inshore and rescue work, and six for attending
      on big monitors.
   Four French Motor Launches, numbers 1, 2, 33, and 34, attending on
      M.24 and M.26.
   Coastal motor boats (40 feet), numbers 2, 4, 10, and 12; (55 feet) 19
      and 20.

46. Navigational aids having been established on the route, the forces from the Swin
and Dover were directed to join my flag off the Goodwin Sands and proceed in
company to a rendezvous, and thereafter as requisite to their respective stations; those
from Dunkirk were given their orders by the Commodore.

47. An operation time-table was issued to govern the movements of all the forces,
wireless signals were prohibited, visual signals of every sort were reduced to a

minimum, and manoeuvring pre-arranged as far as foresight could provide. With few and slight delays the programme for the passage was carried out as laid down, the special aids to navigation being found of great assistance.

48. The Harwich Force, under Rear-Admiral Sir Reginald Tyrwhitt, K.C.B., D.S.O., was posted to cover the operation and prevent interference from the northward, which relieved me of all concern on that score.

49. On leaving the Goodwins, the Main Force was disposed in three columns. The centre column was led by "Vindictive," with "Iris II." and "Daffodil" in tow, followed by the five blocking ships and the paddle minesweeper "Lingfield," escorting five motor launches for taking off the surplus steaming parties of the blocking ships. The starboard column was led by the "Warwick," flying my flag, followed by the "Phoebe" and "North Star," which three ships were to cover the "Vindictive" from torpedo attack while the storming operations were in progress; "Trident" and "Mansfield," towing submarines C.3 and C.1; and "Tempest," to escort the two Ostend blockships. The port column was led by "Whirlwind," followed by "Myngs" and "Moorsom," which ships were to patrol to the northward of Zeebrugge; and the "Tetrarch," also to escort the Ostend blockships. Every craft was towing one or more coastal motor boats, and between the columns were motor launches.

50. The greater part of the passage had to be carried out in broad daylight, with the consequent likelihood of discovery by enemy aircraft or submarine. This risk was largely countered by the escort of all the scouting aircraft under my command. On arrival at a certain position (C), it being then apparent that the conditions were favourable, and that there was every prospect of carrying through the enterprise up to programme time, a short pre-arranged wireless signal was made to the detached forces that the programme would be adhered to.

51. On arrival at a position 1½ miles short of (G), at which Commodore Boyle's force was stationed, the whole force stopped for fifteen minutes to enable the surplus steaming parties of the blockships to be disembarked and the coastal motor boats slipped. These and the motor launches then proceeded in execution of previous orders. On resuming the course the "Warwick" and "Whirlwind," followed by the destroyers, drew ahead on either bow to clear the passage of enemy outpost vessels.

52. When the "Vindictive" arrived at a position where it was necessary for her to alter course for the Mole, the "Warwick," "Phoebe" and "North Star" swung to starboard and cruised in the vicinity of the Mole until after the final withdrawal of all the attacking forces. During this movement and throughout the subsequent operations "Warwick" was manoeuvred to place smoke screens wherever they seemed to be most required, and when the wind shifted from north-east to south-west, her services in this respect were particularly valuable.

VI. – BOMBARDING FORCES.

53. *Zeebrugge.* – The monitors "Erebus" (Captain Charles S. Wills, C.M.G., D.S.O.) and "Terror" (Captain Charles W. Bruton), with the destroyers "Termagant,"

"Truculent" and "Manly," were stationed at a position suitable for the long-range bombardment of Zeebrugge in co-operation with the attack. Owing to poor visibility and an extraordinary set of the tide the opening of bombardment was delayed slightly behind programme time; otherwise the operations of this force were carried out according to plan. During the operation enemy shell fell in the vicinity of "Erebus" and "Terror" but neither was hit. On completion of the bombardment the vessels of this force took up patrolling positions to cover the retirement from Zeebrugge. Aerial photographs show the good effect of this bombardment.

54. *Ostend.* – Similarly, the monitors "Marshal Soult" (Captain George R.B. Blount, D.S.O., "General Craufurd" (Commander Edward Altham), "Prince Eugene" (Captain Ernest Wigram, D.S.O.), and "Lord Clive" (Commander Reginald J.N. Watson, D.S.O.), and the small monitors M.21 (Commander Oliver M.F. Stokes), M.24 (Acting Commander Claude P.C. de Crespigny), and M.26 (Lieutenant-Commander Arthur C. Fawssett) were stationed by Commodore Hubert Lynes, C.M.G., in suitable positions to bombard specified batteries. These craft were attended by the British destroyers "Mentor," "Lightfoot," and "Zubian," and the French "Capitaine Mehl," "Francis Garnier," "Roux," and "Bouclier." The Commodore reports that the bombardment was undoubtedly useful in keeping down the fire of the shore batteries. These returned the monitors' fire about five minutes after the latter opened, the ships being hit by fragments of shell, but no material damage being done.

55. *Siege Guns.* – Co-operation by R.M.A. siege guns (Colonel Pryce Peacock, R.M.A.) on given enemy targets was arranged by the Commodore Dunkirk to which the enemy replied without causing any casualties or any damage of importance.

VII. – ATTACK ON ZEEBRUGGE MOLE.

56. *General.* – The attack on the Mole was primarily intended to distract the enemy's attention from the ships engaged in blocking the Bruges Canal, its immediate objectives were, firstly, the capture of the 4.1 inch battery at the sea end of the Mole[†], which was a serious menace to the passage of the blockships, and, secondly, the doing of as much damage to the material on the Mole as time permitted, for it was not the intention to remain on the Mole after the primary object of the expedition had been accomplished.

The attack was to consist of two parts; (*a*) the landing of storming and demolition parties, and (*b*) the destruction of the iron viaduct between the shore and the stone Mole.

57. The units detailed for the attack were:-

(*a*) H.M. Ship "Vindictive," Acting Captain Alfred F.B. Carpenter (late "Emperor of India"); the special steamers "Iris II," Commander Valentine Gibbs ("Tiger"), and "Daffodil," Lieutenant Harold G. Campbell ("Emperor of India"); the latter detailed to push the

"Vindictive" alongside the Mole and keep her there as long as might be requisite.

(b) Submarines C.3 and C.1, commanded by Lieutenants Richard D. Sandford and Aubrey C. Newbold respectively, attended by a picket boat under Lieutenant-Commander Francis H. Sandford, D.S.O.

58. Besides the above, a flotilla of twenty four motor launches and eight coastal motor boats were told off for rescue work and to make smoke screens or lay smoke floats, and nine more coastal motor boats to attack the Mole and enemy vessels inside it, &c.

At 11.40 p.m. the coastal motor boats detailed to lay the first smoke screen ran in to a very close range and proceeded to lay smoke floats and by other methods produce the necessary "fog." These craft came under heavy fire, and only their small size and great speed saved them from destruction.

59. "*Vindictive*" – At 11.30 p.m. the Blankenberghe light buoy was abeam, and the enemy had presumably heard or seen the approaching forces, as many star shells were fired, lighting up the vicinity, but no enemy patrol craft were sighted. At this time the wind, which had been from the north-east, and therefore favourable to the success of the smoke screens, died away, and at a later period came from a southerly direction. Many of the smoke floats laid just off the Mole extension were sunk by enemy fire, and this in conjunction with the changes in the wind lessened the effectiveness of the smoke screen.

60. At 11.56 the ship having just passed through a smoke screen, the Mole extension was seen in the semi-darkness about 300 yards off on the port bow. Speed was increased to full, and course altered so that allowing for cross tide the ship would make good a closing course of 45 degrees to the Mole. The "Vindictive" purposely withheld her fire to avoid being discovered, but almost at the moment of her emerging from the smoke the enemy opened fire. So promptly, under the orders of Commander Edward O.B.S. Osborne, was this replied to by the port 6-inch battery, the upper-deck pom-poms, and the gun in the fore-top, that the firing on both sides appeared to be almost simultaneous. Captain Carpenter was conning the ship from the port forward flame-thrower hut. Lieutenant-Commander Robert R. Rosoman, with directions as to the handling of the ship should the captain be disabled, was in the conning tower from which the ship was being steered.

61. At one minute after midnight on the 23rd April, St. George's Day – the programme time being midnight – the "Vindictive" was put alongside the Mole, taking gently on the special fenders of the port bow, and the starboard anchor was let go. At this time the noise was terrific. During the previous few minutes the ship had been hit by a large number of shell and many casualties caused. Lieutenant-Colonel Bertram H. Elliot, D.S.O., and Major Alexander A. Cordner, the two senior officers of the Royal Marine storming parties, and Captain Henry C. Halahan, D.S.O., commanding the naval storming parties, all ready to lead the men on to the Mole, had been killed; Commander Patrick H. Edwards, R.N.V.R., and many other officers and men killed or wounded.

62. As there was some doubt as to the starboard anchor having gone clear, the port anchor was dropped close to the foot of the Mole and the cable bowsed-to with less than a shackle out. A three-knot tide was running past the Mole; and the scend alongside the Mole created by the slight swell caused much movement on the ship. There was an interval of three or four minutes before "Daffodil" could arrive and commence to push "Vindictive" bodily alongside. During this interval the ship could not be got close enough for the special mole-anchors to hook, and it was a very trying period. Many of the brows had been broken by shell fire, and a heavy roll had broken up the foremost mole-anchor as it was being placed. The two foremost brows, however, reached the wall and the naval storming parties, led in the most gallant manner by Lieutenant-Commander Bryan F. Adams ("Princess Royal") ran out along them closely followed by the Royal Marines, gallantly led by Captain and Adjutant A.R. Chater. Owing to the rolling of the ship a most disconcerting motion was imparted to the brows, the outer ends of which were "sawing" considerably on the Mole parapet. Officers and men were carrying Lewis guns, bombs, ammunition, etc., and were under heavy machine-gun fire at close range, add to this a drop of 30 feet between the ship and the Mole and some idea of the conditions which had to be faced may be realised. Yet the storming of the Mole by these two brows, and later by two others which were got into position, was carried out without the smallest delay, and without any apparent consideration of self-preservation. Some of the first men on the Mole did splendid work with the object of hauling one of the large mole-anchors across the parapet. Lieutenant-Commander Rosoman assisted in this on board, encouraging and directing the men with great coolness and ability.

"Daffodil" arrived three minutes after "Vindictive," closely followed by "Iris II". Both suffered less in the approach, "Vindictive" occupying practically all the enemy's attention. As already stated "Daffodil's" primary duty was to push "Vindictive" bodily on to the Mole, to enable her to be secured, after which "Daffodil" was to come alongside and land her parties over that ship. In the end her men had to disembark from her bows on to "Vindictive," as it was found essential to continue to push "Vindictive" on to the Mole throughout the action. This duty was magnificently carried out by her Commanding Officer, Lieutenant Harold G. Campbell ("Emperor of India"), who, during the greater part of the time, was suffering from a wound in the head which for the time deprived him of the sight of one eye. Without the assistance of "Daffodil" very few of the storming parties from "Vindictive" could have been landed or re-embarked; and the greatest credit is due to Mr. Campbell for the skilful manner in which he handled his ship.

63. The landing from "Iris II." was even more trying. The scend alongside made her bump heavily, and rendered the use of the scaling ladders very difficult, many being broken up. Lieutenant Claude E.V. Hawkings ("Erin") ascended the first ladder, secured the mole anchor, and was then shot and fell on to the Mole. Lieutenant-Commander George N. Bradford ("Orion") got to the top of a derrick with a mole anchor on it, leaped on to the Mole, secured the anchor and was shot, falling into the water between "Iris II." and the Mole. Gallant attempts to recover his body were made, Petty Officer M.D. Hallihan being killed while so employed. The gallantry

and devotion to duty of these two officers was of the highest order. In the end, so impossible was it to get the mole anchors to hold, that the cable was slipped and "Iris II." went alongside "Vindictive" to enable "D" Company and her Royal Marines to land across her, but only a few men had got to the "Vindictive" when the withdrawal signal was sounded.

64. On board the "Vindictive" the fore most 7.5-inch Howitzer's Marine crew were all killed or wounded in the very early part of the action. A naval crew from a 6-inch gun took their place, and were almost entirely wiped out. At this period the ship was being hit every few seconds, chiefly in the upper works, from which the splinters caused many casualties. It was difficult to locate the guns which were doing the most damage, but Lieutenant Charles N.B. Rigby, R.M.A., with his Royal Marines in the foretop, kept up a continuous fire with pom-poms and Lewis guns, changing rapidly from one target to another. Two heavy shells made direct hits on the foretop, killing Lieutenant Rigby and killing or disabling all in the top, except Sergeant N.A. Finch, who, though severely wounded, continued firing till the top was wrecked by another heavy shell. Captain Carpenter reports that before going into the foretop Lieutenant Rigby had displayed fine courage and ability, and that the success of the storming of the Mole was largely due to the good work of this officer and the men under his orders.

65. Acting Captain Reginald Dallas Brooks, R.M.A., was in command of the R.M.A. gun detachments in "Vindictive." He not only set his men generally a splendid example of devotion to duty, but commanded the crew of the 11-inch Howitzer in its exposed position in a very fine manner.

66. Half an hour after the storming of the Mole had been commenced, the Captain visited the decks below and found Staff-Surgeon James McCutcheon and the staff under him working with great energy and care. A constant stream of casualties were being brought down every hatch, yet there appeared to be no delay in dealing with each case.

67. *The Mole.* – The attack on the Mole was designed to be carried out by a storming force to prepare the way for, and afterwards to cover and protect, the operations of a second force which was to carry out the actual demolition, damage, &c. Both these forces comprised Royal Naval ranks and ratings under the command of Captain Henry C. Halahan, D.S.O., and Royal Marines under the command of Lieutenant-Colonel Bertram N. Elliot, D.S.O.

68. The storming force was composed of Naval Companies – A. (Lieutenant-Commander Bryan F. Adams, "Princess Royal"), B. (Lieutenant Arthur G.B.T. Chamberlain, "Neptune"), and D. (Lieutenant-Commander G.N. Bradford, "Orion"), all under the command of Lieutenant-Commander Arthur L. Harrison ("Lion"), and the 4th Battalion, Royal Marines, organised as follows:-

"A" (Chatham) Company: Major Charles E.C. Eagles, D.S.O.
"B" (Portsmouth) Company: Captain Edward Bamford, D.S.O.
"C" (Plymouth) Company: Major Bernard G. Weller, D.S.O.
Machine Gun Company: Captain Charles B. Conybeare.

On the death of Lieutenant-Colonel Elliot D.S.O., and Major Alexander A. Cordner (Second in Command), Major Weller assumed command of the battalion. Captain A.R. Chater was battalion adjutant.

This force was embarked mainly in "Vindictive," but partly in "Iris II."

69. The demolition force was composed of C. Naval Company, under the command of Lieutenant Cecil C. Dickinson ("Resolution"), and was divided into three parties, Nos. 1 and 3, under Sub-Lieutenant Felix E. Chevallier ("Iron Duke"), being conveyed in the "Daffodil," and No. 2, under Lieutenant Dickinson, in the "Vindictive."

70. The objectives of the storming forces had been communicated to the officers, and specific duties allotted to the different units, who had been exercised on a replica of the Mole, described to the men as "a position in France."

71. This specialised preparation was necessary, but it handicapped the leaders of the storming parties, for, owing to the difficulty in recognising objects on the Mole, the "Vindictive" overran her station and was berthed some 300 yards further to the westward (or shore end of the Mole) than was intended (see plan). It was realised beforehand that "Vindictive" might not exactly hit off her position, but the fact that the landing was carried out in an unexpected place, combined with the heavy losses already sustained by "Vindictive," seriously disorganised the attacking force. The intention was to land the storming parties right on top of the 4.1 inch guns (see footnote to para. 56) in position on the seaward end of the Mole, the silencing of which was of the first importance, as they menaced the approach of the blockships. The leading blockship was timed to pass the lighthouse twenty-five minutes after "Vindictive" came alongside. This period of time proved insufficient to organise and carry through an attack against the enemy on the seaward end of the Mole, who were able to bring heavy machine-gun fire to bear on the attacking forces. As a result the blockships came under an unexpected fire from the light guns on the Mole extension[‡], though the 4.1 inch battery on the Mole head remained silent (see paragraphs 73 and 94).

72. Lieutenant-Commander Adams, followed by the survivors of "A" and "B" Companies, were the first to land, no enemy being then seen on the Mole. These two companies had suffered severely before landing, especially "B," both of whose officers were casualties. They found themselves on a pathway on the Mole parapet about 8 feet wide, with a wall 4 feet high on the seaward side, and an iron railing on the Mole side. From this pathway there was a drop of 15 feet on to the Mole proper. This raised portion of the Mole will in future be referred to as the parapet. Followed by his men, Mr. Adams went along the parapet to the left (towards the lighthouse extension), where he found a look-out station or control, with a range-finder behind and above it. A bomb was put into this station, which was found clear of men. Wing Commander Frank A. Brock here joined the party, and went inside to investigate. He was not seen again by Mr. Adams, but from other accounts it is believed he was seen alive later.

73. Near this look-out station an iron ladder led down to the Mole, and three of Mr. Adams' party descended it and prevented a few of the enemy from reaching the

harbour side of the Mole. Two destroyers alongside the Mole showed no activity up to this time, nor did Mr. Adams see the three-gun battery at the Mole end fire at any time whilst he was on the parapet, but a machine gun about 100 yards to the westward of these guns was firing on his party. It appeared at this time that the enemy were firing at the "Vindictive" from the shore end of the Mole, but no gun flashes were seen, as everything was so well illuminated by enemy star shell and the rockets fired by "Vindictive." After capturing the look-out station Mr. Adams advanced to the eastward about 40 yards, where he left his party in position and himself returned to collect more men.

74. Returning to the look-out station, Mr. Adams found only some wounded, but later collected two Lewis gunners and a small party under Petty Officer George E. Antell, O.N. 232634 ("Lion"). These he sent to the eastward and the Petty Officer inboard, as he had been wounded in the hand and arm before landing, and although in great pain had carried on most gallantly.

75. The situation now was that Mr. Adams' few men and the two Lewis gunners were beyond the look-out station protected from the machine-gun fire from the direction of the Mole Head, but exposed to that from the destroyers alongside the Mole, and the men were being hit apparently by machine guns and pom-poms. Lieutenant-Commander Harrison arrived at this time; this gallant officer was severely wounded in the head on board "Vindictive" before coming alongside, but directly he recovered consciousness he joined his section on the Mole; on receiving Mr. Adams' report he directed him to try and get more men. Major Weller, Commanding the Royal Marines, on receiving Mr. Adams' report, despatched Lieutenant G. Underhill with reinforcements to assist Mr. Harrison. Whilst this party was being collected, Mr. Adams returned to the look-out station, where he was informed that Mr. Harrison had led a rush along the parapet and that he and several of his men had been killed by machine-gun fire. Able Seaman McKenzie, one of B Company's machine gunners with Mr. Harrison, did good execution with his gun, though wounded in several places, and Able Seaman Eaves was killed in attempting to bring in Mr. Harrison's body.

76. About this time the recall was sounded, and Mr. Adams therefore withdrew his men from the parapet and Mole, collected the wounded, and sent them to the "Vindictive." He himself went along the parapet in search of Mr. Harrison, but not finding him, returned to assist in the re-embarkation. As originally planned, Mr. Harrison's bluejacket storming parties were to deal with the battery on the Mole head and Mole extension only, but for the reasons given, in paragraph 71 they started 400 yards further from their objectives than was intended with the intervening ground fully exposed to machine-gun fire. Mr. Adams and his men, and later Mr. Harrison, pressed their attack most gallantly, and, though denied a full measure of success, it appears probable their fire prevented the 4.1 inch battery at the Mole head coming into action, as these guns did not open fire at the blockships (see paragraph 94).

77. *Marine Storming Party*. – The Royal Marines of this expedition were drawn from the four divisional headquarters and the Grand Fleet. The battalion was to provide the officers and men of the storming force: the crews of four Stokes guns,

one 11-inch howitzer, five pom-poms, and some Lewis guns of the "Vindictive's" armament, and a few men to work with the Naval demolition party. It was carried to Zeebrugge in the "Vindictive," except A Company, two Vickers guns of the machine-gun section, and two Stokes guns, which went in "Iris II." All had taken part in the special training and practices already referred to, the howitzer crews having been put through a course at Shoeburyness.

78. The first objective of the Royal Marine Battalion was a fortified zone situated about 150 yards from the seaward end of the Mole proper; its capture was of the first importance, as an enemy holding it could bring a heavy fire to bear on the parties landing from "Vindictive." This objective being gained, the Royal Marines were to continue down the Mole and hold a position so as to cover the operations of the demolition parties from an attack by enemy troops advancing from the landward end of the Mole. The destruction of the Viaduct by Submarine "C.3" was intended to assist in this, by preventing reinforcements reaching the Mole from the shore. Owing to "Vindictive" coming alongside to landward of this zone, the Royal Marines were faced with the double duty of preventing an enemy attack from the shore end and of themselves attacking the fortified zone. The casualties already sustained and the fact that "Iris II." could not remain alongside to land her company of Royal Marines (see paragraph 63) left insufficient men in the early stages of the landing to carry out both operations. The situation was a difficult one, for to attack the fortified zone first might have enabled the enemy to advance up the Mole and seize positions abreast "Vindictive" with the most serious consequences to the whole landing force, whereas by not attacking the fortified zone the guns at the Mole head could not be prevented from firing at the blockships. As will be seen in subsequent paragraphs, the Royal Marines first secured the landward side, after which an assault was organised against the fortified zone, but the unavoidable delay prevented this attack from being carried through before the blockships had passed in and the recall sounded. Major Weller's action was correct; lack of men prevented him reinforcing the bluejacket storming parties under Mr. Harrison and Mr. Adams, who had in consequence to attempt an assault on a very strong position with the depleted A and B Companies, and without the assistance of D Company, which could not be landed in time from "Iris II." (see paragraph 63). How heroically they failed has been related in paragraphs 72 to 75.

79. No. 5 Platoon (Lieutenant T.F.V. Cooke) was the first to land, and proceeded to the right (west) along the parapet. They silenced a party of snipers who were firing from near No. 2 Shed into the men landing. Captain and Adjt. A.R. Chater initiated this, which Major Weller considers greatly assisted the disembarkation. Captain Bamford now joined, and with Lieutenant Cooke and this platoon reached a position some 200 yards from the "Vindictive"; their action greatly assisted the advance along the Mole, they themselves being exposed to a galling fire. Lieutenant Cooke, who set a fine example, was twice wounded, and was rendered unconscious; he was most gallantly carried back to the "Vindictive" by Private John D.L. Press, R.M.L.I., who was himself wounded.

80. No. 9 Platoon and the remnants of No. 10, under Lieutenant C.D.R. Lamplough, were the next to land. They descended from the parapet to the Mole (a

drop of 15 feet) by means of ropes, and proceeded to establish a strong point at the shoreward end of No. 3 Shed, to prevent possible attack from that direction. This unit later attacked a destroyer alongside the Mole, inflicting damage on the craft and crew.

81. Units were now rapidly landing, and No. 7 Platoon (Lieutenant H.A.P. de Berry) succeeded in placing their heavy scaling ladders in position, and then formed up to support Nos. 9 and 10 Platoons. The successful placing of the scaling ladders was largely due to Sergeant-Major C.J. Thatcher. Major Weller then received information that the naval storming party needed reinforcements. He therefore despatched No. 12 Platoon and the remnants of No. 11, under Lieutenant G. Underhill, to their assistance. These platoons advanced to the left (east) along the parapet, and reached the look-out station, where they were checked by machine-gun fire; Mr. Adams and his men were some 40 to 50 yards ahead of them, and both parties could make no headway along the exposed parapet. Meanwhile No. 5 Platoon, which had been recalled from its advanced position, with Nos. 7 and 8 Platoons, all under Captain Bamford, were forming up on the Mole for an assault on the fortified zone and the 4.1 inch battery at the Mole head. This attack was launched, but before it could be developed the general recall was sounded. The units fell back in good order, bringing their wounded with them. The passing of the men from the Mole on to the parapet by means of the scaling ladders was rendered hazardous by the enemy opening fire at that portion of the Mole, several ladders being destroyed; the men were sent across in small batches from the comparative shelter afforded by No. 3 Shed, such rushes taking place as far as possible in the intervals between the enemy's bursts of fire.

82. *The Demolition or C Company.* – This company was under the orders of Lieutenant Cecil C. Dickinson ("Resolution"), and was divided into three parties, Nos. 1 and 3 consisting of Sub-Lieutenant Felix E. Chevallier ("Iron Duke") and twenty-nine ratings in the "Daffodil," and No. 2 of Lieutenant Dickinson and twenty-one ratings in the "Vindictive." Twenty-two rank and file, R.M.L.I., were attached for the transport of the explosive equipment.

83. Lieutenant Dickinson and No. 2 party landed after the Naval Storming Parties and assembled on the pathway of the parapet, which became somewhat crowded before the scaling ladders could be got into position to enable the men to descend on to the Mole. No. 2 party then proceeded to No. 3 Shed. The heavy fire from the destroyers alongside the Mole prevented any advance towards the shore, and the demolition of this shed was therefore impracticable; charges were, however, placed and everything prepared in case an opportunity for its destruction occurred. An attempt was made to place a charge alongside the destroyers, but was repulsed by their fire. Some bombs were therefore thrown on board. The enemy's shell fire at this portion of the Mole became very heavy, and the recall being sounded the party re-embarked under the conditions related in para. 81.

84. The demolition party was on the Mole about 55 minutes, and it was solely on account of the proximity of our own storming parties that no destruction took place. This party, ably led by Lieutenant Dickinson, behaved in a most cool and undisturbed manner both during the approach (when they suffered severely) and on the Mole.

After returning on board the extra explosives, etc., were jettisoned, as they were then only a danger to the ship. The preparation of the demolition scheme and organisation of the company for carrying it out was very efficiently planned by Lieutenant-Commander Francis H. Sandford, D.S.O., borne for special service on my Staff.

85. *Experimental Party.* – The account of the attack on the Mole would not be complete without reference to the contribution in officers and men made by a detachment from the Admiralty Experimental Station at Stratford, and the work done by them. This detachment was commanded by Lieutenant Graham S. Hewett, R.N.V.R., with Lieutenant A.L. Eastlake, R.E., second-in-command. It contributed thirty-four men, all volunteers, for the working of the fixed and portable flame-throwers, phosphorus grenades, etc., either on board "Vindictive," "Iris II.," and "Daffodil," or with the various naval and marine parties landed on the Mole. The fixed flame-throwers in "Vindictive" were put out of action by enemy shell fire. The portable ones accompanied the seaman and marine landing parties, the personnel of the experimental party sharing the difficulties and dangers of the assault. Lieutenant Hewett specially mentions Air-Mechanics W.H. Gough and W.G. Ryan for good service during the attack on the Mole.

86. *Destruction of Viaduct.* – The object of this part of the attack on the Mole was to prevent reinforcements from the land passing on to the Mole during the operations. It was proposed to do this by exploding one or two old submarines in contact with the iron piers and cross-ties of the viaduct. It was calculated that a C class submarine at a speed of 6 knots would penetrate the light bracing of the piers up to her conning tower.

87. To enable the submarine to be abandoned and continue her course automatically, C.1 and C.3 were fitted with gyro-control. A picket boat was provided for the escape of the crew, and each submarine had two motor skiffs, they also carried a light scaling ladder each, so that in case all other means of rescue failed, they might climb on to the Viaduct and escape along it from the effects of the explosion. Exploding charges, primers, battery and switch gear were devised and fitted. These three craft were towed by T.B.D.s "Trident" and "Mansfield" to certain positions, whence they proceeded under their own power.

88. Submarine C.3 (Lieutenant Richard D. Sandford) proceeded on the courses laid down, and duly sighted the viaduct right ahead, distance about a mile and a half. Shortly after this, by the light of star shell, fire was opened on C.3, apparently from 4-inch guns, but was not long maintained. When the viaduct was about half a mile off, a flare on the far side silhouetted the Mole and viaduct, which appeared about two points on the port bow. Two searchlights were then switched on to C.3, and off again, possibly in order that the submarine might run into the viaduct and be caught. By this time the viaduct was clearly visible. One hundred yards away, course was altered to ensure striking the viaduct exactly at right-angles. C.3 struck exactly between two rows of piers at a speed of nine and a half knots, riding up on to the horizontal girders of the viaduct, and raising the hull bodily about two feet; she penetrated up to the conning tower.

89. The crew having mustered on deck before the collision, lowered and manned

the skiff. The fuses were then ignited, and the submarine abandoned, the skiff's course being set to the westward against the current. Her propeller having been damaged, oars had to be used. Immediately the skiff left the submarine, the two searchlights were switched on, and fire was opened with machine guns, rifles, and pom-poms, the viaduct being lined with riflemen firing under the wind screen, and the houses on the inner end of the Mole opening on her with pom-poms. The boat was holed many times, but was kept afloat by special pumps which had been fitted. Mr. Sandford (twice) and two of the crew were wounded at this time. As only slow progress could be made against the current, the charge exploded when the skiff was but two or three hundred yards from the viaduct. The explosion appeared to have great effect, much débris falling into the water around. Both searchlights immediately went out, and firing became spasmodic. The picket boat was then sighted, and the skiff's crew taken on board, the wounded being finally transferred to the T.B.D. "Phoebe." Mr. Sandford describes the behaviour of all his crew as splendid, and worthy of the high traditions of the submarine service. He selects his next in command, Lieutenant John H. Price, D.S.C., R.N.R., for mention, and states that his assistance was invaluable, and his conduct in a position of extreme danger exemplary. To this modest praise of the exploit, I would add that the officers and men, who eagerly undertook such hazards, are deserving of their Lordships' highest recognition. They were all well aware that if their means of rescue failed them, as through untoward circumstances it nearly did, and they had been in the water at the moment of the explosion, they must almost inevitably have been stunned and drowned, or killed outright, by the force of such an explosion. Yet they disdained to use the gyro-steering which would have enabled them to abandon the submarine at a safe distance, and preferred to make sure, as far as was humanly possible, of the accomplishment of their duty.

90. Submarine C.1 (Lieutenant Aubrey C. Newbold), owing to delay caused by the parting of the tow, did not arrive in the vicinity of the viaduct till the retirement had commenced. He had previously seen a big flash, but had not heard any sound, and was therefore in doubt as to what the force in general had done, but realised that his boat might be required for another occasion. He therefore retired, though he and his crew immediately volunteered for similar service. They were naturally disappointed, but in my opinion Lieutenant Newbold was perfectly right, and their Lordships will not lose sight of the fact that they, equally with the officers and men of C.3, eagerly embarked on the enterprise in full realisation of what the consequences might well be.

91. The picket boat employed for rescuing the crew of C.3 was commanded by Lieutenant- Commander Francis H. Sandford, D.S.O., who had organised the method of attack on the viaduct. The picket boat displayed bad qualities when towed above a certain speed in the prevailing conditions of wind and sea. She was steered only with great difficulty, and was twice on her beam ends, being saved from total capsize by the tow parting. She then proceeded under her own steam, and endeavoured to reach the viaduct before the explosion. Her speed was not as much as was expected; still she arrived in time to pick up the motor-skiff very shortly after the explosion, and transferred the officers and men to the "Phoebe." This boat subsequently returned

to Dover under her own steam, as her fore compartment being holed and full of water made towing inadvisable. From first to last she had made a voyage of 170 miles to and from the Belgian coast in unpleasant conditions, and effected the rescue in the face of almost insurmountable difficulties, due to enemy action, weather, and tide. I have already recommended Lieutenant-Commander Francis Sandford for promotion on this and previous grounds. His boat's crew were all volunteers, and I am including them in my general list of recommendations to their Lordships' notice.

VIII. – BLOCKING OPERATIONS.

92. The blocking of the Bruges Canal and the entrance to Ostend Harbour was the principal part of the whole objective, the damage to the Zeebrugge Mole being subsidiary thereto. To the "Intrepid," "Iphigenia," and "Thetis" was assigned the duty in the Bruges Canal; "Brilliant" and "Sirius" being detailed for Ostend.

93. *Zeebrugge.* – The orders to the blockships were to proceed into the canal. If her two consorts were seen to be following, the leading vessel ("Thetis") was to ram the lock gates; the second and third ("Intrepid" and "Iphigenia") were to be run ashore near the entrance at the southern end of the piers, this being the narrowest part of the channel and the position best calculated to block the channel by silt. This opinion as to the best position was based on local knowledge, and the decision to attempt the project in this way was come to after much consideration, and bearing in mind the fact that if the leading vessel should fail to block the lock gates, and should sink in the channel short of the gates, she would have been no obstruction; whereas two ships well athwart the channel at the entrance would be certain to set up silt and cause great inconvenience to the enemy.

94. The proceedings of these ships were as follows:-

"Thetis" (Commander Ralph S. Sneyd, D.S.O.). – Sighted the Zeebrugge Mole ahead, and signalled the fact to the ships astern. She was greatly assisted by rockets fired from "Vindictive," which showed up the Mole extension and the lighthouse, and also by Captain Ralph Collins in a motor launch, who hailed the "Thetis" and gave her the bearing of the lighthouse. After rounding the latter the barge-boom came into view, and "Thetis" was steered for the barge furthest from the Mole, opening fire at the lighthouse, and then at the barge, which is reported from subsequent observation to have been sunk. The ship was under a fairly heavy fire from the light guns on the Mole extension, but her captain did not see any firing from the 4.1-inch battery at the Mole head. As the ship approached what appeared to be an opening between the barges and the net obstruction extending to the south-eastward from them she commenced to swing to port. She was given full port helm, but ran into the nets between the two end buoys, and continuing to forge ahead, took the nets with her. The piers of the canal entrance were in sight when both engines were reported to have brought up. "Thetis" had thus cleared the net obstruction away enough to enable the ships following to pass to starboard of her, and she signalled to them to do so. Being then about 300 yards from the eastern pier-head, and having drifted slightly to

port (shoreward), she appears to have grounded. She had a list to starboard, and was settling down, having been frequently holed along the starboard side by gunfire. She continued to be hit from the Mole, from craft alongside it, and from guns on shore east of the canal. One or two machine guns were also firing at the ship, her 6-inch forecastle gun engaging these guns until her own smoke made it impossible to see. Communication with the engine-room having broken down, a messenger was sent, and Engineer Lieutenant-Commander Ronald C. Boddie ("Hercules") succeeded in starting the starboard engine, which moved the ship ahead; and being still aground aft, her head swung to starboard into the dredged channel. As she appeared to be sinking, the commander cleared the boiler rooms, sent the boat-keepers to their boats, ordered the smoke to be turned on and the ship to be abandoned. Owing to the death of the petty officer in charge of them, the forward firing keys were not in position; smoke and shell fumes prevented their being found, so that the charges were fired by the after keys; they detonated well, and the ship then quickly sank. The ship's company manned the one remaining cutter and pulled to M.L. 526 (Lieutenant Hugh A. Littleton, R.N.V.R.), which was lying near. Although crowded and holed in two or three places, the cutter was got away without confusion, due to the exertions of Lieutenant George A. Belben ("Penelope"), Commander Sneyd and Lieutenant Francis J. Lambert ("Sir John Moore") being at this time disabled by gas.

95. *"Intrepid"* (Lieutenant Stuart S. Bonham-Carter, "Emperor of India"). – This ship had been unable to get rid of her spare watch of stokers, owing at first to the delay in her motor launch getting alongside, and apparently to the disinclination of the surplus crew to miss the coming fight. She therefore proceeded to the canal with 87 officers and men on board instead of 54. On approaching the Mole she came under heavy shrapnel fire. She rounded the lighthouse and, directed by "Thetis," aground on her port hand, steered for the canal, very few enemy guns firing at her, as they were concentrated on the Mole – doubtless at "Vindictive" – and on "Thetis." On reaching his position in the canal, Lieutenant Bonham-Carter went full speed ahead with the starboard engine and full speed astern with the port helm hard a starboard. He then waited for the crew to get into the boats, but finding the ship was making stern way he had to blow the sinking charges before the steaming party could get out of the engine-room. Engineer Sub-Lieutenant Edgar V. Meikle, with his men, got into a cutter, of which he took charge, proceeding out past the "Thetis" till picked up by motor launch. Another cutter was picked up by the T.B.D. "Whirlwind," and the skiff by M.L. 282. With the two officers and four petty officers, Lieutenant Bonham-Carter launched a Carley raft and went down the canal until picked up by motor launch 282. This motor launch came right into the canal under the stern of the "Iphigenia" – the next blocking ship – under a heavy fire. She was commanded by Lieutenant Percy T. Dean, R.N.V.R., whose conduct Lieutenant Bonham-Carter describes as "simply magnificent." I have had the pleasure of recommending this officer to their Lordships for promotion, and I consider his gallant conduct is well worthy of the Victoria Cross. With the exception of Stoker Petty Officer Harold L. Palliser (O.N. 226201), who was killed while in the motor launch by a machine gun, the whole crew got away. Lieutenant Bonham-Carter reports the exceptionally fine behaviour of the whole of

his crew – deck and engine-room alike – and specially mentions Lieutenant Alan Cory-Wright ("Ramillies"), Sub-Lieutenant Dudley A. Babb ("Sarpedon"), and Engineer Sub-Lieutenant Meikle. In another letter I have recommended Lieutenant Bonham-Carter and the two last-named officers for promotion. I may say here that I regarded the chances of escape from any of the blocking ships as very slender, and this was well known to those who so readily volunteered for this hazardous service and to the volunteer crews of the motor launches who ran equal risks in their work of rescue.

96. *"Iphigenia"* (Lieutenant Edward W. Billyard-Leake, "Fearless"). – This ship, like the preceding one, did not discharge all her engine-room ratings, because some managed to avoid it in order to take part in the fight, and they therefore joined up with the rest of the crew. The "Iphigenia" was the third and last of the Zeebrugge blockers to undertake her duty, and it is no disparagement to the predecessors, who made her task the easier by their example, to say that she was, as I believe, completely successful. On approaching the Mole she came under shrapnel fire, and was lighted up by two searchlights on the western (or land) end of the Mole, and by flares, these latter being rendered useless to the enemy by the smoke-screen, and facilitating navigation for the attacker. On rounding the lighthouse the "Iphigenia" went full speed, a star shell showing up the "Intrepid" headed for the canal and the "Thetis" aground. As she approached "Thetis" that ship showed a green light on her starboard side which enabled Lieutenant Billyard-Leake to find the canal entrance. The ship was now hit twice on the starboard side, one shell cutting the siren steam-pipe and enveloping the fore part of the ship in steam.

97. As "Iphigenia" approached the canal entrance it became obscured by smoke, and her captain found that she was heading for the western pier. Going full speed astern he brought his ship in between a dredger and a barge, severing them. He then went ahead with his starboard engine and drove the barge into the canal. When clear of the barge he went ahead with both engines. Seeing that the "Intrepid" had grounded on the western bank of the canal, with a gap between her and the eastern bank, he steered to close the gap, and collided with the port bow of "Intrepid." He then rang the alarm-gong to signify the imminent blowing of the sinking charges, but finding that he was not completely blocking the channel he telegraphed to the engine-room to go astern, which was done. As soon as his ship was clear he sent Lieutenant Philip E. Vaux ("Marvel"), the First Lieutenant, to the engine-room with an order to go ahead, which was promptly obeyed. The entire entrance was then covered in smoke. As soon as he considered the ship had headway, he put the port engine astern, the starboard ahead, and his helm hard-a-starboard, and grounded on the eastern bank. He then abandoned ship and fired his charges, which all exploded. The company left the ship in one cutter, as the other one was badly damaged. While in the cutter the crew came under more shrapnel and machine-gun fire, which caused some casualties. When trying to pull clear of the ship, M.L. 282 (Lieutenant Percy T. Dean, R.N.V.R., whose conduct in rescuing the officers and men from the "Intrepid" has already been described) was sighted across the "Iphigenia's" bows, and the cutter pulled to her. The majority of the crew got into the motor launch, which then went astern. The

cutter also pulled round the stern of the ship and the launch took the rest on board, except three, one of whom was killed. The cutter was made fast to the stem of the motor launch, which went out of the harbour stern first at full speed. Lieutenant Billyard-Leake reports that this motor launch was entirely responsible for saving the survivors from the "Iphigenia." Heavy machine-gun fire was concentrated on her while on passage out, at which time Sub-Lieutenant Maurice C.H. Lloyd, D.S.C. ("Dominion"), was mortally, and Lieutenant James C. Keith Wright, R.N.V.R., of M.L. 416, dangerously wounded, and two of the motor launch's crew of four killed. I trust that the Lords Commissioners, who have so many claims to judge, will consider that this recital of the part played by the "Iphigenia" well justifies my mention of Lieutenant Billyard-Leake and of Mate (E) Sydney Greville West ("Benbow"), who throughout the preparations and operation worked his department in an admirable manner.

98. *"Brilliant" and "Sirius."* – I regret that the effort to block Ostend did not succeed. The "Brilliant" (Commander Alfred E. Godsal, "Centurion"), with "Sirius" (Lieutenant-Commander Henry N.M. Hardy, D.S.O., "Patrol"), in her wake, was approaching the charted position of the Stroom Bank Buoy, but did not sight it as expected. Deducing from the positions of other navigation marks already passed that the ships were to the northward of their supposed position, they continued on their original course for an extra two minutes, sighting the buoy to the north-eastward. They steered to pass to the northward of the buoy, at which time they first came under fire from the enemy's batteries, and then shaped a course for the deduced position of Ostend. No marks were visible owing to smoke, which made it necessary for "Sirius" to keep very close station on "Brilliant." When the Ostend Piers should have been seen by "Brilliant," breakers were observed on the starboard bow, and though the helm was starboarded, the ship grounded. "Sirius," observing this, immediately put her helm hard over and her engines full speed astern, but the ship being already badly damaged by gunfire and sinking, did not answer the helm, and collided with the port quarter of the "Brilliant." In the end, both ships being practically fast ashore, "Brilliant," with her port engine immovable, and "Sirius," in sinking condition, were blown up where they stranded, as observation has since shown, about 2,400 yards east of the canal entrance. Lieutenant A.C. Crutchley ("Centurion"), Sub-Lieutenant Angus H. Maclachlan ("Temeraire"), and Engineer Lieutenant Wilfred Long ("Dublin"), all serving in the "Brilliant," were reported by their captain as having set a fine example to their men. Commander Godsal also mentions Petty Officer Joseph J. Reed (O.N. C230360), who behaved with conspicuous coolness.

99. The rescue of the crews by motor launches which had been standing by under heavy fire of every calibre, was carried out in the gallant manner which distinguished the work of the crews of the motor launches and coastal motor boats throughout the action. Commander Ion Hamilton Benn, R.N.V.R., attempted to go alongside in Motor Launch No. 532, but owing to thick smoke she was damaged by collision with the ship. Lieutenant Roland Bourke, R.N.V.R., in M.L. 276, repeatedly went alongside "Brilliant" in the difficult circumstances of her starboard engines still going astern, while M.L. 283, under the command of Lieutenant Keith R. Hoare, D.S.C.,

R.N.V.R., embarked practically all the men from the "Sirius," and sixteen from the "Brilliant's" whaler, sunk by gunfire.

100. After leaving the "Sirius," Lieutenant-Commander Hardy found that Engineer Lieutenant William R. Maclaren ("Iron Duke") and some men were missing. He therefore hailed C.M.B. 10 (Sub-Lieutenant Peter B. Clarke, R.N.R.), and with Lieutenant Edward L. Berthon, D.S.C. ("Viceroy"), went alongside the ship under a heavy and accurate fire from 4.1-inch and machine guns to search for them, but found no sign of life in either ship. The officer and men were subsequently picked up by the "Attentive" in a boat, in which they had pulled thirteen miles out to sea after the sinking of their ship.

101. Their Lordships will share with me and the commanding officers of these ships the disappointment due to the defeat of our plans, as we may believe, by the legitimate ruse of the enemy in shifting the buoy. As the Commodore at Dunkirk remarks in the despatch to which their Lordships will refer for details on this point, the location of buoys by aircraft is a high art, and can only be done with accuracy in relation to closely surrounding land or shoal features, but aerial photographs have since established the fact that had the buoy been in its original position the vessels would have made the entrance accurately.

102. Both Commander Godsal and Mr. Hardy immediately and repeatedly asked me for other ships, to be allowed to try again. They report that all their officers, and Petty Officer Joseph Reed have volunteered to make another attempt, sanguine that with the experience gained it would succeed.

IX. – THE RETIREMENT.

103. The viaduct explosion having duly taken place, and the blocking ships having been seen proceeding shorewards, the main object of storming the Mole had been accomplished; and the only reason for prolonging the operation till the programme time for retirement was that of continuing the work of demolition. On the other hand, the only guns in "Vindictive" bearing on the Mole had been put out of action; the upper works of the ship and men in exposed positions were presenting an easy target to the shore guns, while, in view of the failure of the Mole anchors, the storming parties would be unable to embark if the "Daffodil" should be disabled. Captain Carpenter, regarding the "Daffodil's" escape up to this time as being almost a miracle, therefore decided to give the order for the retirement, and in this I consider he acted with good judgment; in fact, I had given orders for the "Warwick" to close the "Vindictive" so that I might inform Captain Carpenter that I had seen the blockships proceeding in, ascertain the conditions on the Mole, and decide on further action, when I saw that she was hauling off.

104. The searchlights, by which twenty minutes' warning was to be given, having been destroyed, as well as the "Vindictive's" syren, by which the executive signal was to be made, the "Daffodil" made the latter signal at fifty minutes past midnight, and the retirement commenced. About fifteen minutes later it was reported to the

Captain that officers and men had ceased coming on board, a large number having already embarked by the same means as they had originally used for storming the Mole. To make doubly sure, Captain Carpenter waited till ten minutes past one, and after repeated assurances from officers and his own observation that no more were returning, he ordered "Daffodil" to tow "Vindictive's" bow away from the Mole, the port cable was slipped, and towing commenced. The hawser parted almost at once, but the ship's head was clear enough to allow her to proceed at full speed with helm hard-a-port under cover of her own smoke screen. A large bumpkin made of her own mainmast, rigged out over the "Vindictive's" port quarter, and taking against the wall, protected the port screw, which nevertheless hung up two or three times, being probably fouled by the débris of the brows. The "Vindictive" reached Dover soon after 8 a.m., on the 23rd.

105. Some of the proceedings of "Iris II" have been reported in connection with the storming of the Mole, and the rest may be told here. Shortly after leaving the Mole she came under a very heavy fire from the Mole and shore batteries, being hit ten times by small shell and twice by large ones. The first large shell came through the port control position and carried away the port side of the bridge, causing a very serious fire amongst the ammunition and bombs under the bridge. It mortally wounded Commander Valentine Gibbs and Major Charles E.C. Eagles, D.S.O. R.M., and seriously wounded Lieutenant George Spencer, D.S.C., R.N.R. Lieutenant Oscar Henderson ("P.19") took a volunteer fire party with a hose on to the upper deck to quench the fire, but seeing the condition of the bridge he ran up on to it and found Commander Gibbs, as he then thought, dead, and Lieutenant Spencer seriously wounded, but still conning the ship. He took command and steadied the ship on her course, the coxswain, Petty Officer David P. Smith, sticking to his post with great gallantry, steering with one hand while holding an electric torch to the compass with the other; it is due to Lieutenant Spencer that the ship was turned away from the land. "Iris II" was again hit by three shells simultaneously, and as the men were packed very closely on the main deck the casualties were very heavy. When the ship was steadied on her course the fire was put out, Able Seaman F.E.M. Lake ("Monarch") being the first man to attack it, which he did with sand, afterwards helping Mr. Henderson to throw bombs overboard, regardless of his own life. A motor launch, No. 558, commanded by Lieutenant-Commander Lionel S. Chappell, D.S.C., R.N.V.R., and with Captain Ralph Collins on board, gallantly came into the heavy fire from the enemy's guns, and throwing a smoke screen around "Iris II" enabled her to get clear, the ship being very badly damaged; she reached Dover at 2.45 p.m., some five hours after the death of her captain, who remained confident and cheerful until his very heroic spirit passed.

106. Although the Lords Commissioners of the Admiralty have most promptly recognised and rewarded the services of Acting Captain Carpenter by promoting him to the Post List, I should not like to end this part of my despatch without putting on record the praise which is due to him. An excellent staff officer, he rendered me invaluable assistance in the drawing up of the final operation orders, the preparations for which involved strenuous work by many officers and a vast amount of necessary

detail. My account of the proceedings of the "Vindictive" outlines his personal share in the attack, but as showing the force which his example had on those under his command, I hear on all sides that the Captain's calm composure when navigating mined waters and bringing his ship alongside the Mole in darkness, and his great bravery when the ship came under heavy fire did much to encourage similar behaviour on the part of the crew, and thereby contributed greatly to the success of the operation.

X. – OSTEND.

107. In arranging the sections of this despatch, I have grouped proceedings of units taking part in the operations off Ostend in their appropriate places, but I submit herewith the report by Commodore Hubert Lynes, C.M.G., Senior Naval Officer at Dunkirk, to whom I am indebted for whole-hearted co-operation and loyal assistance at all times. I share his regret as to the alteration by the enemy of the position of the Stroom Bank Buoy not having been discovered, but I feel that the consequence must be accepted as one of the misfortunes of war.

108. The Lords Commissioners will notice that five French torpedo craft co-operated at Ostend with our big monitors, and four French motor launches with our small monitors. I should like to be allowed to express my gratification at this co-operation, and my thanks for the valuable assistance these vessels gave are due to Vice-Admiral Pierre Alexis, M.A. Ronarc'h, K.C.B., C.M.G., Commandant Superieur de la Marine dans la zone des Armées du Nord, Dunkerque, and to Capitaine de Vaisseau Breart de Boisanger, D.S.O.

109. Commodore Lynes has recommended for special recognition several officers and men, and the rest their Lordships will have an opportunity of considering in the list which I am forwarding as soon as it can be prepared.

XI. – TORPEDO BOAT DESTROYER FORCE.

110. I desire to relate the proceedings of some of the vessels of the 6th Destroyer Flotilla under the command of Captain Wilfred Tomkinson, and the "Warwick" flying my flag, which came under my own observation, or are of special interest or merit.

111. The "Trident" and "Mansfield" after parting company from their submarines, covered the western flotilla of smoke-screening small craft. The "Whirlwind," "Myngs," "Velox," "Morris," "Moorsom," and "Melpomene" covered the eastern smoke flotilla. The "Warwick," "Phoebe," and "North Star" cruised off the Mole to protect the assaulting craft from torpedo attack. These duties took the destroyers close in shore, and they were frequently under a heavy fire from guns of all calibres at short range. When the assaulting craft were leaving the Mole, the "Warwick" followed them for a few minutes, and then returned to assist the withdrawal of the small craft, picking up four motor launches, including No. 282, commanded by Lieutenant P.T.

Dean, R.N.V.R. This launch had on board one hundred and one people from "Iphigenia" and "Intrepid," some of whom had been killed in the launch, and others who were wounded. As the motor launch was dangerously overloaded and full of wounded, I ordered them to be transferred to the "Warwick," which took more than half an hour to do. I was much struck with the gallant bearing of Lieutenant Dean and the survivors of his crew. They were all volunteers, and nearly all had been wounded and several killed.

112. While the "Warwick" was engaged as stated in the preceding paragraph, the "North Star," having lost her bearings in the smoke, emerged from the smoke screen to the south-eastward of the lighthouse. Seeing some vessels alongside the Mole, she fired all her torpedoes at them and withdrew; but coming under very heavy fire at point-blank range she was immediately disabled, and soon in a sinking condition. The "Phoebe," commanded by Lieutenant-Commander Hubert E. Gore-Langton, was handled with conspicuous gallantry while under this heavy fire. She repeatedly circled round the "North Star," making smoke screens and attempting under their cover to tow her out of action. She was twice successful in getting her in tow, the hawser being shot away once and parted once. "Phoebe" then went alongside "North Star," and endeavoured to tow in that way. "North Star," however, was in a sinking condition, and being continually hit. In these circumstances, Mr. Gore-Langton ordered the abandonment of the "North Star," standing by her, and taking off all of her company who were left alive.

113. I regret that the "North Star" was lost, but the conduct of Lieutenant-Commander Kenneth C. Helyar and his company was all that could be desired, the "North Star" not being abandoned until all possibility of salving her was gone. The Lieutenant-Commander of "Phoebe" states that Mr. Helyar by his coolness and calm devotion to duty set a splendid example to all, though his ship was totally disabled and constantly being hit. He would not leave his bridge until ordered twice to abandon his ship when she was obviously sinking under him, and could not be saved. He also did his utmost to assist the "Phoebe" in every way to take him in tow.

114. "Tempest" and "Tetrarch," of the Harwich force, accompanied the Ostend blockships from the Goodwins until they reached the inshore smoke screen off Ostend, after which they co-operated with the Dunkirk destroyers "Faulknor," flying the broad pendant of Commodore Lynes, "Lightfoot," "Mastiff," "Afridi," "Swift," and "Matchless" in supporting the small craft inshore, within close range of the enemy's heavy batteries.

115. I wish to record my entire satisfaction with the good work done by the torpedo-boat destroyer force throughout the operations. The part taken by the "Phoebe" in protecting and endeavouring to tow out of action the "North Star," and in the final rescue of her people, is a conspicuous example of the fine qualities of this branch of the service, and is highly creditable to Mr. Gore-Langton, his officers, and crew. I have already recommended that officer for promotion, as I consider that his personal and professional conduct on this occasion marks him as likely to be valuable in the higher ranks of His Majesty's service.

XII. – SMOKE SCREENS, MOTOR LAUNCHES, AND COASTAL MOTOR BOATS.

116. The orders for smoke-screening the approach and operations of the forces attacking Zeebrugge and Ostend, and the reports from the numerous motor launches and coastal motor boats employed on that duty, are necessarily too detailed to be recapitulated in a despatch of this general nature. Apart from the smoke apparatus supplied to the larger craft for self-protection, the duty of making smoke screens and laying smoke floats was imposed on a large fleet of motor launches and coastal motor boats. Without the services of these little vessels for this duty, for rescue work and for inshore work generally, an attack of this nature could hardly have been considered.

117. *Smoke Screens.* – While the wind favoured the screens were efficacious. Captain Ralph Collins, who commanded the motor launches, reports that in some units in which the smoke screens were maintained, and in which most of the boats were under fire, there were no boats hit; whereas, in one instance, which came under my own observation, the absence of a screen led to preventably heavy punishment. As to the smoke floats, the enemy sunk many of them directly they were laid, especially if, as happened in many cases, they emitted flame. Those which remained were effective.

118. *Motor Launches.* – These craft were under the command of Captain Ralph Collins at Zeebrugge and Commander Hamilton Benn at Ostend. As to the handling of these craft, great credit is due to the leaders of sections for the way in which they led their boats up to the objectives. When the wind shifted, the commanding officers proceeded closer inshore to give as much protection to the attacking ships as possible. One unit, under Lieutenant Gordon S. Maxwell, R.N.V.R., went close inshore, and by dropping three floats without baffles succeeded in inducing the enemy to concentrate his fire on these floats. Lieutenant-Commander Dawbarn Young, R.N.V.R., was in command of M.L. 110. He had volunteered to precede the blockships and light the entrance of the harbour and canal with calcium buoys. Whilst approaching the entrance M.L. 110 was struck by three shells, which killed and wounded half the crew and wrecked the engines. Lieutenant-Commander Young, hit in three places, was mortally wounded, but stuck to his post and gave orders to abandon ship, until he collapsed. This very gallant officer died before reaching Dover. Ever the first to volunteer for any dangerous work, the Dover Patrol has sustained a great loss by his death.

119. Of the meritorious work reported from the motor launches, I have already selected the instances of Lieutenant P.T. Dean, R.N.V.R., in No. 282, and Lieutenant H.A. Littleton, R.N.V.R., in No. 526, who brought off the crews of the sunken blocking ships. There is no doubt that these boats were handled in a magnificent manner, and that the highest praise is due to their officers and men. From Ostend reports of the motor launch flotilla are of the same high character. Commander Ion Hamilton Benn reports that M.L. 283 (Lieutenant Keith R. Hoare, R.N.V.R.) took on board the entire crew of "Sirius" and some of "Brilliant's" people, and was seriously overloaded, but was able to reach harbour safely. He cannot speak too highly of the

conduct of Lieutenant Hoare and Lieutenant Rowland Bourke, R.N.V.R. (M.L. 276), who both showed remarkable coolness and good judgment throughout the operation. He also mentions Lieutenants, R.N.V.R., Sidney D. Gowing (M.L. 551), Rawsthorne Proctor (M.L. 556), and Malcolm S. Kirkwood (M.L. 11).

120. *Coastal Motor Boats.* – I have been greatly impressed with the administrative capacity of Lieutenant Arthur E.P. Welman, D.S.C., R.N., the young officer in charge of the coastal motor boats of the Dover Patrol. In the Zeebrugge operation he had seventeen of these vessels under his orders. Besides their screening duties, several of them undertook attacks an enemy vessels and against the Mole, the seaplane shed, &c., with success, Lieutenant Welman always being in the most exposed position. Sub-Lieutenant Cedric R.L. Outhwaite, R.N.V.R., in C.M.B. 5, reports that he attacked an enemy destroyer which was under way, and observed his torpedo hit below her forward searchlight, the light shortly afterwards going out, and her fire diminishing. Sub-Lieutenant L.R. Blake, R.N.R., in C.M.B.7, reports hitting a destroyer alongside the Mole with a torpedo which struck below the fore bridge. No. 32A fired a torpedo at the steamship "Brussels." An explosion followed, but the result was hidden by smoke.

121. The zest of most of the young officers in the coastal motor boats, like that of those in the motor launches, compels one's admiration. I can select only one of many instances which show the eagerness of the officers to take part in a fight from which circumstances tried to exclude them. Lieutenant Edward E. Hill in C.M.B.35A had the misfortune to foul his propellers on the evening of the 22nd April when already 18 miles on his outward voyage. He got a tow from a drifter, and arrived at Dover at 8 p.m. His boat was immediately hoisted and the propellers cleared, but as there was other damage he was not afloat again till 9.40 p.m. He then made his way to the Belgian coast, and was off Zeebrugge – about 70 miles – by 11.50 p.m., taking up his smoke-float patrol at once, and continuing it for an hour, in the course of which he came under rather heavy fire from a battery at Blankenberghe. The chapter of accidents amongst such small craft is naturally a long one, but the resource developed in overcoming them is more than compensation. The daring way in which the crews of these boats approach the shore, drawing the beams of the searchlights and the fire of the guns, then escaping in their own smoke is splendid. Lieutenant Francis C. Harrison, who commanded the Ostend section of C.M.B.'s, mentions the names of Sub-Lieutenant Peter B. Clarke, R.N.R., Midshipman N.S. Herbert, R.N.R., and Chief Motor Mechanic G.H. Hebblethwaite (C.M.B. 10) for the dangerous work which that boat undertook in searching for the engineer of the "Sirius," who was thought to be on board that ship after she had been sunk, in the course of which the boat came under very heavy fire; and Sub-Lieutenant Frank A.W. Ramsay (C.M.B. 19) for his coolness and quickness in laying the inshore calcium buoys under heavy machine-gun fire. Lieutenant Welman also mentions the names of several officers and men in coastal motor boats; these will be forwarded for Admiralty consideration shortly.

XIII. – DOVER TRAWLER PATROL.

122. Captain William V. Howard, D.S.O., of the Trawler Patrol, accompanied the expedition in the paddle minesweeper "Lingfield," and did valuable work in keeping touch with the force, giving assistance by towing, and otherwise helping small craft in trouble while on the passage to and from Zeebrugge, also in receiving the surplus crews from blockships, and escorting motor launches. This veteran officer has been on patrol work off the south-east coast of England during the whole of the war. His energy and example are great incentives to the officers and men of the Trawler Patrol which he commands.

XIV. – MEDICAL ARRANGEMENTS.

123. In conclusion I desire to make a special reference to the praiseworthy manner in which the medical officers and their staff, and volunteer helpers, devoted their skill and sympathy to those who were wounded in these operations. Fighting at such close quarters, the casualties were bound to be numerous, and the wounds likely to be severe. Staff Surgeon James McCutcheon, M.B., was the senior medical officer of the force. In an able report that officer outlines the work of his staff, and the circumstances in which it was done, and I trust that the Lords Commissioners will agree with me in thinking that no branch of the naval service surpassed in zeal and ability the efforts of the medical branch to prove itself worthy of its profession, and of the occasion. I have selected with difficulty from a number of very deserving officers the names of three to be representative recipients of such promotion as their Lordships may be able to award for these operations to the medical branch of the Royal Navy.

I have the honour to be,
Sir,
Your obedient Servant,
ROGER KEYES,
Vice-Admiral.

Enclosure.

PROCEEDINGS AT OSTEND.
REPORT FROM COMMODORE, DUNKIRK.

Office of Commodore, Dunkirk,
April 30, 1918.

Sir,-

I have the honour to forward the following report on Operation Z.-O., carried out on the night of the 22nd-23rd April.

1. A brief preliminary report was 'phoned to Vice-Admiral, Dover Patrol, on the 23rd April, since which photographs and air reconnaissances have established the facts (as reported)
   that:-

   (*a*.) "Sirius" and "Brilliant" are not inside Ostend Harbour, but lie stranded about 2,400 yards to eastward of eastern pier.

   (*b*.) The Stroom Bank Buoy is not in its charted position, but is a little to eastward of the prolongation of eastern pier, approximately lat. 51 15 50 N., long. 2 53 20 E.

2. (*b*) accounts for (*a*); supposing, as is almost certain, that the buoy was in this position on the night of 22nd-23rd.

3. The location of *buoys* by aircraft is, of course, a very high art, and can only be done with any degree of accuracy with relation to closely surrounded land (or shoal) features.

   Captain R. Graham, D.S.O., D.S.C., R.A.F., and Captain L.H. Slater, D.S.C., R.A.F., obtained the present position of Stroom Bank Buoy by coming down to 100 feet and fixing the buoy with reference, for direction, to the line of eastern pier.

4. The organisation detailed in my 0/53, of the 21st April, was carried out for Ostend operation, which I conducted with the assistance of Commander J.L.C. Clark, D.S.O. R.N., from on board "Faulknor," leader of the Off-Shore Destroyer Force.

5. The operation was carried out according to programme. There were no hitches, the times were kept precisely, and I have complimented the senior officers of units, and all, on the care with which they both studied and carried out my necessarily rather voluminous orders.

6. (*a*.) The wind, on starting out, was light north-westerly, and continued thus until about 10 minutes before "Sirius" and "Brilliant" arrived at Stroom Bank Buoy, when it most unluckily shifted round to the south-westward, causing all the smoke to go wrong at the critical moment.

(*b*.) The M.L.'s and C.M.B's strove with resolution and good judgment to compete with this reverse, but all their efforts were overpowered by the enemy's smoke screen blown to seaward, while they themselves became subjected to a heavy, but happily ill-directed, gunfire.

7. The blockships made the Stroom Bank Buoy (which was alight and marked the whole time), but after that the adverse smoke prevented them seeing anything by which they might have retrieved the error of the buoy's position.

8. (*a*.) Since the Captains of the blockships, Commander A.E. Godsal, R.N., and Lieutenant-Commander H.N.M. Hardy, D.S.O., R.N., will have made their full reports to you, I say little more, since, after what has been said, it is needless to remark that the failure to find the entrance was no fault of theirs; on the contrary, the newly discovered position of the buoy only too plainly shows that their course, after rounding the buoy, ought to have brought them right in.

(*b*.) I may add that on my return to harbour about six hours later, the bitter disappointment of these two gallant officers showed itself chiefly in begging for another blockship apiece to have another try.

9. The low clouds and drizzle put all aircraft participation out of the question.

10. The monitor and siege gun bombardments were undoubtedly useful as a blind, and to keep the fire of the shore batteries down.

The shore batteries commenced to return the monitors' fire about 5 minutes after the latter opened. A number of shell fragments were picked up on board the monitors, but there were no hits. Photographs show a number of hits around the German batteries, but none on the guns.

11. (*a*.) This time the enemy took longer to be alarmed than on the night of 11th/12th. He seemed to take but a desultory interest until the monitors opened fire, *i.e.*, ¼ hour after the C.M.B.'s arrived at the Stroom Bank Buoy, and, as on the previous occasion, he cannot have had a single patrol out.

(*b*.) Very few shells fell near us in the offshore destroyers. Enemy's fire was evidently either directed against the inshore boats, at the monitors, or barrage fire into the smoke areas.

(*c*.) His star shell, as before, averaged about 7,000 yards from the shore; when we closed to that range they dropped alongside of (one on) the division.

(*d*.) At intervals the enemy's star shell showed up to us the M.L.'s busily engaged with their smoke screens, and at 11.50 also the blockships with their escort to the E.N.E. steering for the Stroom Bank Buoy. It was at this moment that we noticed the shift of wind to south-westward.

(*e*.) About 10 minutes later the blockships disappeared abreast the buoy into the smoke, and we saw no more of them, but picked up "Tempest" and "Tetrarch."

(*f*.) C.M.B.'s 12 and 19 report a "M.L. blew up" about 00.15, E.S.E., 2 miles from Stroom Bank Buoy; this apparently refers to the blockships being hit by shell.

(*g*.) About 00.25 bursts of firing became more frequent, and more searchlights switched on than before, evidently the result of the blockships' emergence from smoke and stranding.

(*h*.) After this there was little more than desultory firing, probably at monitors, with the exception of two 3-minute bursts of barrage fire at 00.42-00.52.

The searchlights continued searching actively until about 01.30 when their numbers reduced to three or four.

(*i*.) At 01.00 the "retirement" red rocket signals and syren "K's" were made by destroyers; this produced a few big shrapnel in our neighbourhood.

(*j*.) A few C.M.B.'s and M.L.'s were seen coming away off and on up to 2 a.m., when we withdrew to fix position by R, R.M.C. Buoy, picking up No. 7 C.M.B., disabled, on the way. ("Tetrarch" towed her home.)

(*k*.) Having fixed by Position R, we continued to cruise between R and Stroom Bank Buoy until daylight, and the shore became visible, when, nothing floating being in sight, all forces were withdrawn; B.C. Patrol being sent out later, and picking up the last straggler, viz., C.M.B. 17, who had run out of petrol near 3 B.C. Buoy.

(*l*.) At 03.20, when near Stroom Bank Buoy, we saw two searchlights, judged about 500 yards apart, concentrated on something burning in the water between them.

At 03.30 this fire culminated in an explosion, and darkness ensued, the two searchlights switched out a few minutes later.

(*m*.) No enemy craft were seen by anyone except that C.M.B. 12 feels sure that she was chased by a destroyer with searchlights, but I cannot think a craft coming out of Ostend could have been seen by no one else or escaped us, for, apart from the star-shell illumination, the diffused moonlight gave quite one mile visibility.

12. On return to harbour about 07.30, I found that:-

(*a*.) All the crews of the blockships had been saved, the majority by M.L.'s 276, 283, and brought to Dunkirk; the few others who had evacuated in a pulling boat were picked up by the Gap Patrol.

(*b*.) This salvage work of M.L.'s 276 and 283 was carried out under heavy, but fortunately not accurate, fire with a courage and coolness that alone could have achieved its wonderful result, for not a man was wounded, and the heavily laden boats returned to harbour safely.

(*c*.) All the M.L.'s had returned intact with very slight casualties, and one damaged bow.

(*d*.) The C.M.B.'s, too, both for Zeebrugge and Ostend, had all returned safely, either to Dunkirk or Dover, with the exception of two or three which were retrieved later. Their personnel casualties were two dangerously wounded and four wounded, considering the work done, a marvellous result, and one which reflects the greatest credit on the C.M.B. officers.

13. *Conclusions*: – (*a.*) The luck of the wind changing, combined with the shifting of the Stroom Bank Buoy, accounts for the failure to block Ostend Harbour. There is no discredit to anyone; indeed, none could have carried out their duties more admirably than did the Ostend forces on this occasion.

(*b.*) I anticipate success in the new endeavour, the undertaking of which has only been waiting favourable weather conditions during the last few days.

(*c.*) The lion's share of the work was, of course, done by the C.M.B.'s, M.L.'s, and blockships.

I have, &c.,
HUBERT LYNES,
Commodore, Dunkirk.
Vice-Admiral Sir Roger Keyes, K.C.B.,
C.M.G., M.V.O., D.S.O., R.N.,
Dover.

OSTEND OPERATIONS.
MAY 10, 1918.

Fleet House, Dover,
June 15, 1918.
(No. 2305/003.)

SIR,

Be pleased to lay before the Lords Commissioners of the Admiralty the following report on the renewed attempt made in the early morning of the 10th May, 1918, to block the entrance of the Ostend-Bruges Canal by sinking the "Vindictive" therein.

2. When I learnt on the 23rd April that the attempt to block Ostend had not succeeded, I represented to their Lordships the desirability of repeating the operation at once. The "Vindictive," the only vessel available at the moment, being placed at my disposal, every effort was made to repair the damage she had suffered and fit her out before the expiration of the period in which the tide and darkness suited, *i.e.*, about four days. This was accomplished at Dover, thanks to the strenuous efforts of Rear-Admiral C.F. Dampier, the Superintendent of the Dockyard, and his small staff; the services of Engineer Commander Henry F. Bell, R.N., and Mr. A.J. Luke being particularly valuable.

Two hundred tons of cement were put into the "Vindictive's" after magazines and upper bunkers on both sides, which was all her draught would permit her to carry, in view of the depth of water in the approaches to Ostend Harbour.

Major-General Sir William Hickey, K.C.B., Commanding Dover Garrison, most helpfully provided men for filling bags with cement and putting them on board.

3. As already reported in my last despatch, Commander Alfred E. Godsal, R.N., and Lieutenant-Commander Henry N.M. Hardy, D.S.O., R.N., of the "Brilliant" and "Sirius" respectively, had begged to be allowed to make another attempt, and had reported that all their officers and Petty-Officer Joseph J. Reed of the "Brilliant," had volunteered for this service. As Commander Godsal had led the previous attack, he was given command of the "Vindictive," and Lieutenant Victor A.C. Crutchley, R.N., Sub-Lieutenant Angus H. Maclachlan, R.N., and Petty Officer Joseph J. Reed, all of the "Brilliant," accompanied him. Engineer Commander William A. Bury, R.N., however, claimed his right to remain in the "Vindictive." This very gallant officer, who greatly distinguished himself on the 23rd April, represented that his knowledge of the engines and boilers of his ship should be utilised. He further begged that Engine Room Artificers Hubert Cavanagh, Norman Carroll, Alan Thomas, and Herbert Alfred Harris, who also volunteered, might be allowed to remain with him. I acceded to his request.

Lieutenant Sir John Alleyne, D.S.C., R.N., of H.M.S. "Lord Clive," who had been most useful in fitting up the navigational arrangements which were destroyed on the 23rd April, asked to be allowed to navigate the vessel during the operation. I approved of this request, feeling that this officer's experience and intimate knowledge of the shoals and currents on the Belgian coast would be of great value to the Commander of the "Vindictive."

The crew were selected from a very large number of volunteers from vessels of the Dover Patrol.

4. The "Vindictive" was in all respects ready by the desired date, but the weather was unfavourable, and the operation had to be postponed until the necessary condition of tide and darkness recurred. This delay made it possible to prepare a second ship, the old cruiser "Sappho," which was taken from Southampton to Chatham and fitted out by Chatham Dockyard with the greatest celerity and thoroughness.

5. Lieutenant-Commander Hardy took command of her, and he was accompanied by all the officers of the "Sirius," Lieutenant Edward L. Berthon, D.S.C., R.N., Sub-Lieutenant Alfred V. Knight, R.N.R., and Engineer-Lieutenant William R. McLaren, R.N. Her crew were selected from a very large number of volunteers in the Royal Naval Barracks at Chatham.

6. Aerial observation on the 9th May showed that many torpedo and submarine craft were still shut up in Bruges, and proved that the effectiveness of the blocking of the Zeebrugge branch of the canal was maintained up to that date. Although the craft so shut up in Bruges have been unable to use the small waterways to Ostend, the latter port was still being used by enemy torpedo craft and submarines.

7. Other information, confirmed by aerial observation, also disclosed the fact that to counterbalance the forced inactivity of the craft in Bruges, and probably to resist any repetition of the April attack, a considerable number of German destroyers had joined those units of the Flanders force which were outside the canal on the night of the 22nd-23rd of that month.

8. Commodore Hubert Lynes, C.M.G., at Dunkirk, having so ably carried out the direction of the former attempt as part of the Zeebrugge and Ostend scheme, I entrusted the conduct of the operations on this occasion to him, placing under his orders all the monitors, destroyers, motor launches, and coastal motor boats required, in addition to the blocking ships "Vindictive" and "Sappho." On the evening of the 9th May, the weather conditions being most promising, the "Vindictive" and "Sappho" sailed in company to join Commodore Lynes at Dunkirk.

His report, which is attached, furnishes the details of the operation.

9. In order to prevent interference from Zeebrugge by the newly-arrived enemy destroyer force mentioned in paragraph 7 H.M.S. "Warwick," flying my flag, and a division of destroyers consisting of H.M. Ships "Whirlwind," "Velox," and "Trident," under Captain Wilfred Tomkinson, R.N., cruised midway between Ostend and Zeebrugge.

10. Meanwhile the operation proceeded in accordance with the plan, except for the unfortunate breakdown of the "Sappho," due to a boiler accident, which reduced her speed to such an extent that she was unable to reach her destination in time to take part. This halved the chances of success, and was a great misfortune.

With regard to the proceedings of "Vindictive," I cannot do better than quote from the report of Lieutenant Victor Crutchley, on whom the command devolved when Commander Godsal was killed and Lieutenant Sir John Alleyne seriously wounded:-

"On arrival at position P, course was altered for the Stroom Bank Buoy. The boat marking the buoy was seen and left close on the port hand; the buoy was not seen. Speed was reduced to twelve knots on passing the buoy.

"At this time the smoke screen was excellent. There was a lane between the eastern and western sections, and the only fire experienced was shrapnel, which I considered was fired at a venture, and did no harm. We ran on for thirteen minutes from the Stroom Bank Buoy, and then, as the entrance was not sighted, altered course to the westward parallel to the shore, and reduced to 60 revolutions (nine knots). As we still failed to see the entrance we altered course 16 points to starboard, and returned along the shore to the eastward. We again failed to find the entrance, and so altered course 16 points to starboard. All this time, owing to fog and smoke, the visibility was not more than 1½ cables. This time the entrance was sighted about one cable on the port beam, and at the same time the ship came under a very heavy fire from shore batteries of all descriptions.

"On sighting the entrance, in accordance with previous orders, I passed the order 'preparatory abandon ship' to the engine-room. As soon as the entrance was sighted the ship was handled from the conning tower. Commander Godsal immediately turned up for the entrance and ordered smoke to be lighted. At about this time communication with the after control failed. Just after the entrance was passed, Commander Godsal went outside the conning tower and gave the order hard-a-starboard from outside.

"Immediately after this a heavy shell burst either on the conning tower or very close to it; Lieutenant Alleyne was knocked out, and Commander Godsal was not seen again, and all the occupants of the conning tower were badly shaken. I then ordered the port telegraph to full speed astern, to try to swing the ship across the channel. She grounded forward on the eastern pier when at an angle of about three points to the pier. As the ship stopped swinging, and at the time I considered that no more could be done, I ordered the ship to be abandoned.

"When the engine-room had been abandoned, Engineer Lieutenant-Commander Bury blew the ship up, by firing the main charges and after auxiliary charges, and I endeavoured to fire the forward auxiliary charges. There was a considerable shock when the first set of charges were fired. I am not positive that the forward auxiliary charges fired, as I could not distinguish the shock from other disturbances.

"When I got on board M.L. 254 I found that the First Lieutenant had been killed by a shell bursting, also one deckhand. The captain, Lieutenant Geoffrey H. Drummond, R.N.V.R., and the coxswain, had been wounded. We went out of the harbour stern first followed the whole way by machine-gun fire. On finally going ahead the forecastle flooded, and the boat was very much down by the bows. The pump and buckets were got under way and all spare hands placed right aft. However, the water was gaining, and 'S.O.S.' was made by flashing lamp continually to seaward. The courses steered from Ostend were north for 15 minutes, and then west by north until picked up by "Warwick."

"I cannot speak too highly of the bravery of the M.L.'s coming alongside inside Ostend; they were under a continuous and heavy fire. M.L. 254 rescued two officers and thirty-seven men.

"The question of recommendations is a very difficult one. Every man, without exception, behaved splendidly."

11. It had been Commander Godsal's intention to ram the western pier with the object of swinging the ship across the channel under port helm, a manoeuvre that would have been greatly assisted by the tide, which was setting strongly through the piers to the eastward. It would appear that when the "Vindictive" eventually found the entrance she was too close to the eastern pier to use port helm without risk of grounding broadside on. This would account for Commander Godsal's order "hard a starboard" a few seconds before he was killed. The "Vindictive" was thus committed to starboard helm when the command devolved on Lieutenant Crutchley, who very promptly put the port telegraph to full speed astern. Unfortunately the port propeller, which was very severely damaged against Zeebrugge Mole, was of little value. Due

to this, and also to the fact that the tide was setting strongly against her starboard side, the ship's stern did not swing across the channel as desired, with the result that she grounded at an angle of about 25 degrees to the eastern pier, leaving a considerable channel between her stern and the western pier.

12. At 2.45 a.m., fifteen minutes after the programme time for the withdrawal of the motor craft, the "Warwick" and her consorts proceeded slowly to the westward parallel to the coast.

13. At 3.15 a.m. a signal of distress was observed from the direction of Ostend. I directed the division to close, and found M.L. 254 (Lieutenant Geoffrey H. Drummond, R.N.V.R.) badly damaged and in a sinking condition, with two officers and thirty-seven men of the "Vindictive's" crew on board. Lieutenant Drummond was very severely wounded, his second in command, Lieutenant Gordon F. Ross, R.N.V.R., and other men killed, and most of her small crew and many of the "Vindictive's," including her gallant Engineer Commander, were wounded. They were transferred to the "Warwick," and this took half an hour to do, on account of the serious condition of some of the wounded.

14. Dawn was now breaking, and H.M.S. "Warwick" and her consorts were within close range of the enemy's batteries. M.L. 254 was too badly damaged forward to allow of her being towed, and was rapidly settling down. I ordered her to be destroyed, and, as soon as this had been carried out, withdrew the division at 25 knots.

15. By this time the tide had fallen so low that it was inexpedient to return by the route inside of the shoals by which the approach had been made, and a course was steered for a gap in the net defence by the deep-draught route from Ostend to seaward.

It would seem that the enemy had mined this route in anticipation of an attack. At 4.0 a.m. H.M.S. "Warwick" struck a mine, which broke her back just before the superstructure of the after superimposed 4-inch gun, and destroyed the after part of the ship. She took a heavy list and appeared to be settling by the stern. H.M.S. "Velox" was ordered alongside H.M.S. "Warwick," and the wounded, of whom there were a large number on board, were transferred to the former. H.M.S. "Whirlwind" then took H.M.S. "Warwick" in tow, and the latter being unable to steer, H.M.S. "Velox" was kept alongside while navigating the channels through the shoals to the open sea.

I arrived at Dover in H.M.S. "Warwick" at 4.30 p.m.

16. I have again to refer to the fine work done by the motor launches and coastal motor boats, as reported in paragraph 29 of the Commodore's letter. Their conduct in the late operation confirms the opinion I expressed of them in my despatch on the previous operations.

17. The co-operation of the Air Force, under Brigadier-General Charles L. Lambe, C.M.G., D.S.O., R.A.F., was of great value during the operation. In spite of the fog the 214th Squadron (Squadron-Commander Herbert G. Brackley, D.S.O., D.S.C.) continued to attack in accordance with the programme until after the completion of the operation.

18. I greatly regret the loss of so fine an officer as Commander Godsal. His zeal to retrieve the failure of the "Brilliant" on the 23rd April impelled him to disregard all protection in order to secure success on this occasion.

19. As on the 22nd/23rd April, I am much indebted to Vice-Admiral Pierre Alexis M.A. Ronarc'h, Commandant Supérieur de la Marine dans la zone des Armées du Nord, Dunkerque, who placed at my disposal all the available vessels under his command, and assisted me in every possible way. The French torpedo craft and M.Ls. performed valuable service in connection with the monitor bombardment.

20. I commend Commodore Hubert Lynes to their Lordships' favourable consideration.

The officers and men mentioned by him are being included in my list of recommendations, which will be forwarded as soon as possible.

I have, &c.,

ROGER KEYES,

Vice-Admiral, Dover Patrol.

Enclosure to Vice-Admiral, Dover, letter No. 2305/003, dated 15th June, 1918. (No. 053.).

Office of Commodore,

Dunkirk,

15th May, 1918.

SIR,

I have the honour to forward the following report on the operations for blocking Ostend Harbour, carried out on the night of the 9th-10th May, 1918.

2. It will be remembered that on the night of the 22nd-23rd April, when the forces under your command so successfully achieved the blocking of the Zeebrugge-Bruges Canal, the Western Squadron, under my Command, was unsuccessful in its attack; simultaneously delivered, and with the same object on Ostend.

3. The failure on that occasion was due, firstly, to the adverse shift of wind that blew all our smoke screens across the harbour entrance at the critical moment, and secondly, to the displacement – whether by design or chance on the enemy's part – of the Ostend Buoy, whose normal position had formed a convenient departure point for the blockships.

4. Our lack of success was the fortune of war, not the fault of anyone concerned; indeed, no one could have carried out their duties more admirably than did the Ostend forces that night, and I am deeply grateful that, in recognition of this fact, you were so considerate as to place the organisation and leadership of another attack in my hands.

5. In the first operation, the blockships had advanced under cover of a smoke screen, guided by the lights and signals made by the small craft (C.M.B.'s and M.L.'s)

working close inshore. I decided to adopt in general a similar plan for the new attack, but previous experience, and the necessity for assuming that the enemy would make counter preparations against an exactly similar attack, called for modification in detail.

6. In preparing for the new attack, particular attention was paid to perfecting the navigational arrangements; numerous small, but important, improvements were introduced into the smoke gear, and the alternatives for guiding the blockships into the entrance were made so numerous as to reduce chance of failure, in that respect, to the smallest possible dimensions.

7. The quicker the delivery of the new attack, the greater the element of surprise, and, consequently, of success. Realising this, special efforts were made both at Dover and Dunkirk, so that within a few days of the first attack, "Vindictive" had been prepared for her new role of blockship, all the small craft had been completed with their smoke-lights and other fittings, and reorganised according to the new plan of attack, which had been promulgated to all concerned.

The alternative plans of attack, "V.O." and "V.S.," were submitted to you in my operation orders 0/54 and 0/58 respectively.

8. For this rapid and satisfactory work of preparation at Dover, I beg particularly to offer my grateful thanks to Commodore the Hon. A.D.E.H. Boyle, C.B., M.V.O., Chief of the Staff, who left no stone unturned to have all my numerous requests carried out; for that at Dunkirk, I am chiefly indebted to the energy of Commander J.L.C. Clarke, D.S.O., R.N., my Second-in-Command; to Lieutenant-Commander F.H. Sandford, D.S.O., R.N., the staff officer you were good enough to lend me, who was mainly responsible for the smoke screen organisation; and to Lieutenant H.F. Witherby, R.N.V.R., my staff intelligence officer, whose knowledge of the enemy's coast and close association with air reconnaissance work of the 61st (Naval) Wing were invaluable

9. The elements were, however, against us – for despite all these preparations, strong northerly winds, with rough seas, precluded all possibility of the enterprise up to a period when the conjunction of darkness and tide, in its turn, demanded postponement until the second week of the present month.

10. This enforced period of inaction was occupied in perfecting and testing the arrangements, and, above all, in the preparation of a second blockship, which on your representation, was ordered to be prepared and fitted out by His Majesty's Dockyard, Chatham.

11. The conjunction of darkness and tides made the night of the 9th-10th May the first favourable night of the new period. By good fortune the weather conditions on the 9th gave every indication of promise, and accordingly on the afternoon of the 9th the operations were put in progress, firstly by the passage of "Sappho" to Dover, and later by the passage of both blockships, with their supporting and escorting forces, from Dover to Dunkirk. It was at first doubtful whether "Sappho" could be completed in time, but Chatham Dockyard made great efforts, and "Sappho" arrived at Dover with several hours in hand.

12. For days preceding the operation, rain, cloud, and mist had prevented more

than the scantiest air reconnaissances, but towards sunset on the 9th, *i.e.*, when the blockships were already steaming eastwards, an air reconnaissance announced that all the buoys off Ostend had apparently been removed. At considerable risk of having to land after dark, Squadron-Commander Ronald Graham, D.S.O., D.S.C., himself at once went out, returned safely, and confirmed the report.

This new move on the enemy's part had to be countered; we accordingly arranged to lay a special (calcic-phosphide) light-buoy of our own, which subsequently made a satisfactory departure point for the blockship and smoke screens.

13. The weather conditions as night advanced continued excellent, wind N. by W., sky clear, atmosphere good, both for air work and navigation, sea smooth, enough for the small craft to operate, barometer steady, and conditions likely to remain stable.

14. "Vindictive" and "Sappho" arrived in Dunkirk Roads in good time, disembarked their surplus crews, and then proceeded with their escorts at the appointed time in the programme. "Sappho," however, had scarcely left the anchorage than a man-hole joint in the side of her boiler blew out, reducing her speed to about six knots, and therefore putting her participation that night out of the question.

15. This very serious reduction of blocking material required consideration whether or not it was advisable to proceed with the operation.

I decided to continue with "Vindictive," and signalled to Commander Godsal that I had every confidence he would do his best without "Sappho." I also informed you by W/T of my decision.

16. This done, I proceeded on board "Faulknor" (Commander Henry G.L. Oliphant, M.V.O., D.S.O.), leader of the off-shore supports, to overtake the other forces, who, in accordance with orders, were already well on their way to their various stations. Commander Clarke and Lieutenant-Commander Sandford accompanied me in "Faulknor" to carry out staff work, and were of great assistance to me in conducting the operations.

17. After the sudden removal of the buoys, and in the knowledge that nine enemy destroyers had been seen in the offing late that evening, I had fully expected enemy interference with our plan before reaching the place off Ostend where we should lay our buoy and spread the small craft. But no, nothing occurred. The enemy star shells and "flaming onions" fired intermittently from the coast during the approach were evidently only part of his new searching routine. Once again his preparations against surprise included no patrol craft in the offing.

By 1.30 a.m. all preliminary dispositions had been completed, and the (advanced) inshore forces, *i.e.*, the C.M.B. and M.L. divisions, sent in to carry out their various duties.

18. One new feature of the present plan was that there should be no *preliminary* bombardments or air raid; we were to make no attacks until our sea force were discovered by the enemy.

19. At 1.35 a.m. there was still no firing from the shore, but a searchlight lit up, and commenced to search. The C.M.B.'s had arrived, and were running their smoke screens. The noise of their engines, and those of the M.L.'s approaching on their heels, was, of course, carried ashore by the breeze.

At 1.43 a.m. I gave the pre-arranged signal to "open fire," which was immediately responded to by the monitors, siege guns, and the air squadrons. Bombs and shells, whose bursts could be seen over the top of our smoke screen, were undoubtedly giving the enemy a warm time, and constituting a protection to the small craft inshore.

20. Shortly before this, I had noticed with some anxiety the gathering of light-drifting "clouds" – but good-sized gaps, through which stars shone, could be seen at 1.45 a.m., when the sky became completely overcast, and five minutes later we were enveloped in a thick sea fog which, for the next all-important hour, reduced our means of keeping in touch with events to sound alone.

21. I felt that we could hope for no more air or monitor bombardments, and that thus deprived of their valuable support, the small craft in-shore would suffer in proportion, but fortunately this was not the case. The fog proves to have been merely a local patch, not extending to the monitors to the westward, and was also sufficiently low-lying to enable the airmen to continue their attacks between it and the true cloud system at some 10,000 feet altitude.

To realise these conditions, and the darkness due to absence of moon, and to know that the Royal Air Force carried out its whole programme is, in itself, a very high tribute to the efficiency of the air squadrons, who, under the orders of Brigadier-General Charles L. Lambe, C.M.G., D.S.O., took part in the operations. All our aeroplanes eventually returned to their aerodromes; some landed well to the westward naturally under difficulties, one crashed so badly that the pilots were both severely injured.

The monitors, too, did good and useful work – particularly "Prince Eugene." Captain Ernest Wigram, D.S.O., led his division well inside range limits, in order that guns of the secondary armament might play a part as well as the big guns. This they did with good effect, and it is really rather wonderful that his division escaped without injury, for his front rank position put him inside the enemy's long-ranged star shells, and brought his division under a heavy fire from the shore batteries.

The R.M.A. siege guns, under Colonel Pryce Peacock, also maintained a valuable fire on the enemy's heavy coast batteries throughout the operation.

22. To return to Ostend. 2 a.m., *i.e.*, "Vindictive's" programme time to arrive at the piers, was signalled by a heavy cannonade of quick-firers and machine-gun fire near the entrance. The enemy had now almost certainly realised the nature of the attack, and since the smoke screens and fog prevented him aiming at definite objectives, except when the small craft ran close alongside to fire torpedoes at, or engage, the pier-heads with their machine guns, he concentrated his effort in a continuous barrage fire across the entrance from the whole of the exceedingly formidable array of batteries in the neighbourhood of Ostend.

23. For the next twenty minutes, the critical period during which "Vindictive" must succeed or fail, the offshore destroyer forces were ordered to fire star shell over the entrance, and shell at the enemy's batteries – the former to light up the pier-heads for "Vindictive," and the latter to divert the enemy's attention further seaward. This firing was useful; the inshore forces were encouraged by having audible proof of our support close behind them, and the enemy diverted a small proportion of his fire.

Very few shells came near us, however, either at this time or later; there were no casualties either to material or personnel among the off-shore forces. I attribute this mainly to the fog and smoke screens.

24. Meanwhile, "Vindictive," after passing our calcic-phosphide buoy, had arrived "on time" at where she expected to find the entrance. The fog, and apparently also some of the smoke borne on an easterly draught of air (the result of wind impinging on the tall houses on the sea front), had reduced the seashore visibility to two or three hundred yards at the most, and nothing could be seen.

"Vindictive" accordingly reduced speed, turned about, and searched to the westward. Still finding nothing, she again turned about, steered slowly eastward, and gave the "last resort" signal to her C.M.B. escort. This signal was obeyed by lighting a million candlepower flare close inshore to the westward of the entrance. In most circumstances, the illumination of the whole sea front by this intensely brilliant flare would probably have brought very heavy casualties to the inshore craft and "Vindictive" herself, through placing them under accurate gunfire, but on this occasion the fog, hitherto our enemy, now proved our friend, for while the flare showed "Vindictive" the piers, the small craft still remained ill-defined or invisible, except at closest range.

25. "Vindictive" now became clearly visible to the enemy's batteries, who concentrated all efforts on her, but she had only two hundred yards to go, and Commander Godsal immediately turned up for the entrance.

Communication between the conning tower and the after control soon failed, and, the entrance being passed, Commander Godsal went outside the conning tower and gave the necessary orders for placing the ship in her blocking position.

At this moment a very heavy shell burst, either on the conning tower or close to it. This must have killed Commander Godsal, for he was seen no more; and later, after the ship had been sunk in the channel, careful search failed to reveal his body.

This very gallant officer must have known before being killed that his efforts were crowned with success. Lieutenant Sir John Alleyne was knocked out, severely wounded in the stomach, and all the occupants of the conning tower were badly shaken by this shell. Lieutenant Victor Crutchley then took command, and endeavoured to place the ship across the channel. The sinking charges were fired by Engineer Lieutenant-Commander William A. Bury, and preparations made to abandon ship.

26. All this time "Vindictive" was continuously fired at, both by heavy and machine guns, and repeatedly hit; the after control had been completely demolished, killing Sub-Lieutenant Angus Maclachlan and all with him, and the whole upper deck was a mass of débris. Notwithstanding this, perfect order was maintained, and a careful search for wounded was made before embarking in the two M.L.'s (Nos. 254 and 276), who had run in through the fire zone to effect the rescue.

27. Motor Launch 254 (Lieutenant Geoffrey H. Drummond, R.N.V.R.), coming alongside "Vindictive's" inshore side, embarked Lieutenant Crutchley, Engineer Lieutenant-Commander Bury, and thirty-seven men. With his First Lieutenant (Lieutenant Gordon Ross, R.N.V.R.) and Deckhand J. Thomas killed, his coxswain

wounded, and himself wounded in three places, Lieutenant Drummond backed his now heavily laden motor launch out of the harbour, still under a tremendous fire, cleared the entrance, and made straight to seaward.

Arriving outside the fire zone, Lieutenant Drummond found his launch gradually filling forward from her injuries. Standing on at slow speed through the fog, and contriving somehow or other to pass close to the offshore destroyers without either getting in touch, M.L. 254 was most fortunately picked up in a sinking condition about forty minutes after leaving Ostend by your flagship "Warwick." Rescuers and rescued were quickly taken on board, and M.L. 254 then sank.

28. M.L. 276 (Lieutenant Rowland Bourke, R.N.V.R.), having followed "Vindictive" into Ostend (engaging both piers with his machine guns *en route*), went alongside "Vindictive" after M.L. 254, with her first-rescued party, had shoved off.

After much search and shouting, and still under a very heavy fire, Lieutenant Bourke and Sub-Lieutenant Petrie managed to find and embark the last three of "Vindictive's" survivors (Lieutenant Alleyne and two ratings), all badly wounded, in the water clinging to a capsized skiff.

This fine rescue effected, M.L. 276, hit in fifty-five places and with three of her crew killed or wounded, cleared the harbour, and was able to continue steering to the westward until picked up and taken in tow by "Prince Eugene."

29. The small inshore craft – C.M.B.'s, under Lieutenant Arthur E.P. Welman, D.S.C., R.N., and Lieutenant Francis C. Harrison, D.S.O., R.N., and the M.L.'s under Commander Ion Hamilton Benn, D.S.O., R.N.V.R., as before, carried out all their duties splendidly; to them must be given the chief honours of having guided "Vindictive" in.

Daring exploits of these small craft all contributory to the general success, are numerous; they are recounted by the senior officers of divisions in their detailed reports, but I would specially mention the following:-

C.M.B. No. 25 (Lieutenant Russell H. McBean, R.N.) escorted "Vindictive" with smoke screen close up to the entrance, where she assisted her with guiding lights, then torpedoed the piers, and finally engaged the machine guns there with his own machine guns with apparently good effect, during which Lieutenant McBean was wounded and Acting-Chief Motor Mechanic G.E. Keel killed. Having seen "Vindictive" inside the piers, and her work being completed, Sub-Lieutenant George R. Shaw, R.N.R. (second-in-command), brought her safely back to harbour, Motor Mechanic A.J. Davies filling Chief Motor Mechanic Keel's place, and keeping the engines running most efficiently.

C.M.B. No. 24 (Lieutenant Archibald Dayrell-Reed, D.S.O., R.N.R.) and C.M.B. No. 30 (Lieutenant Albert L. Poland, R.N.), both carried out successful torpedo attacks on the pier ends, afterwards laying and maintaining good smoke screens close inshore throughout the remainder of the operation.

C.M.B. No. 26 (Lieutenant Cuthbert F.B. Bowlby, R.N.) escorted "Vindictive" close up to the entrance, then ran ahead, and, finding one of the piers, fired his torpedo at it. The water being shallow, and range short, the explosion shook the boat so severely as to damage her engines and open her seams. She commenced to sink, but by his presence of mind, and the cool perseverance of Chief Motor Mechanic G.W. McCracken, Lieutenant Bowlby got the leak stopped, engines going again, and brought his boat out of the fire zone, where Commander Bertram H. Ramsay, leader of one of the offshore divisions, took her in tow.

C.M.B. No. 22 (Lieutenant William H. Bremner, R.N., with Lieutenant Arthur E.P Welman, D.S.C., Senior Officer of C.M.B.'s, aboard), when carrying out her smoke screening of the shore batteries, encountered close inshore an enemy torpedo boat, who switched on her searchlight and opened fire. C.M.B. No. 22 had no better weapon than her Lewis guns, but with these she attacked and peppered the torpedo boat to such good effect as to drive her away from the harbour entrance, and prevent her interfering with the blocking operation.

C.M.B. No. 23 (Lieutenant the Hon. Cecil E.R. Spencer) escorted "Vindictive" close inshore, and kept touch with her until "Vindictive" gave the "last resort" signal, on which C.M.B. No. 23 laid, and lit, the million candle-power flare, by whose light "Vindictive" eventually found her way in.

30. To recount the foregoing exploits of the small craft is in no way to detract from the praise due to all, particularly to the senior officers of units, for the care and precision with which they carried out my necessarily rather elaborate orders.

31. The general retirement was well executed, and without further casualties or incident, the supporting forces remaining out until daylight to pick up any disabled small craft who might still be out. There were none, however; those who were unable to return by their own power had already been towed home.

32. No interference by enemy craft was experienced throughout the operation, but from subsequent reports of some of the inshore craft it appears that several German torpedo boats were lying close under the shore batteries the whole time, and made no move to come out.

33. Our casualties were remarkably light – 2 officers and 6 men killed, 5 officers and 25 men wounded, 2 officers and 9 men missing, believed killed. Our only loss in material is M.L. 254. A number of the small craft were considerably damaged by gunfire, but all these are, or will be shortly, ready for action again. The light casualty list must be attributed to the efficient smoke screens, and probably also to the fog.

34. Of the "Sappho," I can but record the bitter disappointment of all aboard her at the accident that prevented her following "Vindictive." One and all, they begged to be given another chance, and when the day comes for their request to be granted, I am sure they will not be found wanting.

I have, &c.,
HUBERT LYNES,
Commodore.
To Vice-Admiral Sir Roger Keyes,
K.C.B., C.V.O., D.S.O.

*NOTE – Some amendments to this despatch of 9th May, 1918, have been made by the Vice-Admiral, Dover Patrol, in the light of information received between that date and 22nd January, 1919.

†NOTE – After the evacuation of Zeebrugge by the enemy it was found that these guns were of 5.9 inch calibre, and subsequent to these operations the battery was moved from the end of the Mole on to the parapet.

‡NOTE – After the evacuation it was found that three of the guns on the Mole extension were of 4.1 inch calibre.

**NOTE – Able Seaman Eaves, it appears, was not killed, but was very severely wounded and taken prisoner.

18

RUSSIAN OPERATIONS, CASPIAN SEA, 21 MAY 1919

THURSDAY, 9 OCTOBER, 1919.

Admiralty,
9th October, 1919.

The following despatch has been received from the Rear-Admiral, Black Sea, on the action in the Caspian Sea off Fort Alexandrovsk, on the 21st May, 1919:-

5th July, 1919.

I have the honour to submit the following despatch on the action off Fort Alexandrovsk on the 21st May, 1919, with an account of the circumstances leading up to it and all subsequent operations:-

At the beginning of May reports were being received from various sources that the Bolsheviks had occupied, or intended to occupy, Fort Alexandrovsk. From reports of refugees, prisoners, etc., it was also apparent that the Naval Authorities at Astrakhan were desirous of carrying out an attack on Petrovsk or Baku with the object, of obtaining oil, of which they were in urgent need.

2. – Commodore Norris determined, therefore, to visit Fort Alexandrovsk and to carry out a reconnaissance by means of the coastal motor boats and by the seaplanes of "A. Yusanoff," supported by the ships of the Caspian Squadron. In accordance with this plan, "Kruger," "Asia," "Emile Nobel," "Sergie," and "A. Yusanoff" left Chechen on 14th May and steered for a rendezvous off Kulaly Island. Early in the morning of the 15th the wind got up from the south-east, and it was impossible to get out C.M.B.'s or seaplanes, and the Squadron therefore altered course direct for Fort Alexandrovsk. Soon after daylight a number of fishing boats and a steamer hull

down were sighted on the starboard bow, and later on a convoy of three steamers towing two barges in sight, escorted by one T.B.D. The convoy made off in the direction of Fort Alexandrovsk and the destroyer kept on the port bow of the squadron out of range. "Emile Nobel" fired a few long range shots at the convoy, and at 07.15 the barges, were slipped. The chase was continued until early noon, when the enemy disappeared into the mist which was lying off shore, and Commodore Norris, being unable to determine his position, drew off. During the afternoon the barges were sunk and their crews made prisoners.

3. – The examination of the prisoners revealed the fact that Fort Alexandrovsk was occupied by a considerable number of Bolsheviks, and that the main part of their fleet was there. Also that the concentration was preparatory to an attack on Petrovsk, with the object of obtaining oil.

4. – On 17th May the wind had gone round to west, so that no lee was obtainable on the eastern shore of the Caspian. Consequently (after an unsuccessful attempt to get the seaplanes away) the seaplane carrier had to return to Petrovsk, escorted by "Emile Nobel," who was running short of fuel. By this time Commodore Norris had news of reinforcements in the shape of "Venture," and he cruised off the eastern shores of the Caspian to the southward to await her arrival.

5. – In addition to "Venture" he was joined by "Windsor Castle" and "Emile Nobel," and on the morning of 21st May was cruising in position lat. 44.57 N., long. 50.02 E. Course S.E., speed 5 knots. Detached squadron, consisting of the C.M.B. carriers and seaplane carrier, had parted company on 20th May, with orders to rendezvous off Fort Alexandrovsk.

6. – At 09.27, in lat. 44.43 N., long. 50.03 E., course was altered to S. 66 E. Two small craft were sighted north of the harbour.

7. – Shortly before 11.00 one T.B.D., two small craft and A.M.C. "Caspie" were sighted under the land west of the harbour steering northward. At 11.00 the destroyer opened fire, but the shot fell a long way short. The enemy craft returned to harbour. It was thought possible to cut them off, and the course was altered accordingly and speed increased to 9 knots.

8. – At 12.03 ranging shots were fired by both sides, and ten minutes later "Venture" was straddled. The general signal to "Open Fire" was made at 12.13.

9. – "Emile Nobel's" third salvo hit a large armed barge, which caught fire amidships, and whose crew were taken off by small craft. From 12.30 to 13.00 all ships were in action with "Caspie," a destroyer of the "Finn" class, and various armed barges. "Caspie" was hit by "Emile Nobel," and the destroyer was probably hit by "Venture," as she was seen to be in difficulties, and appeared to run ashore among the fishing boats.

10. – By this time the enemy's fire was both accurate and heavy. "Asia" was repeatedly straddled, and at 12.57 a shell hit "Emile Nobel" in engine room, killing five and seriously wounding seven, and causing considerable damage to the engines. "Emile Nobel" hauled out of line, but eventually followed the squadron into the harbour and continued to engage the enemy.

11. – At 13.03 course was altered down harbour in single line in the following

order: "Kruger," "Venture," "Asia," "Windsor Castle," "Emile Nobel." The enemy had retired to the southern end of the harbour and taken shelter behind barges and small craft, so that only the flashes of his guns could be seen, and it was difficult to get good points of aim. At this time a shore battery situated on the cliffs opened fire on the squadron, and was engaged by "Kruger," "Venture," and "Asia." A few minutes later "Kruger" was hit aft, but, beyond cutting away the telegraphs, little damage was done.

12. – All the enemy ships were now packed together at the south end of the harbour, and it was estimated that five or six separate ships were firing at the British Squadron; these included "Caspie" and the "Finn" class T.B.D. "Caspie," who had been hit repeatedly, was on fire, but was continuing to fire with one gun. A very large fire was started ashore at the south end of the harbour, and many of the ships and small craft were observed to be on fire. This rendered all control very difficult, as there was so much smoke and so many splashes from the various ships. At times the enemy were seen landing from their ships and running up the hillside.

13. – About 13.30, in view of the difficulty in manoeuvring and "Emile Nobel's" condition, Commodore Norris decided to haul off. The shore battery had been silenced and did not fire at the Squadron on its way out. When well clear of the harbour speed was eased to 5 knots, but at 14.30 "Emile Nobel" reported she could steam 8 knots, and speed was accordingly increased.

14. – While still in sight of Fort Alexandrovsk the smoke on shore was seen to be increasing; one very large explosion was observed at 15.00 and two others at 15.15 and 15.43, besides several smaller ones. It was known that "Caspie" and one steamer were on fire during the action, and it was presumed that the enemy was destroying his stores and fuel.

15. – At 17.00 the Squadron stopped and surgeons were sent to "Emile Nobel." Squadron then proceeded N.N.W. in the direction of Astrakhan, as Commodore Norris intended, if possible, to remain on the enemy's line of retreat.

16. – At 20.10 "Emile Nobel" was forced to stop, and the Squadron so remained till midnight. At midnight course was shaped S. 37 W., speed 4 knots, but during the night "Emile Nobel" worked up to 7 knots.

17. – In the early morning two more heavy explosions were observed in the direction of Fort Alexandrovsk.

18. – At 10.00, on 22nd May, the men who had been killed in "Emile Nobel" were buried at sea, after which "Emile Nobel" and "Windsor Castle" were detached to Petrovsk.

19. – In the meantime the detached squadron of C.M.B. and seaplane carriers had arrived at rendezvous, and a seaplane had been sent up to bomb Alexandrovsk. Unfortunately, he had to return owing to engine trouble, and was out of action for 12 hours. He again went up at 15.35, and returned two hours later. Bombs were dropped, but no direct hits were obtained. He reported that a large oil steamer was burning as a result of the bombardment of the afternoon.

20. – In the evening some fishing boats were observed from "Sergie" and searched by a C.M.B., and their cargoes thrown overboard.

21. – At 05.25 the seaplane again started for Fort Alexandrovsk, and dropped bombs on the shipping in the harbour and small craft machine-gunned. During the 22nd May five raids were carried out by this one seaplane with the following results:-

First Raid – Shipping and Eastern Pier bombed and machine-gunned. No direct hits, but probably some damage done as bombs fell close.

Second Raid – Shipping bombed. Direct hits obtained on large destroyer of "Finn" class, which sank. One hit on armed merchant cruiser. Ships and piers machine-gunned.

Third Raid – Barges at eastern and western piers bombed. No direct hits, but bombs fell very close, and damage was probably inflicted.

Fourth Raid – Shipping bombed. No direct hits. T.B.D. bombed in second raid now completely sunk.

Fifth Raid – Southern pier bombed. Bombs fell very close. Shipping machine-gunned.

A sixth raid was attempted, but machines failed to rise. Photographs were taken on second and fifth raids.

22. – On the evening of 22nd and on the morning of 23rd a deserted appearance of ships and town was noticed, no one being seen in streets nor on decks of ships. No armed forces or encampments were seen in vicinity. On the first day heavy A.A. fire was experienced, but on the evening of 22nd and morning of 23rd there was none.

23. – Commodore Norris had every hope of carrying out a final attack with C.M.Bs. on the morning of 22nd May, but was unable to get into W./T. communication with the carriers. In view of the fact that the remainder of the enemy did not leave until night of 22nd May this lost opportunity is very much to be regretted.

24. – On 23rd May, after a night of thick fog, "Kruger" and "Venture" were attacked by two enemy destroyers, who had the range and speed of them, so that they were forced to withdraw. The carriers were informed of the presence of the enemy by W./T., and a seaplane was again got out to attack the enemy. Unfortunately the seaplane was unable to locate the enemy destroyers, and finally carried out another raid on Fort Alexandrovsk.

It is probable that the enemy sighted the carriers, as they suddenly turned towards "Kruger," and then made off to the northward. The seaplane ran into a fog on her way back from Fort Alexandrovsk and fell in the water. The officers were not picked up until 32 hours later (see par. 25 below).

25. – On 24th May Commodore Norris in "Kruger," who was short of fuel, with "Sergie" and "Edinburgh Castle," parted company, and proceeded to Petrovsk, leaving Captain Washington in charge of the squadron, which now consisted of "Windsor Castle," "Asia," "Venture," "Bibi-Abat" and "A. Yusanoff," with orders to cruise to the northward and search for the missing seaplane, to ascertain that Chechan was safe, and, when the carriers returned, to make an extended reconnaissance of Port Alexandrovsk. The seaplane was picked up on the evening of 24th May, after which the squadron cruised between Port Alexandrovsk and Chechen until the carriers arrived.

26. – On 28th May Captain Washington, with "Windsor Castle," "Venture," "Slava," "Bibi-Abat," "Sergie," "Edinburgh Castle," and "A. Yusanoff," made a close reconnaissance of Fort Alexandrovsk. The 1st and 2nd Divisions (1st Division "Windsor Castle" and "Venture," 2nd Division "Slava" and "Bibi-Abat") took up positions for covering the approach of the C.M.Bs. who were got out and proceeded up harbour under the command of Commander Eric G. Robinson, V.C. On their way up harbour they torpedoed a large barge, and on arrival up harbour a white flag was hoisted ashore and a deputation came off. The deputation consisted of the Chief Engineer of the "Leila" and some of her crew, and some Persians and agents of the K-M Company.

From these men full details of the Bolshevik occupation were obtained, and also information concerning the capture of the "Leila" and the death of General Almaroff. The attached lists show the details of the ships which were sunk and which escaped.

27. – From the reports of Commodore Norris, Captain Washington and other officers in command of vessels, and also from the Royal Air Force reports, the conduct of the officers and men appears to have been in accordance with the traditions of the service. I would specially draw attention to the following:-

Commodore David T. Norris, C.B., in command of the Caspian Flotilla. Quite apart from the successful conduct of this action, Commodore Norris deserves the highest praise for the unfailing tenacity with which he has overcome many and great difficulties and eventually succeeded in getting his Squadron in such a state of efficiency as to make this successful action possible. He has been handicapped all through the winter by want of efficient officers, by frequent and serious strikes in the various works at Baku, by delay in the arrival of material and also personnel, by the serious accident he met with in the autumn of 1918 and from which he is by no means recovered, his arm causing him continual discomfort. The way in which he has risen superior to all these and many other difficulties is beyond all praise. He had to take serious risks in attacking an enemy which was known to be efficiently manned and to possess ships with superior gun-power, including several destroyers. He has taken these risks, and has succeeded, by the latest reports, in driving the superior enemy from the Caspian.

Act. Captain Basil G. Washington, C.M.G. He commanded the "Windsor Castle" with great ability, and was the only British officer on board during the action. He did admirable work whilst temporarily in charge of the Caspian during Commodore Norris's illness from 9th October, 1918, to 5th February, 1919.

Commander Kenneth A.F. Guy. Handled the "Emile Nobel" with great ability under difficult circumstances.

Lieutenant-Commander Richard Harrison, R.N.R., of H.M.S. "Venture."
Lieutenant Alexander G.B. Wilson, commanding the "Asia."
Both handled their ships well.

Lieutenant Robert M. Taylor, D.S.C., of the "Emile Nobel." By his admirable control of fire was responsible for much damage to the enemy.

Engineer Lieutenant Thomas Gardner. The manner in which this officer kept his engines running after considerable heavy losses in personnel and severe damage to the complicated machinery reflects the greatest credit on his ability and resource.

Commodore Norris reports that Commander Edward L. Grieve's services on his Staff were of greatest assistance to him. This officer's services in the Caspian have been very valuable.

Lieutenant Bolinsky, R.N.V.R., of "Emile Nobel." was of great service in attending the wounded.

Petty Officer John William Thompson, O.N. 239958. G.L. II., "Windsor Castle." This petty officer was of greatest assistance during the action to Captain Washington, who had no British officer with him.

J.E. Pether, Ch. E.R.A., O.N. 270497, "Emile Nobel." was of greatest assistance in refitting repairs and in keeping the engines running after they were damaged.

The conduct of the following ratings is specially mentioned:-

Sabin, Percy Robert, S.B.S., O.N.351617, "Kruger."
Collins, William Frank, P.O., J.2387, "Emile Nobel."
Bell, Mark, Lg. Smn., 238463, "Emile Nobel."
Crofts, Albert Ernest, Lce.-Cpl., Ply./8538, "Emile Nobel."
Hansler, James Henry William, Cpl., Po./14568, "Emile Nobel."
Young, Reginald George, S.B.A., M.21585, "Emile Nobel."
Hall, Henry Amos, Lce.-Sgt., Ply./ 15471, "Emile Nobel."

and also the Russian Rating Nikolai Samliteoff, who I consider it is very desirable should be included in any awards that may be given.

28. – I have the honour to call particular attention to the services rendered by the following officers of the Royal Air Force who between them carried out 5 raids in one seaplane on the same day with excellent results, and attempted a sixth, and also the services of Lieutenant Chilton, R.N.R., commanding "A. Yousanoff," for his able handling of the ship and organisation which allowed this to be done.

Pilots-

2nd Lieutenant Howard Grant Thompson.
Captain John Archer Sadler.
2nd Lieutenant Robert George Kear Morrison.

Observers-

Lieutenant Frank Russell Bicknell.
2nd Lieutenant Frank Leslie Kingham.
2nd Lieutenant Henry Godwin Pratt.

(Signed) M. SEYMOUR,
Rear-Admiral.

Vessels Sunk in Alexandrovsk Harbour.
Name of Ship and Details.

"Barge No. 2" (properly an oil barge). Two 6 in. guns (reported). Hit by shell when outside the Harbour. Twelve men killed. Abandoned on fire. Hit again. Later towed inside and afterwards sunk.

Reval." – S/M Depot Ship. Fitted with machine gun. Set on fire by us, and abandoned. Blew up. Reported all the crew escaped. Two mines or torpedoes on board. It is stated that this ship had all the Bolshevik money and valuables in gold on board.

"Tuman" or "Kuman." – Store ship carrying ammunition. Unarmed. Burnt and sunk. Not clear if by us or by their own action.

"Galema" (?).– Small tug. No gun. Burnt and sunk.

"Muskvityanise." – T.B.D., 2/4 in., 2/3 in., two tubes, two pom poms. Damaged in action, and either sunk by Bolsheviks or by seaplane bomb on 22/5. The latter most likely from photographs.

Small Barge. – No details. Sunk.

"Zoroaster" (old). – Depôt ship now. Formerly carried Mazout. Torpedoed 28th May.

"Ruvik." – Steel barge. Very strong. Fresh water and Mazout (now mixed). Torpedoed 28th May.

"Demisthene." – Baltic M/S or M/L. Two 4 in., and probably being used as ordinary fleet unit. Sunk, probably as result of gunfire.

Small Barge. – No details. Sunk.

Coal Barge (Wooden). – Large and laden. Torpedoed 28th May.

Ships that Escaped from Alexandrovsk after the Action.

"Caspie." – Damaged in boilers ? by bombs. Reported could only steam 5 knots.

"Martin" or "Meshty." – Mine carrier. Ninety-nine mines on board.

"Alehper." – Ammunition carrier. Unarmed.

"Communist." – Tug. ? 2/4 in.

"Baku." – Coal transport.

"Spartacus." – Tug. 2/2½in. Hit but got away.

Two submarines. – One had fouled propeller and had to be towed.

This is exclusive of the various groups of enemy destroyers and armed merchant vessels that were in action with our vessels outside.

19

RUSSIAN OPERATIONS, NORTH RUSSIAN EXPEDITIONARY FORCE, 1919

WEDNESDAY, 19 MAY, 1920.

Admiralty,
1st January, 1920.

Sir:- With the cessation of hostilities against the Bolsheviks in North Russia, consequent upon the final withdrawal of all British and Allied forces from Archangel and Murmansk on 27th September and 12th October, 1919, respectively, I have the honour to submit the following despatch relating to the Naval side of the operations during the period of my command as Senior Naval Officer, White Sea, from November, 1918, to October, 1919.

2. A short *résumé* of the Naval events in North Russia during the months preceding my arrival is, however, necessary in order to explain the situation as it developed during the time I was in command:- All British men-of-war, except the icebreaker "Alexander," were withdrawn from Archangel before the winter of 1917/18. In April of 1918 H.M.S. "Attentive" (Captain (actg.) E. Altham, R.N.) was selected, on account of suitability of size and draught, to go to Archangel as the ship of the Senior British Naval Officer at that port, when ice conditions should permit.

On leaving England Captain Altham had been given instructions that he was not to take warlike action to prevent munitions and stores being railed away from the port, but was invested with wide discretionary powers. At the beginning of June, 1918, when the "Attentive" arrived at Murmansk, the political situation was already beginning to change. Whereas the local Government had hitherto been in agreement with both that at Archangel and the Central Government at Moscow as regards their attitude to the Allies, with the declaration of peace between Russia and Germany, the Central Government under pressure from Germany became hostile to the continued Allied occupation of Murmansk, and resented any proposal to send Allied forces to Archangel.

It was essential that we should remain in occupation of Murmansk and the Kola Inlet to prevent their use as a probable hostile submarine base. The same remark applied to the Pechenga Gulf, and to Archangel when the White Sea opened. Further, it was to the interest of the local population of these places that we should remain, as they were largely dependent on the Allies for food supplies. The Murmansk Government therefore decided to throw in their lot with the Allies and reject the authority of the Central Moscow Government.

In order to secure the port of Murmansk, it was necessary to hold the railway to the southward, and as soon as ice permitted the "Attentive" passed into the White Sea, and co-operated with the Russian-Allied forces on its western shores during the month of July until they were firmly established as far down the line as Soroka. The damage done to the railway line to the south of Soroka by the retreating Red troops had already caused much distress, and prevented refugees returning to their homes and fishermen from travelling North for the season's fishing. Under the direction of the Captain of "Attentive," shipping in the White Sea was commandeered and diverted as necessary to assist in reaching their destinations the large number of people who would otherwise have been homeless and destitute. Soroka, which was in the hands of the Bolsheviks until the arrival of "Attentive," was secured by a Naval detachment from that ship on 7th July. A junction was subsequently effected with the Military forces at Kem.

It will also be recalled that in view of the attitude of the local Government at Archangel it was decided to postpone sending a ship until additional troops were available to occupy the town. By the end of July these troops had arrived, and "Attentive" and H.M. Seaplane Carrier "Nairana" (Commander C.F.R. Cowan, R.N.) were recalled to Murmansk from the White Sea to prepare for the expedition to Archangel. The "Nairana" had joined "Attentive" soon after the latter ship's arrival at Soroka, and the seaplanes had already performed most useful service in that vicinity.

The situation in Archangel developed unexpectedly, and necessitated the early despatch of the "Attentive" and "Nairana," together with the French cruiser "Amiral Aube," to secure the approaches to the port and support an anti-Bolshevik rising. The "Amiral Aube" having been delayed on passage, the attack on the fort of Modyuski Island and reduction of the defences there was accomplished by the guns of "Attentive" and bombs from "Nairana's" seaplanes. French troops embarked in these two ships were subsequently landed for the occupation of the island, and on the 2nd August, 1918, the ships entered Archangel without further resistance. The following day the troopships arrived and the Allied occupation was secured.

It was this which initiated our obligations on the Archangel front, and in order to secure further the approaches to the port, operations, details of which are described in the report of the Senior Naval Officer (Captain E. Altham, R.N.) had to be undertaken up the Dwina River. H.M. ships "Attentive," "Glory IV." (ex-Russian cruiser "Askold") and the French cruiser "Amiral Aube," were at Archangel. H.M. Monitor "M.23" (Lieutenant-Commander St. A.O. St. John, R.N.) was detached for service in the White Sea to assist in the occupation of Onega, and with "Nairana" co-operated with the forces on the west coast of the White Sea in the vicinities of Kem and Soroka.

Before the closing of the White Sea for the winter of 1918/19 the "Attentive" and "Nairana" were withdrawn and sent home. Monitors "M.23" and "M.25" (Lieutenant-Commander S.W.B. Green, D.S.O., R.N.) were laid up at Archangel for the winter. My predecessor (Rear-Admiral T.W. Kemp, C.B., C.M.G., C.I.E.), having represented the necessity for a stronger river flotilla in the spring of the following year, the large river gunboats "Glowworm," "Cockchafer," "Cicala," and "Cricket," which were then in home waters, were despatched in time to arrive at Archangel before that port closed. They were laid up for the winter, and their crews, together with those of the two monitors, were accommodated in barracks ashore.

During the winter months a small Russian-Allied force was raised at Archangel, under the command of Lieutenant-Commander H.E. Rendall, D.S.O., R.N., and subsequently provided a useful personnel for manning flotilla auxiliaries.

H.M.S. "Cochrane" had arrived at Murmansk on 7th March, 1918. Whilst at Murmansk 50 Royal Marines were landed to assist in defending the place. On 2nd May she proceeded to Pechenga, and there landed a Naval Brigade of 100 seamen and 50 Royal Marines, to prevent its occupation by White Finns, who were being supported by Germany.

On 11th and 12th May actions took place between "Cochrane's" Brigade and a force of "White" Finns, which latter were finally beaten off and retired across the frontier. More seamen were subsequently landed, together with Royal Marine reinforcements from "Glory," altogether a total force of about 350 men being maintained.

This force was finally relieved by the Military on 29th September.

"Cochrane" left Pechenga for Murmansk to turn over to "Glory IV." on 1st November, and left Murmansk for England on 3rd November.

3. My instructions were to assist the Military with all available resources at my disposal.

On my arrival at Murmansk on 13th November, 1918, the following were the Naval forces under my orders:-

At Archangel.

Monitors: "M.23," "M.25."

River Gunboats:- "Cricket," "Cicala," "Glowworm," and "Cockchafer." (Laid up and frozen in for the winter.)

French Cruiser "Gueydon" (Capitaine de Vaisseau J.E. Hallier, C.M.G.), which was relieved in July by French Cruiser "Condé" (Capitaine de Vaisseau J.R. Lequerré), the latter remaining till final evacuation.

At Murmansk.

H.M.S. "Glory" (Captain G. Hopwood, C.B.E., R.N., who was invalided and relieved by Captain J.F. Warton, C.M.G., C.B.E., R.N., in April, 1919).

"Glory IV.," late Russian Cruiser "Askold" (Captain (actg.) A.W. Lowis, R.N.), returned to England in April, 1919.

"Sviatogor" and "Alexander," Ice-breakers; and various Drifters and Trawlers.

These vessels were reinforced during summer of 1919 by H.M.S. "Cyclops," Repair Ship (Captain A.C. Bruce, D.S.O., R.N.); H.M.S. "Fox," (Captain E. Altham, R.N.) (S.N.O., River Expeditionary Force); Hospital Ship "Garth Castle"; H.M.S. "Nairana," Seaplane Carrier (Commander H.R.G. Moore, O.B.E., R.N.); H.M.S. "Pegasus," Seaplane Carrier (Commander O.M.F. Stokes, D.S.O., R.N.); River Gunboats "Moth" and "Mantis"; Monitors, "Humber," "M.24," "M.26," "M.27," "M.31," "M.33"; "Erebus" (Captain J.A. Moreton, D.S.O., R.N.); and in addition numerous and miscellaneous Auxiliaries and Hospital Carriers.

4. During the winter months no Naval operations were possible except the arduous and difficult work of keeping up communications between Murmansk and Archangel by passing various troops and Storeships under escort of the Ice-breakers through the ice, and also in preparing the Monitors and Gunboats for the summer campaign.

5. *The U.S. Navy* was represented by Rear-Admiral Newton A. McCully, U.S.N., who lived ashore at Murmansk till March, 1919, when he transferred his flag and was accommodated on board U.S. Yacht "Yankton."

In June, 1919, U.S. Cruiser "Des Moines" (Captain Zachariah H. Maddison, U.S.N.), U.S. Cruiser "Sacramento," and 3 Eagle boats arrived, Rear-Admiral McCully returned to England in "Sacramento" in July.

U.S. Cruiser "Des Moines" remained at Archangel until all the U.S. troops had left in September.

6. With the clearing of the ice at the end of April, 1919, Naval operations on the River Dwina were commenced. Captain Altham, who had been appointed by the Admiralty as S.N.O., River Expedition, narrates their exploits in the attached report.

7. During the summer months of 1919 the water in the River Dwina ran very low. Water transport, which was the only means of carrying troops and stores, &c., for the expedition, therefore became most difficult, and strained to the utmost the capabilities and resources of the Naval Transport Service, which was working under Commodore R. Hyde, C.B.E., M.V.O., R.N. Every sort of local craft that was of light draught was commandeered for use either as a troop, store, or hospital carrier. The transport difficulties inseparable from such operations were most successfully undertaken by Commodore Hyde and his staff.

8. The medical arrangements for the transport afloat of the sick and wounded, both naval and military, British or otherwise, were carried out entirely by the Navy under the very able organisation of Surgeon Commander D.W. Hewitt, C.M.G., M.B.. F.R.C.S., R.N., with much success and the greatest credit to all under his orders.

9. In July it was decided to withdraw all Allied troops from North Russia before the arrival of the winter.

During the summer monitors and gunboats were operating in the White Sea in conjunction with the military, for which purpose the "Nairana" was based on Kem and the "Pegasus" at Archangel.

On 25th July "M.26" (Lieutenant-Commander A.O. Fawssett, R.N.) rescued the small British garrison at Onega, which was in the hands of Russian troops who had mutinied and joined the Bolsheviks.

On 1st August "M.26," "M.24," H.M. Auxiliary "Walton Belle" and a small Russian steamer carrying a mixed force of Russians, supported by British Gunners, entered the Onega River to retake Onega, but after a hot engagement failed to do so.

Onega was shelled by "Erebus" (Captain J.A. Moreton, D.S.O., R.N.), assisted by "Nairana" with her seaplanes on 28th August, and the town was re-occupied by the Russians.

10. The final evacuation of Archangel took place on 27th September, when some 8,000 British troops were embarked without a hitch.

"Erebus," "Nairana" and "M. 23" operated from Kem and in the Gulf of Kandalaska during the time troops were being evacuated from the Murmansk front.

The final evacuation of troops from North Russia took place from Murmansk on 12th October, when I left for England in the "Glory."

11. The Naval transport arrangements generally, under the abnormal conditions obtaining in North Russian Waters and on the Dwina River, and the organisation for evacuation reflect the greatest credit on Commodore Hyde and all concerned under him.

12. H.M.S. "Glory" was the depôt ship at Murmansk during 1917-'18-'19, and her presence there was essential both as an armed support for the military and for the safety of the town. The repair work, administration, &c., of all the many small craft, both those permanently attached to her and those visiting the port, was undertaken by "Glory," and her officers and men deserve high commendation for their valuable work, which was carried out continuously throughout the hardships and discomforts of a rigorous Arctic winter.

H.M.S. "Cyclops," acting as repair ship at Archangel during the summer of 1919, rendered invaluable service by the efficiency with which her staff performed the repairs, &c., required by the vessels employed on the expedition.

13. I wish to place on record the very cordial relations which always existed between the Naval and Military Services, without which good feeling all these varied operations could not have been successfully undertaken.

14. I wish to make mention of the following Officers:-

Commodore R. Hyde, O.B.E., M.V.O., P.N.T.O., at Archangel.
Captain A.C. Bruce, D.S.O., R.N., H.M.S. "Cyclops," repair ship, who acted as S.N.O. at Archangel during my absence from that port.
Capt. J.F. Warton, C.M.G., H.M.S. "Glory," my Chief of Staff.
Captain E. Altham, R.N., S.N.O., River Expedition.
Engineer Captain R.W. Skelton, D.S.O., R.N., on my staff. Acting at Archangel.

Surgeon Commander D.W. Hewitt, C.M.G., M.B., F.R.C.S., R.N., S.M.O., in charge of medical arrangements on Dwina River.
Tempy. Hon. T. Major W.C.T. Hammond, R.M. In charge of Naval stores.
A list of the Officers and men whose services were considered specially deserving of recognition has already been submitted to Their Lordships.

I also desire to endorse Captain Altham's commendations of the work of the various officers and personnel mentioned by him in the accompanying report, with which I concur.

15. My thanks are due to the following Officers of our Naval Allies:-

Rear-Admiral N.A. McCully, U.S.N.;
Captain Z.H. Maddison, U.S.N., U.S. Cruiser "Des Moines";
Capitaine de Vaisseau J.E. Hallier, C.M.G., French Cruiser "Gueydon";
Capitaine de Vaisseau Lequerré, French Cruiser "Condé,"
whose cordial co-operation and assistance were at all times of much value.

I have the honour to be,
Sir,
Your obedient Servant,
John F.E. Green,
Rear-Admiral.
Late Senior-Naval Officer,
White Sea.

Admiralty, S.W. 1,
1st January, 1920.

SIR,-

I have the honour to submit the following report on the Operations of the Naval flotilla employed in the Archangel River Expedition:-

It will be recalled that on 1st August, 1919, H.M.S. "Attentive," then under my command, assisted by the seaplanes of H.M.S. "Nairana," attacked the forts on Modyuski Island which formed the chief defences of Archangel.

These were silenced by bombardment and bombing after a short but hot engagement, in which the "Attentive" sustained damage by shell-fire.

Archangel was subsequently occupied without opposition.

2. In the subsequent pursuit of the enemy up the Dwina River it at once became evident that armed ships would be essential to co-operate with the Russian-Allied forces ashore and counteract the fire of the enemy's ships. A river flotilla was evolved mainly out of local paddle steamers, which were armed and equipped with an expedition and ingenuity which reflected much credit on the technical Officers of the "Attentive."

3. Later in the month the flotilla was strengthened by the addition of the small

monitor "M.25" (Lieutenant-Commander S.W.B. Green, D.S.O., R.N.). The fighting developed, and by desire of the General Officer Commanding-in-Chief, Allied Forces, I went up-river and took command of the force which originated our naval obligations on this front.

4. The flotilla successfully countered the attacks of the enemy ships, sinking two of them. With our support the shore forces were established some 200 miles up river. The lateness of the year then necessitated the withdrawal of the ships before the ice set in.

5. In October, 1918, the "Attentive" returned to England, H.M. Gunboats "Glowworm," "Cockchafer," "Cicala" and "Cricket" were sent out, and together with H.M. Monitors "M.23" and "M.25" wintered at Archangel in readiness for the opening up of the river in spring.

6. In February, 1919, it was decided that the situation on the Archangel front necessitated the provision of a strong Naval flotilla, more particularly in view of the part the Navy might be called upon to play in an evacuation.

7. The ships composing this force were:-

(*a*) *Up-River Force.*

> Monitors "Humber," "M.24," "M.26," "M.27," "M.31" and "M.33."
> Gunboats "Moth" and "Mantis."
> 4 Tunnel Minesweepers.
> 6 Coastal Motor-boats.
> River Depôt Ship – H.M.S. "Hyderabad."
> (*b*) *Flying force attached to above.*
> 8 Seaplanes (number subsequently increased).
> 1 Kite balloon.

(*c*) *Ships at base.* (Archangel.)
> H.M.S. "Fox" as flotilla depôt ship.
> H.M.S. "Pegasus" – Seaplane Carrier.
> H.M.S. "Cyclops" – Repair Ship.

The flotilla was organised solely for active operations, the whole of the transport work being undertaken by the Naval Transport Service.

8. Having been appointed in command of the flotilla, I reached Archangel in H.M.S. "Fox" on 16th May.

The majority of the ships of the up-river force arrived during the month of June.

The monitors and gunboats which had wintered at Archangel had already proceeded upriver, and were under command of Commander (Act.) S.W.B. Green, D.S.O., R.N., until my arrival.

I. – *Commencement of Operations.*

"M.23" (Lieut.- Commander St. A.O. St. John, R.N.) left Archangel on the 3rd May, and, forcing her way through thick ice in the lower reaches of the river, reached Pless on 5th May.

2. The first Naval offensive of the year was opened on 6th May by "M.23" in co-operation with a scouting party, when Tulgas was bombarded.

"Cricket" (Lieut.-Comdr. F.A. Worsley, D.S.O., R.D., R.N.R), and "Cockchafer" (Lieut.-Comdr. C. Hester, R.D., R.N.R.) arrived off Pless on the afternoon of 6th May, and the following day the "Glowworm" (Commander (act.) C. Ackland, R.N., Retd.) and "Cicala" (Lieut. E.T. Grayston, R.N.R.) entered the Vaga River and bombarded Nijni Kitsa.

3. The prompt arrival of our ships at the front when the ice broke, and the good seamanship displayed in getting them up-river, prevented what might have proved a critical period when the enemy's ships could have come down and bombarded our positions without having their fire returned by heavy long-range guns which only the ships could bring to bear.

4. The Allied forces at this time held Kourgamen and Shushuga, the enemy Topsa and Tulgas, on the right and left banks of the river respectively.

5. On 18th May the flotilla co-operated in an attack on the enemy's positions at Tulgas. The attack was completely successful, and resulted in the enemy being driven out with the loss of 30 prisoners and 12 machine-guns. Our forces sustained no casualties.

Heavy fire from the enemy gunboats was countered by our ships.

One of the enemy ships was observed to be hit, but was not sink.

From now onwards the enemy flotilla frequently employed "tip-and-run" tactics, coming down river, firing a few shots and retreating directly fire was returned.

On 27th May a lowest depth of 12 feet of water was found on Chamova Bar. On 31st May it was reported to have fallen to 10 feet.

6. I arrived up-river on 3rd June in the local paddle steamer "Borodino," which henceforth became Naval Headquarters and accommodated the flotilla staff.

7. The relief of the troops who had been out during the winter was in progress at this time.

8. *Intention to Advance.* – The success of Koltchak, and our obligations to leave the North Russian troops in a sound position when we withdrew before the winter, decided the policy of an endeavour to enable the Russians to reach Kotlas and join hands with Koltchak, who was at that time reported to be at, or near, Perm.

9. *Effect on Naval Plans.* – This decision materially affected the Naval considerations, as the flotilla had not been intended for an advance far up-river; some of the ships were of too deep draught and the river was already low and falling. Further, the gunboats had suffered from contact with the ice and constantly firing their guns at extreme elevation, and required refitting.

10. Guns mounted on shallow-draught barges would have been invaluable, but the base was unable to undertake the work. The heavy-draught monitors had therefore to be retained, at much risk, to ease the strain on the gunboats, which alone might be able to operate later.

11. By the middle of June the flotilla was complete with the exception of "Moth"

and "Mantis," which had not then arrived from England, and "M.24" and "M.26," which were detached for service in the White Sea.

II. – *Capture of Topsa and Troitsa.*

On 19th June a more extensive operation was undertaken with the object of capturing the high ground between Topsa and Troitsa, and the flotilla co-operated with Graham's Brigade, bombarding heavily prior to the attack and countering the fire of the enemy ships.

2. H.M.S. "Cockchafer" (Lieut.- Comdr. Q.B. Preston-Thomas, R.N.) did particularly good work in getting up the narrow Kourgamen channel to within a mile of Topsa when that place was taken, and materially assisted in repulsing a counter-attack which threatened the success of our undertakings.

3. H.M.S. "Glowworm" (Commander (actg.) S.W.B. Green, D.S.O., R.N.) was actively engaged with the enemy flotilla in the main channel.

4. H.M. Monitors "Humber" (Lieut.- Comdr. A. Johnstone, R.N.), "M.27" (Lieut.-Comdr. G.H.I. Parker, R.N.), and "M.33" (Lieut.- Comdr. K. Michell, D.S.C., R.N.) also assisted in this operation, which marked the first stage of the advance, and materially improved our positions.

In the course of this fighting a barge on which the enemy had mounted two heavy long-range guns was holed by our fire and abandoned.

5. *Mine-sweeping.* – This brought the ships to the edge of the enemy minefield, and for the next week mine-sweeping had to be carried out under most difficult conditions. The river water was so thick that it was impossible to see to any appreciable depth, even from a seaplane. Instead of being able to sweep in comparative safety on the rise of the tide, as at sea, the river was of course tideless and falling.

6. It was necessary to explore channels with small steamboats, clear mines where discovered, buoy a passage, and then send up the heavier-draught tunnel mine-sweepers to sweep up the heavier and deeper-moored mines. The whole of the work had to be carried out within range of the enemy flotilla, and the minesweeping craft were daily exposed to heavy fire from his guns, and at times even came under direct machine-gun and rifle fire.

7. The exploratory sweeping in steamboats was most gallantly performed by parties of British seamen and the Russian boats' crews under the orders of Lieutenant R.H. Fitzherbert-Brockholes, R.N., and Lieutenant C.E. McLaughlin, R.N. The tunnel minesweepers were under the command of Lieutenant A.K. McC. Halliley, R.N.

8. I cannot speak too highly of the gallantry and devotion to duty displayed by the minesweeping party in their tireless endeavours to clear the river for the safe navigation of the flotilla and water transport.

Their efforts were crowned with success after a week's most arduous work, and over 40 mines had been cleared from the river. This had not been achieved, however, without the loss of the mine-sweeper "Sword Dance," which was mined and sunk on

24th June. Subsequently a second mine-sweeper, the "Fandango," also struck a mine and was lost.

9. *Flotilla passed through mine-field to Troitsa.* – On 27th June I went on board H.M.S. "Cricket" (Lieutenant I.W.G. White, R.N.), and that ship passed safely through the swept channel, and running the gauntlet of a heavy barrage of enemy fire arrived off Troitsa. Here the high cliffs gave some measure of protection, and a gunboat, once established, could drive the enemy's ships back and secure the anchorage for the flotilla.

10. The remainder of the ships and transport moved up the following day, and from then onwards this became our advanced base and Brigade headquarters.

11. *Situation on 7th July.*

On the right bank we held Topsa, Troitsa and advanced positions north-west of Selmenga River, the enemy having strong blockhouses on the opposite bank, with artillery in support.

On the left bank we occupied Yakolevskoe and advanced positions on the Nyuma River, the enemy holding Seltso.

The enemy flotilla was based on Puchega, with advanced gunboats between that place and Lipovets.

Enemy mines. – Three new lines of deep-sea mines were reported off Seltso.

12. *Mutiny of Russian Troops.* – On 7th July a mutiny broke out amongst the Russian troops of Dyer's Battalion, and the 4th North Russian Rifles also became affected. Fifty seamen under Commander F.G. Bramble, R.N., and a small Royal Marine Detachment under Lieutenant C.M. Sergeant, R.M., were landed at the request of the General Officer Commanding to assist in securing our position until the arrival of more British troops.

The enemy, who was evidently fully conversant with the situation, seized the opportunity to attack.

On the night of 7th/8th July the situation was critical, as British reinforcements had not arrived, and the enemy's gunboats were pressing hard in support of an advance along the right bank.

13. *The Seaplanes' good work.* – Very valuable assistance was rendered by the seaplanes bombing and machine-gunning, but by the forenoon of the 8th July they had "run out" and had to be given a brief rest and overhaul.

14. *The Flotilla.* – The situation about this time was that the enemy ashore was reported within 1,200 yards of the flotilla anchorage, with the Russians slowly retiring. The auxiliary craft were therefore moved back, and H.M. Monitor "Humber," which had been covering Topsa during the mutiny, came upriver and I embarked in that ship.

A telephone cable was run to the shore to keep in close touch with the General Officer Commanding (Brigadier-General L.W. de V. Sadleir-Jackson, C.B., C.M.G., D.S.O.), who had by now taken over the command.

"M.33" was hit by a heavy shell, fortunately without casualties, and continued in action. "M.27" did useful service with her triple 4-inch mounting.

The "Cicala," which had been heavily engaged as advanced gunboat, developed defects due to the continual firing at high elevation, and was relieved by "Cricket." The latter ship came under heavy machine-gun fire from the woods in the vicinity of Selmenga, but replied to it with her own machine-guns, and continued to engage the enemy ships until hit on the waterline with a heavy shell and obliged to come down-river and secure alongside the repair barges, as there appeared to be risk of the ship sinking.

The gap had to be filled promptly to prevent the enemy profiting by his success. The "Humber" slipped her cable and telephone and proceeded up-river at full speed. The fire of her twin 6-inch turret was so effective that, with the further assistance of seaplane bombing, the enemy flotilla's fire was silenced and it withdrew.

That evening a counter-attack was organised to be carried out by our Russian troops, and four heavy bombardments were carried out by the monitors; but very little progress was made.

As there were still no signs of the British reinforcements the naval paddle steamers and "Borodino" were despatched to assist in bringing them up, and on the morning of the 9th July they arrived and the position was stabilised.

15. *Floating mines and net defences.* – The enemy now endeavoured to damage the flotilla by floating mines down on to it.

One of these mines was sighted very early on the morning of the 2nd July approaching the hospital barge. Lieutenant R.H. Fitzherbert-Brockholes, R.N., jumped out of his bunk and into a skiff which happened to be alongside and reached the mine before it could do any damage. He was in the act of securing it, when it exploded, instantly killing him and the three men forming the crew of the boat.

The death of this very gallant young officer was a great loss to the flotilla.

All ships promptly set to work, and in a few days a complete net defence had been laid out above the flotilla anchorage.

16. *Fall of the river.* – The movements of the ships, and the water transport in particular, were seriously handicapped for the ensuing seven weeks by the abnormally low state of the river. Bars at several places limited the load draught to 3 feet 6 inches for some time, and this greatly increased the difficulties of supply.

III. – *Change in the Situation.*

On the 18th July a mutiny of the 5th North Russian Rifles at Chinova spread on to Onega, and by the 22nd July that place had been lost. This caused considerable anxiety to the Military Command on account of the threat to our line of communications on the railway front, and orders were received to prepare for immediate withdrawal on the Dwina front and to mine the river.

However, the position was stabilised, and such premature withdrawal avoided.

2. *A marked change had now taken place in the whole situation.* – Koltchak, who had completely failed, was retiring.

Our advance on Kotlas would therefore be purposeless.

3. The evacuation of our forces was governed by various factors, including the

provision of shipping to enable persons whose lives might be endangered by our withdrawal to be given the opportunity of leaving the country first, and the collection up-river of the necessary water transport. This latter undertaking was affected to a great extent by the state of the river, as was also the withdrawal of the flotilla. A number of the ships of the flotilla were of such deep draught that at one time they could not have crossed the bars, and would have had to be destroyed.

4. *The main considerations preparatory to withdrawal* became therefore:-

(*a*) To strike a blow at the enemy to obtain freedom of movement.

(*b*) To mine the river to obstruct his advance after our withdrawal.

(*c*) To pass as many ships of the flotilla as possible down the river when the depth of water permitted.

IV. – *Battle of* 10*th August, and Subsequent Events.*

An extensive plan of attack was prepared and carried into effect on 10th August.

2. The troops detailed having completed their enveloping movements and arrived in position for assault, the flotilla, in conjunction with the shore artillery, opened a heavy bombardment on Terekovskaya, Leushinskaya, Gorodok and Seltso.

3. H.M. Monitors "Humber," "M.31" (Lieut.-Comdr. F.L. Back, R.N.) and "M.33" were engaged. Seaplanes assisted in bombing and spotting. The kite balloon, working from its barge, was moved up close to the ships to assist in spotting and reconnaissance.

4. After a forty minutes' bombardment fire ceased, and the shore attacks were launched.

5. On the right bank the attack on Gorodok succeeded at once. A further bombardment on Borok was called for and carried out by "Cicala" (Lieut.-Comdr. J.H.L. Yorke, R.N.) and "Humber," when that place fell.

6. On the left bank the attack on Seltso failed at first, and a new attack had to be organised. "Humber," "M.27" and "M.33" bombarded in conjunction with the shore artillery, and Seltso was taken that evening.

7. During these operations the Navy also assisted the Army ashore.

Thirty-five seamen under Lieutenant M.S. Spalding, R.N., and thirty-nine Royal Marines under Lieutenant C.M. Sergeant, R.N., were landed to reinforce at the base.

Twenty seamen under Lieutenant R.P. Martin, R.N., manned two 60-pounders, one of which had been rescued from the bottom of the river by a naval salvage and diving party. The 60-pounders were actively engaged during the bombardments; the Royal Marines subsequently assisted to garrison Seltso, and the seamen detachments were at Takolevskoe.

8. The successful operations on 10th August, and during the next few days, secured the banks of the river up to Borok on the right bank and Puchega on the left bank. In addition to the large number of prisoners taken, the enemy's flotilla sustained severe damage, including one gunboat sunk.

9. *Further minesweeping operations.* – An extensive enemy minefield was discovered off Seltso and a passage cleared for the transport of Army supplies up to Nijni Seltso.

While sweeping this passage one of the steamboats was mined and Lieutenant (actg.) C.E. McLaughlin, R.N., was killed. This officer had been employed in the advanced minesweeping steamboats on every occasion, and had rendered very gallant service.

In view of the fact that no further advance was intended, minesweeping was stopped, as the risk outweighed the convenience of water transport.

10. *Advanced minelaying.* – The enemy's mines precluded sending mine-laying craft above Seltso, but fifteen small "whisker" mines, which the enemy had floated down river, were caught, prepared for service, taken up by road on country carts, and laid in the river off Lipovets. Subsequently eight small horned mines were pulled out of the enemy mine-field and similarly transported and laid at night above Puchega.

These lines of mines effectively prevented the enemy ships coming down and attacking our bases at Troitsa during the evacuation and after our own ships withdrew.

This work was carried out with much enterprise and ability under Lieutenant-Commander A.J.L. Murray, O.B.E., R.N.

11. *Accident to H.M.S. "Glowworm."* – On the evening of 24th August a serious accident occurred off Beresnik, resulting in the death of Commander S.W.B. Green, D.S.O., R.N., and four other British officers and seventeen men, and two Russian officers, and injuries to two other officers and thirteen men.

A barge filled with ammunition caught fire. The Captain of H.M.S. "Glowworm," being unaware of its contents, was placing that ship close to it to play the ship's fire hoses on to the fire when it exploded, and put out of action practically everyone on deck. The ship's upper works were riddled with splinters.

V. – *Preparations for Evacuation.*

Mining the Dwina and Vaga Rivers. – As the enemy flotilla retired up-river whenever we advanced, and could lay mines faster than we could sweep them up, it was impossible to bring about a decisive engagement. It only remained, therefore, to bottle him up.

2. Between 28th August and 2nd September sixty large sea mines were laid in the river above the flotilla anchorage, and subsequently the Vaga River was also effectually mined.

3. Owing to the shallow water the ships fitted for mine-laying could not be used, and the work involved much ingenuity in fitting up barges locally for the purpose. Credit is due to Lieutenant H. Babington, R.N., and Lieutenant G.E. Coker, R.N., for the very satisfactory way in which it was performed.

4. *Withdrawal of advanced flotilla.* – The rapid rise of the water brought about by the August rains stopped at the end of that month, and as soon as this was seen as many ships as possible were sent down-river.

This called for exceptional efforts, as it entailed removing heavy guns, mountings, ammunition and stores, and in some cases even the main engines, to lighten them sufficiently.

By the 30th August all the ships had passed down except "M.25," "M.27" and the yacht "Kathleen," which were of too deep draught.

5. Subsequently efforts were made to clear the bars, which prevented the three remaining heavy-draught ships from passing down-river, by dredging and exploding a large number of depth charges. The latter were successful in getting "M.25" across two bars and "M.27" across one, and the yacht "Kathleen" got right through.

The river continued to fall, however, time cut short further work on the bars, and "M.25" and "M.27" had to be destroyed in accordance with my orders from S.N.O., White Sea. This was done very thoroughly on the 16th September after the last convoy had passed them.

6. *A reserve flotilla* was organised on 8th August and placed under the command of Commander H. Boyes, C.M.G., R.N., in H.M.S. "Fox" for the local defence of Archangel until the Naval Command up-river returned.

VI. – *Miscellaneous Services and Events.*

The naval 12-*pounders* under Lieutenant R.P. Martin, D.S.C., R.N., of "M.27," with crews which had previously manned the 60-pounders, were hotly engaged in an advanced position at Chudinova, where they were responsible for supporting the line and countering the fire of the enemy's gunboats and their efforts to sweep out advanced mines.

2. *The coastal motor-boats* under the command of Lieutenant C.C. Dickinson, D.S.O., R.N., were of great value in support during the fighting of 10th August and subsequent evacuation. 3. *Seaplanes.* – The admirable work of the seaplane squadron under the command of Lieutenant-Colonel L. Tomkinson, D.S.O., R.A.F., was a factor of very great importance in the success of the operation. Although working as a unit of the naval flotilla, both Navy and Army benefited by the close co-operation they maintained at all times.

4. *The Kite-Balloon* was useful in giving early information of enemy movements.

VII. – *The Evacuation.*

The date for commencing the evacuation was postponed until the refugees had been shipped away and the troop transports were ready at Archangel and water transport collected upriver. Also, it was hoped that the river would continue to rise and facilitate the passage of the last of the heavy-draught ships, but this hope, as has been seen, was not fulfilled.

2. The whole force moved back from the Troitsa base to Pless on 10th September, the embarkation being carried out in perfect order without enemy interference. The final start down-river commenced on 17th September, when the convoy left Pless.

3. *Attack off the Vaga.* – Owing to the Russian forces failing to hold the Vaga front, part of the convoy came under machine-gun fire off the mouth of that river.

An armed naval launch and coastal motor-boats were at once despatched to counter this, and a Royal Marine Detachment under Lieutenant C.M. Sergeant, R.M., was landed. A spirited attack dispersed the enemy machine-gunners, killing three of them, and the safety of the remainder of the convoy was thus secured.

4. *Remainder of the passage down-river.* – This was uneventful save for a delay due to the grounding of several barges in the shallow and intricate channel off Khorobritskoe.

The convoy was covered by C.M.B.'s and an armed launch until reaching H.M.S. "Mantis" (Lieutenant H.T.C. Walker, R.N.), off Siskoe. That ship acted as escort to Ust Pinega, where H.M.S. "Moth" (Lieutenant H.A. Simpson, D.S.C., R.N.) was stationed.

Lyavlya was reached on the 22nd September, and here the line was established until the day of the final evacuation of Archangel.

5. *The final withdrawal.* – On the morning of 27th September the British troops left the Lyavlya front and, escorted by "M.31" and "M.33," arrived at Archangel to embark in the sea transports.

With the exception of these two ships, "M.26" and H.M.S. "Fox" the whole of the River Flotilla had already sailed for England.

The final stages of the evacuation were completed in perfect order.

VIII. – *Conclusion.*

The flotilla underwent many vicissitudes and was called upon to perform as many and varied services as perhaps have ever fallen to the lot of a Naval force of its size.

2. I owed the success it achieved to the unfailing loyalty and support I received from the Captains, officers and men of the ships I had the honour to command and no less to my excellent Staff, whose work in overcoming all difficulties I cannot praise too highly.

3. Lastly, I beg to record the exceptionally cordial relations which existed between the flotilla and our comrades-in-arms of the Sister Service, especially the Volunteer Brigade, under the command of Brigadier-General L.W. de V. Sadleir-Jackson, C.B., C.M.G., D.S.O., with which we were most closely associated.

I have the honour to be,
Sir,
Your obedient Servant,
E. ALTHAM,
Captain, R.N.,
Late Senior Naval Officer,
Archangel River Expedition.
Rear-Admiral
Sir John F.E. Green,
K.C.M.G., C.B.

APPENDIX I.

APPRECIATIONS.

1. Major-General Sir Edmund Ironside, K.C.B., C.M.G., D.S.O., expressed his appreciation of the work of the Flotilla in the following message to the Senior Naval Officer, River:-

"Will you accept on behalf of myself and the Army our thanks for the co-operation of the Royal Navy? The Army feels that you have never failed to respond, even in our troubles on land, and that a great deal of our success has been due to the efforts of you and your men.

"Will you please be so good as to give my thanks to all ranks of the Royal Navy?"

2. On the return of H.M.S. "Fox" to England, their Lordships caused the following message to be sent to Captain Edward Altham, R.N.:-

"Their Lordships wish to express to you and the officers and men of the Archangel River Expeditionary Forces their satisfaction at the successful conclusion of the operations and the manner in which they were carried out."

3. The Army Council signified their appreciation of the work of the Navy in North Russia in War Office Letter 0149/8281 (c.I) of 31st October, 1919:-

"I am commanded by the Army Council to request that you will convey to the Lords Commissioners of the Admiralty the Council's appreciation of the valuable services rendered by the Royal Navy in connection with the operations in and the withdrawal from North Russia. I am to refer particularly to the work of the river expedition on the Dwina, which rendered the greatest possible assistance, not only by the provision of landing parties and heavy artillery support, for which, owing to the nature of the country, the military forces were almost entirely dependent on the monitors and gunboats of the Royal Navy, but also by constant and effective minesweeping, and subsequently by the laying of a minefield, which effectively prevented the enemy's pursuit. The Council recall that the Naval Transport Service was responsible for carrying stores and supplies from Archangel to the front, a distance of 200 miles, for the movement of troops up and down the river, for the transport of the special stores required during the preparations for the Dvina offensive, and for the conveyance of troops down the river. The Council also desire especially to express their appreciation of the highly efficient arrangements made for the embarkation of the troops at Archangel and Murmansk.

"Throughout the campaign and during the evacuation the assistance and co-operation of the Royal Navy has been indispensable, and the Army Council desire to take this opportunity of recording their sense of its efficiency and value. Without it, in the Council's opinion, the success of the operations, and especially of the withdrawal, would have been impossible."

20

RUSSIAN OPERATIONS, THE BALTIC, 1919

FRIDAY, 9 APRIL, 1920.

Admiralty, 9th April, 1920.
"Delhi" at Devonport,
9th February, 1920.

SIR,

I have the honour to forward herewith this my report on my year's Service in Command of His Majesty's Naval Forces in the Baltic, where I relieved Rear-Admiral Sir Edwyn S. Alexander-Sinclair, K.C.B., M.V.O., on the 6th January, 1919.

2. When I arrived the German situation was as follows:- German Troops were nominally in occupation of Latvia, with Headquarters at Libau.

The Bolsheviks were in Riga, and gradually advancing South and West.

The German Troops were of low morale, and in a poor state of discipline – and wherever the Bolsheviks advanced the Germans fell back, in many cases handing over arms and munitions to the Bolsheviks on their retirement.

3. The Bolsheviks had by the middle of February advanced so far as Windau, and were also within forty miles from Libau from the Westward.

4. I therefore in "Caledon" (Commander Henry S.M. Harrison-Wallace, R.N.) shelled them out of Windau; and made what preparations I could to evacuate the refugees from Libau, as I did not consider an indiscriminate shelling of the town in the event of its occupation by the Bolsheviks would be advisable if no troops were available to land for its reoccupation.

5. Shortly after this (at the end of February), large German reinforcements began to arrive by sea, and General-Major Graf Von der Goltz assumed command at Libau, and very soon afterwards stabilised the situation, and drove the Bolsheviks well East again – and this, so far, was satisfactory.

6. In the meantime the Letts – under the direction of M. Ulmanis, the Acting President – were making every endeavour to raise and equip a sufficient military

force – aided by a limited quantity of small arms, machine guns and ammunition supplied by His Majesty's Government – to enable them to undertake the defence of their own country against the Bolsheviks when the time should come for the Germans to withdraw.

It soon became evident, however, that it was not the Germans' intention to permit any Lettish Force being raised, and constant cases of friction, oppression and disarmament of Lettish Troops began to occur.

7. The climax was reached on the 16th April, when at the Naval Harbour – where the Headquarters of the Lettish Troops were – German troops raided these Headquarters, arrested and disarmed all the Officers, and looted money and documents, killing and wounding several Lettish soldiers.

Simultaneously with this, in the town of Libau itself, Baltic-German troops arrested those members of the Lettish Government who were unable to escape them, whilst the rest took refuge on board His Majesty's ships, and M. Ulmanis, the Acting President, with the British Mission, which consequently was surrounded by Baltic-German sentries.

8. That night two young Baltic-German Officers came off to my ship and announced that they were the Heads of the Committee of Safety until the formation of a new Government, and asked me if I could guarantee them the support of His Majesty's Government in this movement.

I pointed out to them that until I had some satisfactory explanation for the events of the day I could listen to and recognise no such proposals.

I then sent them on shore again and heard nothing more of them.

9. On my requiring an explanation from Von der Goltz for these happenings, he denied all responsibility or knowledge for them, saying that his troops were out of hand, and that the Baltic-Germans were not under his orders.

10. In consequence of this I called a meeting of the Allied representatives, and with them demanded the following from Von der Goltz:-

First. – That the unit which raided the Lettish Headquarters should be at once removed from the Libau district.

Second. – That the Commanding Officer of the offending Baltic-German Unit be relieved of his command.

We also gave him the time and date by which we required the fulfilment of these demands.

11. Both were complied with within the time, but Von der Goltz stated that as he considered the Lettish Government to be Bolshevik and a danger to the district he was administering by order of the Allies, he could not agree to their release from arrest, or the continuance of their functions.

12. This state of affairs was reported to Paris accordingly, and a very few days afterwards, owing to the melting of the ice, and signs of activity by the Bolshevik Fleet, I had myself to proceed to the Gulf of Finland, and Commodore Arthur A.M. Duff, C.B., arrived on the 29th May and took charge of affairs in the Western Baltic; and thereafter, by his quick and accurate grasp of the whole German situation there, freed me from a very considerable portion of my preoccupations.

It is hard for me to do justice on paper to the adequacy and effectiveness of his administration until he left for England again on the 28th September.

I have now transferred to him the duties of Senior Naval Officer in the Baltic.

13. On arrival in the Gulf of Finland and reviewing the situation, my hope and intention was – as soon as ice conditions allowed it – to move as far East as possible in order to support the left flank of the Esthonian Front, and to protect it from any attempt at being turned from the sea.

14. After getting into touch with the Esthonian Naval and Military Authorities, I went over to Helsingfors to call on the Regent (General G. Mannerheim), and also to congratulate the Finns on the recognition of their independence, which had been announced the previous day. Circumstances then obliged me to return to Libau for a day on the 12th May.

15. I had previously – on the 7th May – shifted my flag from "Caledon" to "Curacoa."

On returning from Libau to Reval on the 13th May "Curacoa" struck a mine, which disabled her from further service and occasioned eleven casualties amongst her personnel.

16. I therefore shifted to "Cleopatra," and left Reval the next morning for the Eastward, and, from the 14th May onwards I lay – first in Narva Bay for a few days reconnoitring as far as Kaporia whilst the Esthonians were landing and operating between there and Louga – and then, as they established themselves further East, I moved forward to Seskar, from which place, with the very good visibility prevailing day after day, I was able from the mast head to keep an effective watch on Petrograd Bay.

17. The situation then was somewhat of an anxiety to me, as the strength of the Bolshevik Naval Forces was known to include Armoured Ships – the Esthonians were lying in Kaporia with unarmed Transport (including the Nekmangrund Light Vessel, so hard up were they for ships), an old, slow ex-Russian Gunboat "Bobr," and one ex-Russian Destroyer, dependent on me for fuel, of which I had then, only a limited supply – and my own Force consisted only of "Cleopatra" and four Destroyers, the Seventh Submarine Flotilla arriving shortly afterwards at Reval.

18. From then onwards I maintained a watch on the Bay, whilst the Esthonians were constantly in contact with the Bolshevik Troops, bombarding and pushing forward here and there, and landing more men, whilst relieving those who needed refit, always under the direction of Admiral John Pitka, who, before the War, was a Shipowner of Reval and Director of a Salvage Company, but who assumed command of the Esthonian Naval Forces last winter, and has always shown a most correct instinct for war, both on land and sea. He has since been decorated by His Majesty.

19. On the 17th May a great deal of smoke was observed over Kronstadt; and on the 18th five Bolshevik craft, led by a large Destroyer of the "Avtroil" type came as far West as Dolgoi Nos, five miles clear of the Petrograd Minefields, and then while still close under the land turned back. So in "Cleopatra" (Captain Charles James Colebrooke Little, C.B.), with "Shakespeare" (Commander – now Captain – Frederick Edward Ketelbey Strong, D.S.O.), "Scout" (Lieutenant-Commander

Edmund F. Fitzgerald), and "Walker" (Lieutenant-Commander Ambrose T.N. Abbay), I went ahead full speed from Seskar on an Easterly course, closing the range rapidly from 20,000 to 16,000 yards when fire was opened, the Bolshevik Destroyer, flying a very large red flag, firing the first shot. I stood on until within half a mile of the mined area, and came under the fire of the Grey Horse Battery, but by this time the range was opening and spotting very difficult, owing to the vessels being close under the land all the time.

20. The speed of the enemy appeared to be reduced to about ten knots, one good hit on the Destroyer at any rate was observed, but under the circumstances I did not consider it advisable to run in over the minefields and under the guns of the shore batteries in order to obtain a decision, and so these craft made good their escape.

21. To the Eastward, but not taking part in the action, was a three-funnelled Cruiser, the "Oleg," and to the Eastward of her again was smoke – and it was reported that the Bolshevik Dreadnought Battleship "Petropavlovsk" was also out.

22. On the 24th May General Sir Hubert Gough arrived in "Galatea" on a special Mission to Finland and the Baltic States, and I accompanied him over to Helsingfors to assist at his ceremonial landing, and to salute him there, and went with him to interview the Finnish authorities, thereafter leaving again for the Eastward, leaving "Galatea" at Helsingfors.

23. On the 31st May, whilst still lying off Seskar in "Cleopatra" with "Dragon" (Captain Francis Arthur Marten, C.M.G., C.V.O.), "Galatea" (Captain Charles Morton Forbes, D.S.O.), "Wallace" (Captain George William McOran Campbell), "Voyager" (Lieutenant-Commander Charles Gage Stuart, D.S.C.), "Vanessa" (Lieutenant-Commander Edward Osborne Broadley, D.S.O.), "Wryneck" (Commander Ralph Vincent Eyre, R.N.), "Versatile" (Commander Gerald Charles Wynter, O.B.E.), "Vivacious" (Commander Claude L. Bate, R.N.), and with "Walker" and two Submarines on patrol, a Bolshevik Destroyer was sighted coming West with a Dreadnought Battleship, and two other small craft behind the minefields. The Destroyer was engaged by "Walker" and chased Eastwards, the Battleship opening a heavy and well-controlled fire at the same time.

24. On the first report I weighed and steamed East, a Bolshevik aeroplane appearing overhead and dropping bombs among my force as it advanced, but it flew off Eastwards on being fired at.

25. The Destroyer fell back on the battleship, which manoeuvred behind the minefields and kept up a heavy and well-disciplined fire on "Walker" as she fell back to meet me; Fort Krasnaya Gorka, having a kite balloon up and fixing also.

26. I stood up and down the edge of the minefield, but the Bolshevik Force showed no intention of coming on, and retired Eastwards after a few salvoes had been fired.

27. "Walker" was hit twice, but no appreciable damage was done, and there was one slight casualty only.

28. It now became apparent to me that with the small forces at my disposal it would be necessary, in order to keep an effective watch on Bolshevik Naval movements, and in particular to, if possible, ensure that no mines were laid to the Westward of

the existing fields across the entrance to Petrograd Bay, that I should have a Base nearer to Kronstadt than Reval.

29. I therefore moved to Biorko, and required certain assistance from the Finns in the way of patrols and accommodation on shore for aircraft, which assistance was at once agreed to by them.

30. It was evident by then that the Bolshevik Active Squadron consisted of:-

2 Battleships (1 Dreadnought "Petropavlovsk"),
1 Cruiser, and
6 Large Destroyers.

31. Up to about the end of June there were constant attempts by Enemy Light Craft to break out on the Northern side at night, and both to sweep and lay mines – and a good deal of shooting, though little hitting, went on between the Patrols – also, there is no doubt more mines were laid by the Bolsheviks to the Southward of Stirs Point, and to the Eastward of the existing Mine Barrier.

32. On the 13th June very heavy firing broke out between Fort Krasnaya Gorka and the forts and ships at Kronstadt – Fort Krasnaya Gorka having suddenly turned over to the "Whites," who, however, were not strong enough to hold it – the forces immediately available being only a hundred or so of badly-armed and much-exhausted Ingermanlanders, who, owing to the fire from the Bolshevik Heavy Ships, were unable to occupy the Fort long enough either to effectively man the guns, or destroy them – and so, after changing hands twice, Krasnaya Gorka remained in Bolshevik hands.

33. These Ingermanlanders were fighting under the direction of the Esthonian Command, and were armed and equipped by them, chiefly from supplies captured from Bolsheviks, and had done very well ever since these operations started, and were fighting with the more enthusiasm as it was their own country they were freeing.

Apparently, however, their successes aroused the suspicion and jealousy of the Russians of the Northern Corps, who, equipped and supported in every way by the Esthonians, had by then begun to become a considerable fighting force, and were holding the line on the right of the Esthonian-Ingermanland Force – whose left flank rested on the sea, and had pushed forward as far as Krasnaya Gorka.

34. In order to deal with any attempt by heavy ships to break out – as well as to maintain an effective patrol on the entrance to Petrograd Bay, I considered it advisable to lay mines so as to restrict the movements of the enemy, and this was done by "Princess Margaret" (Captain Harry H. Smyth, C.M.G., D.S.O.) and the 20th Destroyer Flotilla (Captain (D) Berwick Curtis, C.B., D.S.O.).

35. On 17th June our lookouts reported a Cruiser ("Oleg") and two Destroyers at anchor West of Kronstadt, and also a Submarine moving Westward.

36. A few minutes after midnight a sudden burst of firing was heard by our outpost Destroyers, which, as suddenly ceased, and next day Lieutenant Augustine W.S. Agar, R.N., informed me that he had torpedoed the Cruiser "Oleg" at anchor, the torpedo hitting her about the foremost funnel, and came under heavy fire from the Destroyers on retiring.

37. On the 6th July "Vindictive," on passage from England to join me in the Gulf of Finland, ran aground outside Reval on the Middle Ground Shoal, and remained there for eight days.

It was a time of some anxiety to me, as she was going fifteen knots at the time of striking, and had slid up half her length, and was in two feet six inches to three feet less water there than her draught, and in a tide-less sea.

"Delhi" and "Cleopatra" made several ineffectual attempts to tow her off before, after lightening her by 2,212 tons, and experiencing a rise of water of about four to six inches due to a Westerly wind, "Cleopatra" at last pulled her clear after eight days of effort and, as we discovered shortly afterwards, all the towing operations were carried out in the middle of a minefield.

38. Early in July strong attacks were made by the Bolsheviks on the Russian front on the southern shore, necessitating frequent bombardments by Light Cruisers and Destroyers of the Bolshevik positions. Bolshevik aircraft were also active; Fort Krasnaya Gorka also occasionally firing at our patrols in Kaporia Bay.

39. Later in the month our Flying Operations started, consisting at first of reconnaissance and photographic flights, and then on the morning of the 30th July a bombing operation against the ships in Kronstadt, the main objective being a Destroyer Depot Ship with five or six Destroyers lying alongside her. The whole was under the command of Squadron Leader David G. Donald, A.F.C., R.A.F. Sixteen bombs in all were dropped, and one hit, at any rate, was registered on the Depot Ship, which disappeared from her accustomed position in the harbour, and was not seen again. All machines returned safely after passing through a heavy anti-aircraft fire from the ships and batteries defending Kronstadt.

40. Thereafter continued a close watch on Petrograd Bay, with frequent bombardments by us of Bolshevik positions on the Southern Shore, and occasional shellings by Fort Krasnaya Gorka and other guns, varied by attacks by enemy submarines on our vessels, and intermittent activity by Bolshevik Destroyers and Minesweepers, with occasional appearances outside the harbour by larger craft.

41. On the morning of 18th August, with the object of removing, as far as possible, the threat which existed to my ships and also to the Left Flank of the Russian advance to Petrograd by the presence of the Bolshevik Active Squadron, an attack on the ships in Kronstadt by Coastal Motor Boats and Aircraft was made.

42. The position of the ships in the harbour had been ascertained by aerial photographs. Frequent bombing raids on the harbour had also been made at varying times in the weeks beforehand.

43. The attack was planned so that all available aircraft co-operated under Squadron Leader D.G. Donald, A.F.C., R.A.F., and that they should arrive and bomb the harbour so as to drown the noise of the approach of the Coastal Motor Boats.

44. The time-table was most accurately carried out, with, the result that the first three Coastal Motor Boats, under Commander Claude C. Dobson, D.S.O., passed the line of Forts and entered the harbour with scarcely a shot being fired.

45. Each boat had a definite objective – six in all. Of these six enterprises four were achieved, the results being gained not only by dauntless disciplined bravery at

the moment of attack, but by strict attention to, and rehearsal of, every detail beforehand by every member of the personnel, both of the boats and also of the Air Force.

46. Of the latter there is this to say, that though all their arrangements for bombing were makeshift, and the aerodrome from which the land machines had to rise in the dark, was a month before a wilderness of trees and rocks, and in size is quite inadequate, not one of the machines (sea and land) failed to keep to its time-table, or to lend the utmost and most effective support during, and after, the attack to the Coastal Motor Boats.

47. After this nothing bigger than a Destroyer ever moved again, but a certain amount of mine-laying and sweeping was observed near the approaches to the harbour.

48. During September our ships constantly bombarded Bolshevik positions on the Southern Shore in Kaporia Bay, in support of the Esthonian Left Flank, whilst the aircraft were employed in bombing Kronstadt and attacking their small craft whenever seen.

49. Early in October the long talked of advance against Petrograd by General Yudenitch began – but as his left flank was not made secure by making the capture of Forts Krasnaya Gorka and Saraia Lochad his first objective – as was repeatedly urged – the attempt failed.

50. The Esthonians, so long as their advance was such that the guns of the light cruisers and destroyers of the Biorko Force could support them, went forward – but thereafter they met with strong and effective resistance and much barbed wire, and were held up within four miles of the land approaches to Fort Krasnaya Gorka and suffered very heavy losses – equal to nearly one-third of their forces, which did not at the beginning exceed two thousand men.

51. It was after this check that "Erebus" (Captain John A. Moreton, D.S.O.) arrived (24th October), which encouraged Admiral Pitka, who was in command of the Esthonian Forces, to try again; but by then the Russians had begun to fall back, thereby uncovering the Esthonian right flank and causing them further distress, and dispersion of their few remaining effectives.

The Russians and Esthonians then fell back with considerable rapidity as far west as the line Narva–Peipus Lake, and I devoted myself to endeavouring to ensure that, from the sea, no further attempt was made to further harass these very war-weary and dispirited troops.

52. Unfortunately the "Erebus" (Captain John A. Moreton, D.S.O.) arrived only after the attempt was doomed to failure, and by that time also the weather had broken, making it very unsuitable for flying in order to direct the firing of "Erebus"; also our machines and many of the pilots were, from hard service through the summer, rather past their best. The type of machine, too (Short Seaplane), was unable to get sufficient height to avoid the very severe and accurate anti-aircraft fire from these two forts.

53. All that could be done by our ships (light cruisers and destroyers) besides "Erebus," in the way of shelling positions and covering the advance, was done, and always within the range of Fort Krasnaya's Gorka's twelve-inch guns, and under the

observation of its kite balloon; these guns, however, though throughout the year they have constantly shelled us, have never succeeded further than to land a few splinters on board.

54. On the 30th October arrived, out from England General Sir Richard Haking and a small staff of officers, who, after investigating and acquiring what appeared to me to be a very complete grasp of the whole Baltic situation and its needs, returned to England after two weeks.

55. Towards the beginning of October and concurrently with the attempt on Petrograd by the Russian North-West Army, the German-Russian threat against Riga became acute, and a bombardment of the town commenced.

"Abdiel" (Captain Berwick Curtis, C.B., D.S.O.) and "Vanoc" (Commander Edward O. Tudor, R.N.) were there at the time, also a French destroyer ("L'Aisne"), "Dragon" (Captain Francis A. Marten, C.M.G., C.V.O.) was on her way out from England and I therefore diverted her there.

56. Owing to the situation in the Gulf of Finland and the necessity of supporting the advance of the Esthonians on the left flank of the Russian Army, I was unable to leave those waters myself, and so requested Commodore Brisson, the French Senior Naval Officer, who had by then proceeded to Riga, to take charge of the operations there, and to open fire on all positions within range on the the the left bank of the Dvina River, at the expiration of the time given in my ultimatum to Prince Avaloff Bermont, who was ostensibly in command of the troops occupying those positions, and attacking Riga.

57. This Commodore Brisson most faithfully and effectively did at noon on the 15th October, apparently much to the surprise of Bermont, who had, in reply to my ultimatum, stated that he was friendly to the Allies and was only resisting Bolshevism, and disowned all connection with the Germans, and whose forces, were in position and with little shelter, in some places less than one thousand yards from ours, and the French ships, Bermont having evidently assumed that his statements and arguments were sufficient to hoodwink me and delay our offensive action.

58. This enabled the Lettish troops to cross the river in strength and with great enthusiasm after twenty-six days' fighting, to sweep away all these Russo-German forces from within striking distance of Riga and out of Mitau – which had been the German main base and headquarters throughout the year – Tukkum and the Windau district.

59. On about the 30th October the threat to Libau by German troops became serious, and I sent directions to Captain Lawrence L. Dundas, C.M.G., the senior naval officer there, to, with the help of the British Military Mission, get into co-operation with the Lettish Defence Forces, establish communications and observation posts and plot targets, and sent "Dauntless" (Captain Cecil Horace Pilcher) down from Biorko to reinforce, and shortly afterwards "Erebus" also, as by this time General Yudenitch was falling back from before Petrograd, and therefore the need for bombarding Fort Krasnaya Gorka had ceased.

60. On the 14th October a very heavy attack on Libau commenced and the Germans succeeded in occupying the outer fixed defences of the town, but after eight

hours hard fighting by the Lettish troops and incessant bombardment by the British ships they were thrown back again with very heavy losses.

61. The ammunition question at the end of this day was of some anxiety to me, two vessels having fired the whole of their outfits and others being very short.

An ammunition ship was on her way down from Riga at the moment – "Galatea," homeward bound with General Sir R. Haking on board, and also two destroyers were in the vicinity, so all were ordered in to replenish the Libau force with their ammunition.

No further attack of any weight however was made, and the crisis passed.

62. With regard to these two attacks on Riga and Libau, it is unquestionable that the German intention was to frustrate by every means in their power any successful attack on Petrograd and Kronstadt, and to gain this footing for the winter in the Baltic Provinces with a view to overwhelming them, and then to drive on to Petrograd.

63. I had constant rumours that the Dreadnought Battleship "Sevastopol" had been prepared for, and was in every way fit for service – also, there was ever-recurring Submarine activity – and by my reckoning there were still two large Destroyers available as well, though two had been destroyed by our mines during the operations in support of Yudenitch whilst attempting to come out and attack our patrols at night.

64. The work of the Destroyers was, as ever, tireless, dauntless, and never ending, and with never the relaxation of lying in a defended port with fires out and full rations, and all their work in cramped navigational waters, necessitating the almost constant presence on deck of the Captain, and, in the case of the Petrograd Bay "Biorko" Patrol, always within the range, and often under the fire, of the twelve-inch guns from Fort Krasnaya Gorka.

65. This patrolling of Petrograd Bay, though generally in smooth water, was arduous and anxious always, because there was no room to manoeuvre East or West – there were mines in each direction – much foul ground, unindicated by the charts, and the charting of the Southern Shore disagreed by a mile of longitude with that of the Northern – also for that small space, (six by twenty miles), bounded on the West by Seskar, and on the East by the minefields, three charts had to be in use.

66. In the whole of that area no shoals (and there are many), were marked by anything better than a spar buoy.

When the winter came on, with incessant snow and fog throughout the long sixteen-hour nights, I scarcely hoped that the Destroyers could succeed in maintaining their stations without frequent and serious groundings or collisions, and the fact that they did is sufficient witness of the spirit that was in these two Flotillas – the First, Captain George W. McO. Campbell, and the Second, Captain Colin K. MacLean, C. B., D.S.O., reinforced by some of the Third Flotilla also, under the command of Commander Aubrey T. Tillard, in "Mackay."

The energy, care and forethought which these two officers constantly displayed in order to maintain the efficiency of their Flotillas, I must always bear in most grateful admiration and remembrance.

The boats were always in "watch and watch" – *i.e.*, as often at sea as in harbour, and very frequently under harder conditions.

67. At the beginning of the campaign the enemy's active Naval Force appeared to be:-

2 Battleships (1 Dreadnought "Petropavlovsk," 1 "Andrei Pervozvanni,")
1 Cruiser ("Oleg"),
5 Destroyers ("Novik" class),
2 to 4 Submarines, and perhaps
4 smaller coal-burning Torpedo Boats, besides – Minesweepers.

68. Of these:-

2 Battleships ("Petropavlovsk" and "Andrei Pervozvanni") were torpedoed and disabled, in Kronstadt Harbour, and have not moved since – except "Andrei Pervozvanni" into dock.
1 Cruiser ("Oleg") was torpedoed and sunk at her moorings off Kronstadt.
3 Destroyers ("Novik" class), "Azard," "Gavril" and "Constantin" were sunk, two of them by our mines, the other either by mine or torpedo.
1 Patrol Vessel (armed), "Kitoboi," which surrendered on the night of 14th-15th June,
and, I think,
2 Submarines, one by depth charge and the other by mine.
Besides this:-
1 Oiler was bombed and badly damaged.
A number of Motor Launches were set on fire and destroyed, and
1 Submarine Depot Ship ("Pamiet Azov") was torpedoed and sunk, all in Kronstadt Harbour.
An Oil Fuel Store and a very large quantity of wood and coal fuel was also burnt.

69. – Against this our losses have been:-

1 Submarine ("L.55") *(above, sister-boat L.52 - Navy Photos)* mined and sunk.
1 Destroyer ("Verulam") mined and sunk.
1 Destroyer ("Vittoria") torpedoed and sunk by enemy submarine.
2 Mine-sweeping Sloops ("Gentian" and "Myrtle") mined and sunk.
3 Coastal Motor Boats sunk during the attack on Kronstadt.
2 Coastal Motor Boats blown up; unserviceable.
2 Coastal Motor Boats and 2 Motor Launches sunk through stress of weather whilst in tow.
1 Store Carrier ("Volturnus") mined and sunk.
1 Light Cruiser ("Curacoa") mined and salved.
1 Paddle Minesweeper ("Banbury") mined and salved.
1 Motor Launch (M.L.156) mined and salved.
1 Admiralty Oiler ("War Expert") mined and salved.
1 Mine-layer ("Princess Margaret") damaged by mine.

70. – The losses of personnel have been:

Killed.

Royal Navy	16 Officers.	97 Men.
Royal Air Force	4 Officers.	1 Man.
Total	20 Officers.	98 Men.

Wounded.

Royal Navy	7 Officers.	35 Men.
Royal Air Force	2 Officers.	- Men.
Total	9 Officers.	35 Men.

Missing.

Royal Navy	3 Officers.	6 Men.
Royal Air Force	- Officers.	- Men.
Total	3 Officers.	6 Men.

Abstract.

Killed.		Wounded.		Missing.	
Officers.	Men.	Officers.	Men.	Officers.	Men.
20.	98.	9.	35.	3.	6.

Total Officers	32.
Total Men	139.
Grand total	171.

71. My aim was throughout the year to prevent any Bolshevik warships breaking out into the Gulf of Finland – and the ice has now relieved me of this responsibility – and also to frustrate by every means the most evident design of the Germans to overrun and dominate the Baltic Provinces and then to advance on Petrograd, and their repulse from both Riga and Libau in October and November by the Lettish troops under cover of the bombardment of our ships has, I think, put an end to this also, and all German troops were back into Prussia by 15th December.

I have the honour to be,
Sir,
Your obedient servant,
WALTER COWAN,
Rear-Admiral Commanding First Light
Cruiser Squadron.

21

RUSSIAN OPERATIONS, NORTH RUSSIA, 1918

THURSDAY, 8 JULY, 1920.

Admiralty, April 29th, 1920.

SIR,-

In accordance with Admiralty letter dated April 19th, 1920, I have the honour to enclose herewith for submission to Their Lordships a despatch dealing with Naval affairs in N. Russia during 1918.

I have the honour to be,
Sir,
Your obedient Servant,
T.W. KEMP,
Rear-Admiral, Retired.
The Secretary of the Admiralty.

SIR,-

I beg you will lay before Their Lordships the following despatch dealing with Naval affairs in North Russia during the year 1918:-

In December, 1917, it was decided to withdraw from Archangel all Naval elements. I therefore embarked these in H.M.S. "Iphigenia" on December 19th, together with as many British subjects as could be induced to leave, arriving at Murmansk next day.

The position, whether regarded from a political or military point of view, was very simple. The complete breakdown of the Russian Military system had left Russia open to German invasion. This reacted on the naval position in Murmansk.

It was, nevertheless, decided to retain an allied footing in Murman Province, which afforded the only means of physical communication with European Russia. This decision in itself involved no ulterior motive with regard to the internal policy of Russia. Such elements of Russian life as were friendly to the above aims were to be welcomed, and such as were hostile were to be opposed. This, put in simple terms, was the gist of my instructions. At the same time I was given plainly to understand that the military situation elsewhere did not admit of the despatch of an expedition, and that I must do my best with the naval forces at my disposal, together with the assistance of such units of Allied Military Commissions, etc., which *rendezvoused* at Murmansk from time to time for despatch home.

The same process applied to Pechenga, the nearest important Russian harbour to the Norwegian boundary. In order to hold Kola inlet it was necessary to hold Pechenga, since the occupation of the latter by a hostile force would have turned it into a German submarine base. Finland was then dominated by Germany, and the possession of Pechenga affording a northern outlet was a Finnish aspiration. All indications tended to show that a German Finnish movement against the place was in contemplation.

With these considerations in view I begged to be sent an armoured cruiser and 500 Royal Marines. Accordingly H.M.S. "Cochrane" was sent and reached me on March 9th. She was to be followed by French and American armoured cruisers, both of which were to come under the British command. Later on, both these ships took their full part in operations ashore and afloat, and I was indebted to their captains for much sound advice on various matters. The detachment of Royal Marines did not reach me until later, but the arrival of the "Cochrane" enabled me to make immediate dispositions for the defence of Kola and Pechenga. A small body of R.E. officers and men which she brought, trained in demolitions work, rendered good service, as the nature of the surrounding country made the Murman Railway the only avenue of hostile approach. In the meantime a force of 300 French Artillerymen had collected at Murmansk, and it was believed that a similar number of Serbians were available at Kandalaksha.

On arrival of "Cochrane" an armoured train manned by "Cochrane" and 150 French Troops was despatched to Kandalaksha under command of Chef de Bataillon Molier of the French Army. Their orders were to hold Kandalaksha, to collect and organise all friendly elements, to regulate the passage of armed men in the direction of Kola, and if unable to hold the position to retire to Murmansk, destroying the line behind them. Though their position was often critical, this force held the post until the arrival of reinforcements in June, and the opening of the White Sea relieved the situation, and their presence at Kandalaksha assured Murmansk against surprise.

At the same time a landing party from H.M.S. "Glory" and "Cochrane" was put ashore at Murmansk, and the necessary arrangements made for the guns of the ships to assist in the defence. The general arrangements were under the Rear-Admiral Commanding, while Colonel Mercier of the French Army was in immediate command ashore. On May 2nd information reached me that a German Finnish attack on Pechenga was threatened. The arrival of the French armoured cruiser "Amiral Aube" on March 19th enabled me to detach the "Cochrane" for its protection. The "Cochrane" arrived at Pechenga on May 3rd, blasting her way through the ice. A landing party was put ashore, and a defensive position prepared. Scouting parties of friendly Finns were organised and sent out to the Norwegian frontier. On May 12th the position was attacked by some 400 Finns on skis, with two guns. The attack was repulsed with loss to the enemy. Later on the defence of Pechenga was taken over by a detachment of the force commanded by Major-General C.C.M. Maynard, C.M.G., under Colonel G.S. McD. Elliot. The "Cochrane," however, remained as a support until her return to England in November.

The above affords a general view of the situation until the arrival on May 24th of Major-General Sir F.C. Poole, K.B.E., C.B., C.M.G., who took over the command on shore. From that date onward the Navy remained in constant co-operation with the military forces under his command. At my request all Naval elements serving ashore came under the Army.

Local Conditions at Murmansk.

On my arrival I found the command invested in Rear-Admiral C.P. Ketlinsky of the Russian Navy. He was assassinated on February 10th, and thereafter things were in the hands of the Murmansk Soviet. The Soviet in its turn was dominated by the Bolshevik element of the seamen and Red Guard, numbering some 1,200 men. The landing of armed parties in March, as above related, stabilised the situation in this respect. The economic situation was very bad. Cut off from the usual sources of supply from the interior, White Sea, and Norway, the province was in danger of starvation.

Steps were taken to relieve the distress from Allied resources. The presence of many hundreds of Allied refugee subjects, who had escaped to Murmansk from the interior and were awaiting transport home, was a constant source of anxiety. The circumstances under which many of them had effected their escape was a very plain indication of the latent hostility of the Central Government.

My relations with the Central Soviet Government may be summarised as follows:-

Early in March I received a message from them asking me to co-operate with the local authorities in preserving the integrity of the Northern Provinces. In June the same Government sent me a peremptory summons to withdraw all Allied warships from Russian waters.

On April 25th I was authorised to make the following official statement to the Murmansk Soviet:-

"Great Britain has no intention of annexing any part of Russian territory, and will continue to assist in defence of district against outside aggression with such forces as can be spared, and will maintain friendly relations on basis of mutual advantage to both sides. Great Britain will view with greatest concern any severance from Russia of the district lying to the north and east of Finland. The Allies have never entertained any annexational intentions either in Siberia or in any portion of the Russian dominion."

Naval Position.

In accordance with the practice of former years, the bulk of the Naval forces on the station had left for England on the closing of navigation. On January 1st, 1918, the following Naval forces were at Murmansk and Kola Inlet:-

British.
> H.M.S. "Glory" (Flag), Captain Robert W. Glennie, R.N.
> 8 Trawlers.

Russian.
> "Chesma," Battleship similar to "Glory";
> "Askold," Cruiser;
> 4 Destroyers;

Several Trawlers, Yachts, etc.

"Chesma" and "Askold" were fully manned and in fighting condition. Their crews were strongly Bolshevik. The "Glory" and "Chesma" were lying at point-blank distance from each other, and the tension at times was so great that the possibility of a sudden attack from the latter could not be overlooked.

Subsequent Allied reinforcements were as follows:-

> Trawler force augmented to 24 by the end of May;
> H.M.S. "Cochrane," Armoured Cruiser, Captain James V. Farie, R.N.,
>   arrived March 9th;
> "Amiral Aube," French Armoured Cruiser, Captain Louis J. Petit, arrived
>   March 17th;
> H.M.S. "Alexander," lightly-armed icebreaker, Acting Captain Henry A. le
>   F. Hurt, R.N., arrived April 1st;
> "Tay and Tyne," special anti-submarine ship, May 20th;
> H.M.S. "Salvator," armed yacht, May 21st;
> "Olympia," United States Armoured Cruiser, Captain B.B. Bierer, May
>   24th;
> H.M.S. "Attentive," Light Cruiser, Captain Edward Altham, R.N., June
>   11th;
> "Nairana," Seaplane-carrier, Commander Charles F.R. Cowan, R.N., July
>   11th;
> "M.23" and "M.25," Monitors, August 9th.

In addition to above, Russian Cruiser "Askold" was commissioned by Captain Charles G. Wills, C.M.G., D.S.O., R.N., on August 3rd with a British crew specially sent out, and renamed "Glory IV."

In addition to their ordinary duties, the above squadron was called upon to provide officers and men for the following services:-

Landing parties at Murmansk, Pechenga, and subsequently at Archangel; armoured trains for Murman and Archangel railways; *personnel* for 4 Russian Destroyers;

Russian armed yachts and trawlers, and improvised river gunboats for the Dwina River Expedition.

In addition to providing *personnel* for above, the Squadron was called upon to carry out with its own resources large machinery and other repairs to all Russian craft taken over before the latter could be ready for sea.

The excellent way in which these services were carried out reflects great credit on the officers and men concerned.

Anti-Submarine Operations.

In former years the White Sea and approaches had been a point of enemy submarine activity as regards both Fighting-submarines and minelayers. I had reason to believe that the Soviet Government had made a strong appeal to Berlin to intensify submarine activities in these waters. The protection of troopships throughout the summer of 1918 taxed to the full the energies of the naval forces on the station. Except for one ship which was mined in an outlying minefield to the north of Ribachi Peninsula, and afterwards salved by the Auxiliary Patrols, there were no losses from submarines. Submarines had made their appearance in the beginning of May, sinking sealers and fishing craft as far east as Svatoi Nos. A small Russian passenger ship, plying between Vardo and Kola, was attacked close to Vaida Gouba, on the Ribachi Peninsula. The survivors, many of them women and children, were shelled in the boats and even after landing. Over 20 harmless civilians were killed and wounded. The effect of these outrages was to weld the people more closely to the Allied cause. I was later on informed by the Vice-President of the Archangel Soviet, who was in close touch with Moscow, that access to Russian waters was granted to German submarines provided that Russian ships flying the Red Soviet flag were not molested.

Arrival of Major-General Poole.

On May 24th Major-General Sir F.C. Poole, K.B.E., C.B., C.M.G., arrived in the "Olympia" and took over the command ashore. On May 29th the Royal Marines previously asked for arrived, and were turned over to the Army.

On June 19th I requested "Amiral Aube" to attempt the passage to Kandalaksha and Archangel Bar. She was forced to return, having sustained some damage from heavy ice, which, even at this late period of the year, was still thick in the approaches to the White Sea.

On July 1st I sent "Attentive," with a detachment of trawlers, to Kandalaksha and Kem, with orders to co-operate with the Army in the southern advance down the railway line.

Ice was encountered, but the passage was practicable. At Kem she found that the Red Army had retreated to the south of Soroka, partially destroying the railway behind them. "Nairana," which had arrived on July 11th, was sent to assist with seaplanes. Both ships did good work in harrying the enemy south of Soroka, enlisting the sympathies of the local authorities, and supplying the needy with food. They remained on this service until recalled to Murmansk late in July to prepare for the Archangel operations.

Position of Archangel.

The position at Archangel was obscure. Communication was difficult, and coded messages were prohibited by the local authority. In consultation with General Poole I decided to visit the place myself, and left in "Salvator" on July 2nd, taking with me Mr. Lindley, British Political Commissioner, and Sir William Clarke, Head of an Economic Commission, both of whom had arrived a few days before and were desirous of joining the Allied Ambassadors at Vologda. I arrived at Archangel on July 4th, after considerable difficulties had been raised as to the passage of the ship. Mr. Lindley and Sir William Clarke left next day for Vologda. I found here H.M.S. "Alexander" and two transports with food supplies. These had left Murmansk on April 17th, and had made their way with much difficulty through the ice. It had been intended that the cargoes of the food-ships should be exchanged for Allied war material landed in Archangel during 1917, which, in spite of protest, had been despatched into the interior by orders of the Central Government.

These negotiations had broken down, and the ships were undischarged when I arrived. In concert with Mr. Douglas Young, British Consul, it was arranged that these food stores should be turned over to the Russians, provided that a large number of Allied refugees, whose safety was a primary consideration, should be sent to Kandalaksha. There was a strong disposition on the part of the Archangel Soviet to hold these refugees as hostages, and send them back to Moscow.

I found the position very strained. Two days before my arrival an unprovoked hostile demonstration had been made against "Alexander." She had been surrounded by armed vessels and field batteries on the shore. The courage and address of Captain Henry A. le F. Hurt, R.N., saved the situation. To save further trouble of this nature I sent her to Murmansk, as her armament was too light to be of practicable use.

The Allied position in North Russia was explained to the local authorities, but all efforts to secure their co-operation failed, and I was given plainly to understand that any attack would be resisted. I was also convinced that active assistance on an organised scale was not to be hoped for from the pro-Ally element, who were very closely watched.

I returned to Murmansk on July 17th, calling at Kem on the way. On my return I was informed by General Poole that the Allied occupation of Archangel had been decided on. This decision entailed the following considerations from a naval point of view. Resistance was probable. The known fixed defences consisted of a battery of eight 6 in. guns on Modjuga Island, and a minefield operated from the shore. The battery covered at close range a narrow dredged channel up which the expedition must pass. The ascent of the river, about forty miles, could be undertaken by only medium-draft ships, and ample field artillery existed to dispute the passage at any point. Lack of pilots, removal of buoys and beacons, and the presence of mines or sunken obstructions in the channel might cause serious difficulty. The garrison was numerically ample, and included at least one Lett regiment, and could be reinforced to any extent from Petrograd at 36 hours' notice. The nature of the ground and the meagre forces at our disposal did not admit of an encircling attack by land.

In our favour were the idle and undisciplined state of the garrison, lack of competent leadership, the moral effect of aircraft – then a novelty in Archangel – and the hope that, though no direct assistance could be expected from the pro-Ally element, they were in a position to help materially by putting obstructions in the way of defence.

Such arrangements as were possible were made to cope with the above, and it was arranged for the expedition to start on August 3rd. An urgent message from the Allied Ambassadors, who had arrived at Kandalaksha on July 30th, made it necessary to modify these arrangements and start at once.

A body of 500, consisting of French Marines and French Colonial troops, with a detachment of British Royal Marines and a small party from "Olympia," in all 600, was distributed between "Amiral Aube," "Attentive," and "Nairana." Brigadier-General R.G. Finlayson, C.M.G., D.S.O., and myself embarked in latter. These three ships left at 9 p.m., July 30th, and proceeded for Archangel at 16 knots. A trawler detachment with "Tay and Tyne," under Captain Henry A. le F. Hurt, R.N., left at 10 knots at 6 p.m. the same day. Another trawler detachment was left behind as an escort to the transports "Stephen," "Asturian," "Kassala," and "Westborough," which it was hoped would leave at noon next day with the main body of the troops in charge of Captain John L. Pearson, R.N., Chief of Staff. These arrived at Archangel on August 4th.

Major-General Poole and staff and Captain B.B. Bierer, U.S.N., of the "Olympia," left in "Salvator" at 10 p.m. at 11 knots.

A thick fog was encountered, in which "Amiral Aube" got separated from the "Attentive" and "Nairana." At 12.6 a.m., August 1st, I received a signal from "Amiral Aube" to say that she was aground at Intzi Point. After consulting with General Finlayson I decided to go on with "Attentive" and "Nairana," telling "Amiral Aube" to come on to a *rendezvous* on the coast 15 miles N.W. of Dwina lightship. "Nairana" and "Attentive" anchored at this *rendezvous* at 3 a.m. on August 1st.

The weather was then fairly clear and blowing strongly from the north-east. Final arrangements were made, and three seaplanes got out, one with orders to demonstrate over Archangel and the other two to work with the ships. "Attentive" was sent on to the lightship (which, contrary to our expectations, was in place), with orders to seize her and any pilots found, and to telephone an ultimatum to the Island. The Island was required to surrender within half-an-hour. "Nairana" followed as soon as the last seaplane was in the air. The Island agreed to surrender, and to hoist the white flag on the battery, "Nairana" and "Attentive" accordingly stood in, and prepared to land troops. A tug then arrived from the lightship with a message from the battery refusing to submit, and saying that landing parties would be fired on. Troops were therefore re-embarked, and "Attentive" and "Nairana" anchored close to the north point of the Island. "Attentive" was ordered to open fire and seaplanes to bomb. The fort, which was about 5,000 yards distance, replied, and made pretty good shooting. "Attentive" was hit through the base of the foremost funnel, putting one boiler-room out of action, but without casualty. "Attentive" made good shooting, and the seaplanes bombed effectively.

The fort gradually ceased fire, and the troops were landed in ships' boats with some difficulty owing to the necessity of finding a channel and the shelving nature of the beach. The troops were under the command of Captaine Alliez, of the French Army, who had orders to work down South and occupy the battery and all mine-firing posts found. It was afterwards found that the battery and minefield arrangements were in good order.

The landing party encountered slight opposition from rifles and machine-guns, and the Island was in our possession by 8 p.m.

Some prisoners were made, but the majority of the garrison escaped in boats. Our casualties were slight. In the meantime the "Amiral Aube" got off and joined me at 3 p.m. on August 1st.

The result of the action at Modjuga was so discouraging to the Red garrison in Archangel that they retreated by rail and river, leaving the town temporarily in the hands of the pro-Ally element. They were afforded no time to rally.

"Salvator," with Major-General Poole on board, arrived at 8 p.m. Next morning the squadron proceeded up the river, leaving the "Amiral Aube" to control the approaches. It was found that two large icebreakers, "Sviatogor" and "Mikula," had been sunk, with the intention of blocking the channel at a narrow point in the river, but fortunately leaving enough room for ships to pass. The two icebreakers were raised shortly afterwards and refitted. The squadron anchored off Archangel, which was occupied, troops having been landed at Solumbola and other places on the way up. The Russian tricolour and naval flag had everywhere replaced the red flag of the Soviet. At 7 p.m. the "Attentive" captured the armed yacht "Gorislava," which was firing on the town, and brought her down. Early on August 3rd I ordered "Attentive" to Bakaritzan to assist the Army in warding off an attack. She took up a good position in shoal and confined waters, and did excellent work both with guns and a landing party in helping to save this important terminus.

Dwina River Expedition.

The decision of the General Officer Commanding to despatch a considerable military force up the Dwina River with a view to co-operation with Admiral Kolchak, who, it was hoped, would take Kotlas, made naval co-operation necessary. This expedition had not formed part of the original intention, and no provision in the shape of river gunboats had been made. The Bolshevik element, in retreating from Archangel, had taken with them the best of the river craft. The river was intricate, with many shallow spots, while pilots, barges and tugs of suitable draft were few and in bad order.

Four river paddle-craft were manned and armed, and, together with "M.25," and two small seaplanes from "Nairana," were placed under the immediate command of Captain Edward Altham, R.N., of the "Attentive," with orders to co-operate with Army. "M.25" drew 9 feet of water, and it was not possible to reduce her draft materially. Only abnormally high water in the river during the summer permitted her employment. During the latter half of August, September and until the advent of ice-conditions in October caused the flotilla to be withdrawn to Archangel, it was in constant action with the enemy gunboats and shore batteries. Three enemy ships were sunk and twenty-four mines swept up. Much zeal and gallantry was shown by the flotilla, and the value of their services in assisting the Army to establish themselves in their advanced positions some 200 miles up the river before winter was warmly appreciated by the General Officer Commanding.

Work of Seaplane Carrier "Nairana."

The "Nairana" did excellent work on all fronts. Her intrepid pilots made many flights where the lack of water surface meant disaster in case of a forced landing. They were constantly in action with the enemy, and generally had tangible marks to show of the latter's attention.

H.M. river gunboats "Glowworm," "Cockchafer," "Cicala," and "Cricket" arrived at Murmansk on October 30th. They wintered in Archangel, ready for work next season. The navigation of these frail craft to the far North in the stormy weather of late autumn was a noteworthy achievement.

On November 15th I handed over the command of the Station to Rear-Admiral John F.E. Green, C.B., and returned to England, having held the command of these waters since September, 1915.

I beg to attach herewith a list of officers specially mentioned for good service in 1918.

I have the honour to be,
Your obedient servant,
T.W. KEMP,
Rear-Admiral, Retired.
The Secretary of the Admiralty.

List of Officers Mentioned for Good Services

During Naval Operations in N. Russia, 1918.
Captain Louis Jules Petit, French Armoured Cruiser, "Amiral Aube."
Captain B.B. Bierer, United States Armoured Cruiser, "Olympia."
Captain John L. Pearson, R.N., Chief of Staff.
Captain James U. Farie, R.N., H.M.S. "Cochrane."
Captain Edward Altham, R.N., H.M.S. "Attentive."
Acting Captain Henry A. le F. Hurt, R.N., H.M.S. "Alexander."
Commander Charles F.R. Cowan, H.M.S. "Nairana."
Engineer-Commander Francis H. Lyon, R.N., H.M.S. "Attentive."
Lieutenant-Commander Edward H. Richardson, A.M., R.N.R., H.M.S. "Glory."
Paymaster Lieutenant Norman H. Beall, R.N., Secretary to Rear-Admiral.
Mr. S. Harrison, Civilian (for special services rendered to Navy).

ABBREVIATIONS

(Ch)	Chatham
(Ply)	Plymouth
(Po)	Portsmouth
AB	Able Seaman
ADM	Admiralty
AFC	Air Force Cross
AM	Albert Medal
AMC	Armed Merchant Cruiser
AMS	Armed Merchant Ship
CB	Companion of The Most Honourable Order of the Bath
Cdr., Cdre.	Commander
CIE	Companion of the Order of the Indian Empire
CMB	Coastal Motor Boat
CMG	Companion of the Order of St Michael and St George
CPO	Chief Petty Officer
CVO	Commander of the Royal Victorian Order
DSC	Distinguished Service Cross
DSO	Distinguished Service Order
ERA	Engine Room Artificer
FMS	Fleet Minesweeping Sloop
FRCS	Fellow of the Royal College of Surgeons
GCB	Knight/ Dame Grand Cross of the Most Honourable Order of the Bath

GCVO	Knight/Dame Grand Cross of the Royal Victorian Order
HIGMS	His Imperial Germanic Majesty's Ship
HM	His Majesty
HMAS	His Majesty's Australian Ship
HMS	His Majesty's Ship
HMT	His Majesty's Trawler; His Majesty's Troopship
KBE	Knight Commander of the Most Excellent Order of the British Empire
KCB	Knight Commander of the Most Honourable Order of the Bath
km	Kilometre
Lce.-Cpl.	Lance Corporal
Lce.-Sgt.	Lance Sergeant
Ldg. DKhnd.	Leading Deckhand
Ldg.Sea, Lg.Smn.	Leading Seaman
MA/SB	Motor Anti-Submarine Boat
M/L	Motor Launch
M/S	Motor Ship; Mine-Sweeping
MB	Motor Boat
MFV	Motor Fishing Vessel
MMR	Mercantile Marine Reserve
MT	Motor Tanker
MV, M/V	Motor Vessel
MVO	Member of the Royal Victorian Order
NOIC	Naval Officer in Charge
ON	Official Number
PNTO	Principal Naval Transport Officer
PS	Patrol Service
QARNNS	Queen Alexandra's Royal Naval Nursing Service

RAF	Royal Air Force
RAN	Royal Australian Navy
RD	Reserve Decoration
RFR	Royal Fleet Reserve
RFR A, B, C, IC	RFR A, men in receipt of a life pension from RN; RFR B, men who served in Royal Navy but who were not in receipt of a pension; RFR C, artisan ratings who have passed through the dockyards as boy apprentices for the Royal Navy; RFR IC (Immediate Class), similar to B, but could be called up for service without a Royal Proclamation.
RIM	Royal Indian Marine
RM	Royal Marines
RMA	Royal Marine Artillery
RMLI	Royal Marine Light Infantry
RNAS	Royal Naval Air Service; Royal Navy Air Station
RND	Royal Navy Department
RNR	Royal Naval Reserve
RNROD	Royal Naval Reserve Officers' Decoration
RNTR	Royal Navy Torpedo Range; Royal Naval Trawler Reserve
RNVR	Royal Naval Volunteer Reserve
Rtd	Retired
S/M, S/m	Submarine
SBA	Sick Berth Attendant
Sea.	Seaman
SGB	Steam Gun Boat
SMO	Senior Medical Officer
SNO	Senior Naval Officer
Sqn.	Squadron

SS	Steamship
TS	Training Ship
TSD	Training Ship Depot
Tr	Trawler
USN	United States Navy

INDEX OF NAVY UNITS

INDEX OF PERSONS